The 1964 Phillies

ALSO BY JOHN P. ROSSI

A Whole New Game: Off the Field Changes in Baseball, 1946–1960 (McFarland, 1999)

The National Game: Baseball and American Culture (Ivan R. Dee, 2002)

The 1964 Phillies

The Story of Baseball's Most Memorable Collapse

JOHN P. ROSSI

McFarland & Company, Inc., Publishers
Jefferson, North Carolina, and London

LIBRARY OF CONGRESS CATALOGUING-IN-PUBLICATION DATA

Rossi, John P.
  The 1964 Phillies : the story of baseball's most memorable collapse / John P. Rossi.
      p.   cm.
  Includes bibliographical references and index.

  ISBN 0-7864-2117-7 (softcover : 50# alkaline paper)

  1. Philadelphia Phillies (Baseball team) — History — 20th century.   I. Title.
  GV875.P45R66   2005
  796.357'64'0974811 — dc22   2005009073

British Library cataloguing data are available

©2005 John P. Rossi. All rights reserved

No part of this book may be reproduced or transmitted in any form or by any means, electronic or mechanical, including photocopying or recording, or by any information storage and retrieval system, without permission in writing from the publisher.

On the cover: The losing Phillies' Roy Sievers is tagged out at home by Cincinnati catcher Johnny Edwards, May 10, 1964

Manufactured in the United States of America

McFarland & Company, Inc., Publishers
  Box 611, Jefferson, North Carolina 28640
  www.mcfarlandpub.com

For Monica and Eric
as they begin their new life together

Contents

Preface	1
1. Philadelphia in the 1950s	5
2. The End of the Whiz Kids	17
3. The Little General	35
4. A Phillies Surprise	52
5. A Long Hot Summer	80
6. The Blue Snow Melts	112
7. What Went Wrong	135
8. Where Are They Now	145
Appendix 1. The 1964 Phillies Statistics	155
Appendix 2. The 1964 Phillies Season	157
Appendix 3. The Ten Game Collapse	166
Chapter Notes	177
Bibliography	183
Index	185

Preface

> I heard the old, old men say,
> "all that's beautiful drifts away
> like the waters."
> — *William Butler Yeats*

In the spring and summer of 1964 I was trying to complete my Ph.D. thesis in history at the University of Pennsylvania. If I finished and got my degree by June 1965, my school, La Salle College, told me that I would be promoted to the rank of assistant professor, with a raise of $1,100 — $20 a week was not to be sneezed at back in those days.

I almost didn't make it. Along with thousands of others in Philadelphia, I was caught up in the Phillies' unexpected run at the National League pennant. I became so involved in the fate of the club that I neglected my own work. There are games from that fateful summer that I still vividly remember and replay in my mind. The entire season is burned indelibly in my memory — from Jim Bunning's perfect game to Johnny Callison's winning home run in the All-Star Game. And of course, most painful of all, Chico Ruiz's steal of home that began the awful ten-game collapse. I finished my thesis, but only after everything turned bitter for the Phillies and their long-suffering fans.

Anyone past 50 knows what happened to that ill-fated team and its brilliant but star-crossed manager, Gene Mauch. Phillies fans had their hearts broken. A pennant that seemed theirs was snatched away in a ghastly ten-game losing streak at the end of the season. "All that's beautiful drifts away" indeed.

For years I have thought about the '64 season, about what went wrong and why. This book is a form of catharsis both for me and for those Phillies fans with memories of that wonderful but ultimately flawed season. I hope to bury the ghost of what catcher Gus Triandos called "the year of blue snow." Sometimes it is necessary to relive events in order to see them more clearly. I hope this book succeeds in that if nothing more.

In 1964 for the first time since the glory days of the Whiz Kids, a Philadelphia baseball team had won the hearts of the city's notoriously difficult fans. The '64 Phillies were the by-product of a chain of events dating back to the late 1950s. Team owner Bob Carpenter brought in a well-known baseball lifer, John Quinn, to put an end to the Whiz Kid era and begin the building of a new contender.

In 1960 Quinn hired a new manager, Gene Mauch, young, dynamic, intense and something of a baseball genius. Over the next four years, Phillies fans watched as the team underwent a painful process of growth. In Mauch's first season as manager, the Phillies finished in baseball's dungeon for the third consecutive season. The next season, 1961, the Phillies not only lost 107 games but they also set a record of futility unmatched in baseball history — 23 consecutive defeats.

Out of the rubble of that disastrous year, the Phillies fans, partly out of perverse pride and love of the underdog, began to embrace their young team. Mauch noted this phenomenon as he watched the awful losing streak begin the process of forging 25 different players into a team.

Beginning in 1962 the Phillies became a respectable team, winning more games than they lost and starting to settle scores with National League teams that had beaten them with regularity. Phillies fans responded in growing numbers, and old Shibe Park began to vibrate with happy, enthusiastic fans again. The city had new heroes in the Phillies young stars: Johnny Callison, Tony Gonzalez, Tony Taylor, and Art Mahaffey. Something like a love affair began to develop between the Phillies and their often fickle fans.

In 1963 the Phillies shocked the baseball world by finishing in the first division for the first time in eight years. They also played some of the best baseball in the National League. Buzzy Bavasi, general manager (GM) of the Los Angeles Dodgers, summed up the attitude of many in baseball when he half jokingly said that the Phillies, and not his Dodgers, should go to the World Series since they were the best team in the National League the last half of the season.

Expectations were high in Philadelphia as the 1964 season approached. The Phillies were regarded as a possible long shot for the pennant although a more realistic assessment was for continued improvement and a pennant a year or two down the road. The team had won 87 games in 1963, it was believed they would better that figure through two dramatic additions: Jim Bunning, to anchor a young and developing pitching staff, and Richie Allen, the first great African American player produced by the farm system.

Led by these two and great years from pitcher Chris Short, Callison and unexpected performances from reserves like Cookie Rojas, the Phillies surprised the baseball world in 1964, took over the National League lead in mid-July and held onto first place for 73 consecutive days. And then, as the team's first pennant in a generation seemed theirs, the Phillies collapsed in the greatest meltdown in baseball history.

My objective in this book is to trace the rise and fall of this particular Phillies team, to try to disentangle what went right and what ultimately cost them the pennant.

A final point. While I was writing this book, William Kashatus published *September Swoon: Richie Allen, the '64 Phillies, and Racial Integration* (Penn State University Press, 2004). I did not read Kashatus' book until I completed my manuscript as I didn't want to be influenced by his interpretation of this seminal event in Philadelphia's baseball history. As it turns out, Kashatus' major interest was not the collapse of the '64 Phillies as much as the role played by racism in ending Richie Allen's career in Philadelphia. I have since read his book and gained a few insights into the 1964 campaign. (I disagree, however, with his view that certain baseball writers in Philadelphia played an instrumental role in driving Allen out of town.)

I want to thank the following people for their help. First and foremost, my wife, Frances, who encouraged me to write the story of this event in the long, sad history of the Phillies. I first met her in August of that year, so at least one good thing came out of the 1964 season. Stephen Breedlove and Eithne Bearden of the Connolly Library of La Salle University answered my many questions and tracked down sources without which I could not have written this book. I also want to thank Sam Pino, director of the duplicating department of La Salle, for helping me to put together a polished version of this manuscript. I thank my companions at lunch, John Rooney, John Reardon and Jon Caroulis, for listening to me relive one year in Phillies history. Their suffering must have been great.

John P. Rossi
La Salle University
Philadelphia

1
Philadelphia in the 1950s

Corrupt and Contented

In 1950 the city of Philadelphia stretched for 131 square miles from the reclaimed swamps of south Philadelphia to Torresdale in the far northeast. The city was packed with block after block of neat, red brick row houses, a feature that made Philadelphia unique among the great urban areas in the nation. William Penn would not recognize his "Greene country town."[1]

A few underdeveloped areas remained within the city limits, mainly in the far northeast and far southwest. Over the next 15 years they would fill up. New developments opened within the city limits as real estate firms tried to attract some of the people fleeing to the far suburbs of southern New Jersey and Bucks and Montgomery counties north of Philadelphia.

Philadelphia's population in 1950 was 2,072,000, the first time the city reached the 2 million mark. It would hover around 2 million throughout the 1950s, dipping slowly during the decade. By 1960, its population down 50,000, Philadelphia would begin a steady decline that would reduce its population by a half million by the end of the century. The year 1960 would also see Philadelphia lose its position as the third largest city in the nation to Los Angeles, confirming a trend that first became apparent by the 1930s.

Philadelphia in the 1950s remained overwhelmingly white, mostly working and lower middle class with scattered islands of middle class professional types. A strong tradition of ethnic and racial neighborhoods remained: Italian in south Philadelphia, African American in north Philadelphia, Jewish in Strawberry Mansion and Logan, Irish in Kensington and Port Richmond, and Polish in Bridesburg. A small WASP enclave existed in Chestnut Hill in the far northwest part of the city. The minority population in 1950, largely African American, was 18.3 percent and growing. The great Puerto Rican migration had just started. They would arrive in significant numbers from the late 1950s on. White flight to the suburbs also was just beginning but would speed up throughout the decade. Philadelphia at mid-century was often described as the "northernmost southern city."

Race relations in the 1950s on the surface seemed normal. Still a form of strict segregation existed in the city, not only in its neighborhoods but also in just about every other area of public and private life: in government, in jobs, in the schools, in churches etc.

Philadelphia in the early 1950s was one of the nation's great industrial, financial and legal centers. Baldwin Locomotive Works, SKF Ball Bearings, Rohm & Haas in chemicals, the Budd Company that built car bodies for Detroit, the John B. Stetson Hat company and numerous textile factories that were dispersed throughout north Philadelphia were all thriving. The Pennsylvania Railroad and the Reading Railroad were still prosperous and linked the city to the booming industrial centers of the Northeast corridor and the Midwest. Already there were signs of trouble for the railroads as the automobile revolution of the post-war era was about to take off. In 1950 you could still park relatively easily in Center City and other parts of the town. Even parking meters were rare in most parts of the city. That was coming to an end.

Philadelphia was one of the oldest banking centers in the nation, a role that it played dating back to the founding of the first National Bank of the United States in the 1790s. The city's banking tradition was serious, sober and unimaginative. One of the leading financial establishments had a name that perfectly reflected the city's stodginess: the Corn Exchange Bank. Most of Philadelphia's working people saved their money not in the big financial houses in Center City, called Downtown, in Philadelphia but in local savings and loans, often ones with an ethnic flavor: the Polonia Federal Savings and Loan Association, the Italian Merchants Savings and Loan Association, and the Berean Savings and Loan Association (which was African American).

Philadelphia's law firms, once famous throughout the nation, retained a reputation for honesty and probity. The term "Philadelphia lawyer," originally coined in honor of one of the nation's first great lawyers in colonial times, Andrew Hamilton, had become a synonym for a shrewd advocate. The term was still widely in use—the folk singer Woody Guthrie even wrote a song (not very flattering) about "A Great

Philadelphia Lawyer." In reality, by the 1950s, the best legal talent was no longer found in the city but had long ago fled to New York or Washington. The University of Pennsylvania had a reputation for maintaining a first class law school, but it was sinking far below Harvard and Yale as the premier law school in the nation. Most of Philadelphia's lawyers went to Temple University, a vast urban complex in the middle of north Philadelphia founded by a famous late-19th-century Baptist preacher, Russell Conwell. Conwell was famous for his oration about "Acres of Diamonds" being there for the city's industrious youth willing to work hard to gather them. In the 1950s, Temple still attracted the industrious urban poor who were seeking to better themselves. The GI Bill was in the process of revolutionizing education in Philadelphia as in the rest of the nation. The city's colleges— many religious, such as St. Joseph's and La Salle — boomed in the decade of the 1950s, attracting mostly first generation students.

In sum, Philadelphia in the early 1950s was a sleepy, somewhat conservative city, a once rich dowager, nursing her resources, but with an eye for propriety, if not excitement or innovation.

The blight on Philadelphia for years had been its reputation for political corruption. "Corrupt and Contented," the term first coined by Lincoln Steffens early in the 20th century, still resonated. Philadelphia was the last of the great urban areas to remain Republican, defying the Democratic racial and ethnic tide that swept through urban America in the late 1920s and 1930s. While other cities had their "little New Deals," Philadelphia remained safely Republican, controlled by a political machine that by the 1940s was beginning to show signs of political and moral dry rot.

The days of the great Republican bosses like Boies Penrose and the Vare brothers of south Philadelphia were long over. The closest thing the Republicans had to a party boss in the years after World War II was Sheriff Aus Meehan, a fat, genial pol who was rapidly becoming an anachronism. The last Republican mayor, Barney Samuel, was a south Philadelphia stalwart and something of a genial party hack. Inarticulate with a sad face and deep dark circles under his eyes that made him look like a basset hound, he was personally honest but presided over a corrupt administration that had lost any sense of direction. Cracks in Republican dominance had begun to appear during the Depression years. Roosevelt carried the city with huge majorities in 1936, 1940 and 1944. John B. Kelly, father of Princess Grace, almost beat the Republicans in the mayoralty election of 1935. In fact, many observers believe that the

Republican machine stole the election by dumping Kelly's votes in the Delaware River, a famous Philadelphia tradition in close elections. A dozen years later Richardson Dilworth, a decorated veteran of the two world wars, ran an effective race against the entrenched Republican machine, losing to Samuel by 70,000 votes, an impressive showing for the reviving Democrats.

Philadelphia's Republican machine was notorious not only for its petty corruption but also its neglect of city services. City hall was run down, its long 19th-century corridors marred by peeling paint and overrun with party hangers-on. Dilworth's name caught the public's attention — they were "drones." The city's water supply was legendary for its odors and awful taste. Civil service was virtually nonexistent. City jobs, including the police and fire departments, were controlled and dispensed by ward leaders. Since the 1920s there had been a hold on any civic improvements. Philadelphia was in need of a complete renovation.

Then, after World War II, a reform movement emerged led by progressive Democrats like Joseph Sill Clark, Richardson Dilworth and Jim Finnegan plus a handful of liberal Republicans mortified by their party's reputation for corruption. Even the staunchly pro-business, pro-Republican daily papers, such as Walter Annenberg's shoddy morning *Inquirer* and the dull but honest *Evening Bulletin*, threw their support behind the reformers. The reformers first won control of key city offices including city treasurer and district attorney in 1949. Dilworth as district attorney used his investigative powers to expose the depths of Republican corruption in the city. The police department was revamped and professional policing adopted. Senior police officials, many of them products of the Republican machine, resigned or retired as Dilworth's probe dug deep. Some of them were charged with crimes, a couple committed suicide.

In 1951 the reformers, with Clark running for mayor, ousted the Republicans. Philadelphia finally got its "little New Deal," 20 years after most other American large cities. An urban Renaissance led by talented city architects such as Ed Bacon began that gradually transformed this sleepy metropolis. Huge construction projects sprouted all over the slumbering city. The so-called Chinese Wall that blocked access to Center City west of Broad Street was torn down. A new area named Penn Center with hotels and high-rise office buildings rose in its place. A large food distribution center was built. The first superhighway linking the city together, the Schuylkill Expressway (known to locals as the Surekill Expressway because of all the accidents that took place), opened toward the end of the decade. The decrepit area around Independence Hall was remodeled to include a large open park that was tourist friendly. In center city dark, narrow streets virtually empty after the closing of business witnessed one of the most impressive housing revivals in the nation. Modeled after colonial Philadelphia and called Society Hill, it was designed to lure young, upwardly mobile professional types to the city. It worked and made the old center of the city one of the most exciting places to live as fashionable restaurants and sprightly new businesses developed around the Society Hill core. Philadelphia was transformed and became a by-word for urban excitement in the 1950s.[2]

Philadelphia's professional sporting teams did not share the city's political success. The Philadelphia Eagles, led by their great Hall of Fame runner, Steve Van Buren, experienced great success in the late 1940s, winning two National Championships in 1948 and 1949. By the early 1950s the Eagles drifted into mediocrity. It didn't matter. At the time, professional football didn't have much of a following in the city or the nation for that matter.

The hottest football team in Philadelphia in the early 1950s was that of the University of Pennsylvania. In those days before the Ivy League did away with football scholarships, Penn attracted major competition and filled Franklin Field most Saturdays in the fall.

The pro basketball team the Philadelphia Warriors also had been successful in the late 1940s led by league scoring champ Joe Fulks. Even more than football, basketball was a minor league sport in the 1950s, with teams often playing their games in run-down arenas before small crowds.

College basketball did have a big following in the city. The rivalry among the so-called Big Five — Temple, Penn, La Salle, St. Joseph's and Villanova — was intense. In the 1950s the Big Five fielded excellent teams with talented players, many of whom, like Paul Arizin, Tom Gola and Guy Rogers, went on to play professional basketball. In the early 1950s La Salle, led by Tom Gola, won both the NCAA and the then more important NIT titles.[3]

In truth, Philadelphia had always been a baseball town. Connie Mack had produced two great baseball dynasties in the past, most recently in the years 1929–31 when great A's teams ended a Babe Ruth led Yankee reign of success. Mack's team won back-to-back World Series in 1929–30. The Depression devastated the A's and attendance sagged. Mack, chronically short of cash, had to sell off his best players, including future Hall of Famers like Jimmie Foxx, Al Simmons, Lefty Grove and Mickey Cochrane to keep the team afloat. From 1935 to 1946 the A's finished in the cellar nine times. Beginning in 1947 the A's became briefly competitive again, reaching the .500 mark for the first time since 1933. Their farm system developed some quality pitchers including Phil Marchildon, who won 19 games in 1947; Alex Kellner, a 20 game winner in his rookie season, 1949; Carl Scheib; Dick Fowler; and Lou Brissie.

Mack showed that he had not completely lost his touch. He made some shrewd purchases, including a talented shortstop in Eddie Joost and a superb defensive first baseman in Ferris Fain, who would later win batting titles in 1951 and 1952. In 1948 the A's were in a tight pennant race with the Yankees, Red Sox and Cleveland until they faded in early September. The 1948 A's record of 84 victories, good enough for a fourth place finish, was the team's best record in 16 years.

In mid-1949 they brought up pitcher Bobby Shantz, a 5'6", 139-pound southpaw. Shantz became one of the best drawing cards in the city's history, capturing the fans hearts with his gutsy style of pitching and his superb fielding skills. He would go on to win eight Gold Gloves for fielding prowess. In 1952, his greatest season, Shantz won 24 games, received the Most Valuable Player Award and was personally responsible for attracting 44 percent of the fans the A's drew that season.[4]

Shantz's success could not postpone the inevitable. The Athletics again fell on hard times. Connie Mack retired in 1950 after a half-century of managing, and his sons, Roy and Earle, took over a declining franchise. They soon drove the team to the edge of bankruptcy. One sportswriter observed that they were a rare example of the sons becoming senile before the father. In 1954, after finishing last in the American League, the team was sold and moved to Kansas City. Philadelphia was now the sole property of the Phillies.[5]

One Hundred Years in the Cellar

Someone once wrote a humorous history of the Phillies entitled *100 Years in the Cellar*. The title wasn't far off the mark. The Phillies have been in the National League since 1883 and carved out a record for futility unmatched in baseball history: only one World Championship and four pennants and more cellar finishes than any other team in baseball history.

The Phillies enjoyed a brief period of success in the mid-teens when led by their great pitcher Grover Cleveland Alexander and power-hitting outfielder Gavvy Cravath; the Phils won the pennant in 1915. They were beaten in the World Series by the Boston Red Sox four games to one. The Phillies remained competitive for two more years but then the team owner, William Baker, a former New York City Police Commissioner, began to sell off his best players. Alexander at the peak of his career — he had won 190 games in seven years with the Phillies and was just 30 years of age — went to the Cubs for two nondescript players and $60,000 in cash. Unlike Connie Mack, Baker was a rich man, but he was reluctant to dip into his own money to finance the Phillies. He also refused to make improvements in the ballpark he named after himself.

To make matters worse, Baker Bowl, nicknamed the "Dump on the Hump" because of the Reading Railroad tunnel that ran underneath center field causing a slight rise, became obsolete by the 1920s. Built in 1887 at the then astronomical cost of $100,000, it quickly became run down, reflecting the performance of the team itself. On two occasions the stands collapsed, the worst occurring in 1903. Twelve people were killed and over 200 were injured when a railing gave way as fans watched a fight in the street outside the ballpark.

Baker Bowl continued to deteriorate all through the 1920s and 1930s. The right field wall, over 60 feet high, was made of tin and rusted badly over the years. Balls that hit the wall hard would shower rust down on the right fielder. A legend has it that the ground rules for right field read as follows: over the wall a homerun, off the wall as many bases as you could get, through the wall a double. One of the signs on the right field wall advertised, "The Phillies Use Lifebuoy Soap." "Yeah, and they still stink" was the retort of the fans.[6]

The Phillies brief success in the mid-teens was followed by 30 years of futility. They finished last 16 times, lost 100 games 12 times and finished over .500 just once between 1918 and 1945. After Baker died the new Phillies owner, a local businessman with limited financial resources, Gerry Nugent, chronically was strapped for cash. Nugent ran the ball club out of his own pocket, and he was always one step ahead of the sheriff. He had practically no staff—his son and daughter helped run what was essentially a family business. Since the team drew poorly during Nugent's tenure (1932–43), he resorted to desperate measures to keep up a steady flow of income. He scheduled high school football games at the ballpark while the professional Eagles team played in Baker Bowl for three years in the 1930s. Nugent also rented the park to Negro League teams and even staged wrestling and boxing matches there. Anything for a dollar.

Nugent eventually gave up on Baker Bowl. By the late 1930s, the ballpark in the words of Red Smith, then writing one of the best sports column in the *Philadelphia Record*, "bore a striking resemblance to a run-down men's room."[7] In 1938 Nugent approached Connie Mack about moving the Phillies to Shibe Park. In July 1938 after 51 years at Baker Bowl, the Phillies became tenants of the A's. The Phillies paid Mack 10 cents for every ticket sold.[8] Given the fact that the Phillies averaged a little over 200,000 in attendance per season, the deal hardly made Mack rich. The Phils drew poorly until after World War II. They averaged just 236,000 fans during Nugent's tenure as Phillies owner. Their best one-season attendance in this period came in the war year 1943 when they drew a surprising 466,000 fans to watch the Phillies finish seventh.

Despite their financial problems, the Phillies consistently developed talented players, including future Hall of Famers Chuck Klein and Lefty O'Doul in the late 1920s. They continued to produce a steady supply of fine players throughout the 1930s, such as pitchers Claude Passeau, Kirby Higbe and Bucky Walters and hitters Dolf Camilli, Danny Litwhiler and Pinky Whitney. But financial considerations led Nugent to trade and sell them to pay the team's bills. By the early 1940s, the Phillies were the laughingstock of major league baseball. Nugent was broke, the National League had been bailing him out for years and he was forced to find a buyer for the team in 1943.

Nugent's successor was millionaire playboy William Cox, who headed a syndicate that bought the Phillies in March 1943 for approximately $240,000. Years later in his memoir, *Veeck As in Wreck*, the iconoclastic baseball owner Bill Veeck claimed that he had a deal with the National League to buy the Phillies but the League reneged when they discovered that he intended to stock the team with players from the Negro Leagues. Veeck claimed that he would not only have integrated baseball before Branch Rickey but also would have dominated the National League for years with Negro Leaguers. It is a good story but a figment of Veeck's vivid imagination.[9]

Cox proved a disaster in his own right. He knew virtually nothing about baseball but made a good move in appointing the knowledgeable Bucky Harris as manager. Unfortunately the two strong willed individuals clashed. When Cox fired Harris midway through the 1943 season, the latter told the Philadelphia baseball writers that Cox had bet on Phillies games. Judge Kenesaw Mountain Landis, in his last year as baseball commissioner, investigated and in November 1943 banned Cox from professional baseball. The Phillies needed a savior.

The Carpenter Era

In 1943 Connie Mack passed on the information that the Phillies were for sale to Robert Carpenter Jr. whose mother was a DuPont and whose father was vice president of the DuPont Company. Carpenter, then 28, had no interest in the family business. He had dabbled in sports promotion ever since his graduation from Duke University. After college, Carpenter promoted sporting events in Delaware, including boxing bouts. He also owned a professional basketball team but found his true love in baseball where he ran the Wilmington Blue Rocks of the Class B Interstate League. The Blue Rocks had a working agreement with Connie Mack's A's.

Carpenter's father, acting on Mack's information, bought the Phillies from Cox for $400,000 and put his son in charge. Young Carpenter's first act was to hire a general manager, the Hall of Fame pitcher Herb Pennock, a fellow Delawarian and then serving as director of the minor leagues for the Boston Red Sox. Pennock was the first GM in the Phillies' history. Carpenter told Pennock that the first priority was to "build up the farm system. We are not going to beat anybody's brains out by trying to get a good club right off the bat. But we are going to start working for one systematically."[10] At the time the Phillies had no farm system to speak of. They had a working agreement with just one team, Trenton.

Acting on a five-year plan and using Carpenter's ample funds, Pennock went about building an organization for the Phillies, something the team never had. By 1950 the Phillies had 11 teams in their system including a Triple A franchise in Toronto.

When Carpenter took over the Phillies, they had three quality players: outfielder Ron Northey in the majors and catcher Andy Seminick and outfielder Del Ennis in the minors. Pennock hired scouts and began immediately signing young players. Before his untimely death in January 1948 at 54, Pennock shelled out $1,250,000 of Carpenter's bonus money securing future stars such as Richie Ashburn, Granny Hamner, Curt Simmons, Robin Roberts, Willie Jones and Stan Lopata.

The Phillies gradually became respectable, rising to sixth place in 1946 and drawing one million fans to Shibe Park, the first time any Philadelphia team had broken the million mark. In 1947 and 1948, they finished tied for seventh and sixth place, respectively, but showed signs of improvement. Older players like Dutch Leonard, Eddie Miller, Jim Tabor and Oscar Judd were let go and replaced by young blood from the farm system. Hamner, Roberts, Curt Simmons and Richie Ashburn became regulars in 1948.

The next year guided by Eddie Sawyer, a young manager Pennock hired from the Yankee organization, the Phillies won 81 games and finished in third place, their highest finish since 1917. Toward the end of the 1949 season, Robin Roberts relates that some of the Phillies players decided that the team had a legitimate chance of winning the pennant the next year. Sawyer thought the same thing.[11]

1950 was the miracle year for the Phillies. The Whiz Kids, as they were christened by the baseball writers, captured the heart of the city and shocked the baseball world by beating out the more highly regarded Dodgers, Cardinals and Braves for the pennant. Behind great seasons by Roberts who became the team's first 20 game winner since Alexander, Del Ennis who led the league in RBIs and Jim Konstanty who appeared in a record 74 games in relief, winning 16 and saving 22, the Phillies seized first place in July beating back challenges from the Cardinals and the Braves.

Despite a near total collapse in September — they had a five game lead over the Dodgers with just eight remaining — they won the last game of the season to capture the pennant. Roberts, pitching on just two days rest, beat Don Newcombe 4–1 in 10 innings behind Dick Sisler's three run homer in one of the most dramatic games in Phillies history.

Philadelphians who hadn't seen good baseball in years were mad about the Phillies. A record 1,200,000 fans turned out to see the team. The World Series was a let down as Casey Stengel's vaunted Bronx Bombers won four straight games as the Phillies' bats suddenly went cold. Still the games were all close — three were one-run victories. The Phillies' pitching staff, exhausted from their struggle with the Dodgers, managed to hold the Yankees to 11 runs and a team batting average of .222. Even this four-game sweep by the New York Yankees in the World Series couldn't dim the enthusiasm that 1950 engendered.

Roberts and many other Phillies expected the team to win several other pennants and compete in the National League for the foreseeable future. But it wasn't to be. The Phillies slipped to fifth place in 1951 and dropped out of contention for a decade. Other than Ashburn who hit .344, Jones who had a decent year and Roberts who won 20 games again, the Whiz Kids were awful in '51. The team's collapse was personified by the fate of Mike Goliat. After helping win the pennant in 1950 by solidifying the infield by taking over an unfamiliar position, second base, Goliat slumped to .225 in 1951. He was sent back to the minors and never played again for the Phillies: another example of too much success, too early.

Later Sawyer would argue that the team peaked too soon. "We built the club to win in 1951 or 1952," he said. "If it is possible to say that you can win a pennant too early ... then we did." The Phillies problems were more deep-seated then just peaking too soon. Part of their difficulties in the 1950s could be traced to a residual racism that plagued the Phillies for years. Neither Carpenter nor Pennock had gone after the African American talent that became available once Jackie Robinson had ended 60 years of baseball segregation. As the National League was transformed by an infusion of players from the Negro Leagues, the Phillies remained pure white. They were the last team in the National League, for instance, to go to the World Series without an African American player on their roster. The Phillies also have the unenviable distinction of being the last team in the Senior Circuit to integrate. Richie Ashburn, a shrewd judge of baseball realities, believed that the Phillies' failure to sign good African American players largely was responsible for the team's decline in the 1950s.[12]

Carpenter, who had run the team since Pennock's death, and Sawyer both overestimated the Phillies' talent level. In many ways 1950 was a freak season with key players having career years. Konstanty, for example, would never approach his success as a reliever again. Curt Simmons, who was the leading Phillies pitcher before going into military service because of the Korean War, returned to the Phillies in 1952 but never achieved the greatness predicted for him. When he went into the army, Sawyer believed he was destined to be a better pitcher than Roberts.[13]

Sawyer was released in mid-1952. The farm system that had been so productive under Pennock dried up as Carpenter proved to be an ineffective general manager. The Phillies' minor league system did not produce a single everyday player until 1957. In 1954 Carpenter recognized his mistake and hired Roy Hamey from the Pirates to take over as GM.

Hamey was supposedly a skilled baseball administrator and he began rebuilding the farm system. But he made a series of disastrous transactions that doomed the Phillies for years. In 1954 he traded catcher Smoky Burgess, who had hit .368, to Cincinnati for outfielder Jim Greengrass. Greengrass had bad legs—he suffered from phlebitis—and never produced for the Phillies. Burgess went on to have a distinguished career with Cincinnati and Pittsburgh for another dozen years. Two years after getting rid of Burgess, Hamey also traded Del Ennis, the teams best RBI producer, to the Cardinals for outfielder Rip Repulski who put in two mediocre seasons for the Phillies.

Hamey's worst Phillies trade was his last. In 1958 he sent pitcher Jack Sanford who had won 19 games in his rookie season, 1957, and led the National League in strikeouts to the Giants for pitcher Ruben Gomez and catcher Valmy Thomas. In his one season with the Phillies, Thomas hit .200 with one homerun and exactly seven runs batted in. Gomez was equally bad. He won three and lost 11 in two seasons with the Phillies. Sanford on the other hand went on to have a distinguished career with the Giants, winning 24 games in 1962 and helping them win the pennant that year. Hamey was let go in 1959. During his tenure the team had not finished above .500 once.

The Phillies dropped to last place in 1958, the first time that had happened since 1945. Carpenter was determined to take drastic action. After firing Hamey, he went out and got one of the most successful general managers in baseball, John Quinn. Carpenter's reasoning was simple: "I wanted the best." In Quinn he got one with a record of success.

Quinn had spent over a decade with Boston, then the Milwaukee Braves and oversaw the development of a franchise that won three pennants and one World Championship. He had overseen a minor league system that produced talent, such as Eddie Matthews, Del Crandall, and Wes Covington, and he had been one of the first baseball executives to see the potential in the African American athletes. He got a young shortstop from the Negro Leagues named Henry Aaron who would become a key figure for pushing the Braves over the top in the National League in the mid-1950s. Carpenter's orders to Quinn were simple: rebuild the Phillies. The task would prove fascinating and ultimately tragic for the team and the city.

2

The End of the Whiz Kids

John Quinn

A case could be made that when Carpenter talked about getting the best general manager in baseball in John Quinn that is exactly what he got. At the very least he was the best GM in the National League at a time when great general managers like Gabe Paul, Buzzy Bavasi, and Bing Devine were molding pennant contenders. Carpenter was tired of the Phillies' mediocrity over the last five years and finally seems to have grasped that the Whiz Kid era was gone for good. As a result, Quinn came to the Phillies with a virtual free hand to revive a franchise in desperate straits.[1]

John Quinn was a baseball lifer, a hard living, hard drinking Irishman who grew up around the game he loved. His father was the president of the Braves for years and had schooled his son in every phase of the game. The young Quinn became secretary to his father and eventually replaced him as the man who made the baseball decisions for the Braves.

The Boston Braves were one of baseball's orphans—a team that constantly was overshadowed by their more glamorous and better financed rivals, the Red Sox. In their long history in the National League, the Braves had won only one pennant and one World Series. The 1914 so-called Miracle Braves team had gone from last place on July 4th to win the pennant and then defeated a heavily favored Philadelphia Athletics team in the World Series. Years of mediocrity followed and the Braves didn't even have a "Curse of the Bambino" to give them a sense of destiny denied. In fact, they got the Babe for a few games in 1935 to add some glamour to an otherwise awful franchise. But the Babe was old and quit a month into the season. The Braves' ambitious owner,

Judge Emil Fuchs, had lured Ruth to the Braves with the promise of taking over as manager in the future. Fuchs had no intention of making Ruth manager. He wanted him solely for his public relations value.

When John Quinn succeeded his father as GM in 1945 at the age of 37, he immediately began constructing a pennant contender. First he hired Billy Southworth, the highly successful manager of the great Cardinal teams of the early 1940s. Under Southworth, improvement immediately took place. The Braves finished fourth in 1946 and third the next season as Quinn quietly built a solid club to compete with the National League's two dominant teams, the Cardinals and the Dodgers.

Building on the nucleus of established Braves players such as pitchers Johnny Sain and Warren Spahn and outfielder Tommy Holmes, Quinn made a series of moves that turned the Braves into pennant winners in 1948. He got third baseman Bob Elliot after the 1946 season from the Pirates, bought slugging outfielder Jeff Heath from the Browns, drafted Al Dark off the campus of LSU and got Eddie Stanky from the Dodgers where he had become expendable when Jackie Robinson moved to his natural position, second base, after the 1947 season.

Along with solid players such as first baseman Earl Torgeson, catcher Phil Masi and veteran pitchers like Bill Voiselle, the Braves fielded a competitive team going into the 1948 season.

Quinn's 1948 Braves, the team of "Spahn and Sain and pray for rain," easily beat out the Dodgers and Cardinals for the pennant only to lose the World Series to Lou Boudreau's Cleveland Indians four games to two. Boston's margin of victory in the National League, 6½ games, was the Senior Circuit's biggest until the Dodgers won by 13 games in 1953.

The Braves slipped badly over the next few years. Southworth had a serious drinking problem — he had never recovered from the death of his son in World War II. After a poor performance in 1949 when the team finished in fourth place with a losing record, Quinn broke up the team. He made one of his few bad trades as he sought to upgrade the offense. He sent Dark and Stanky to the New York Giants for outfielders Willard Marshall and Sid Gordon. The trade made the Giants a pennant contender and did nothing for the Braves. By 1952 the team wound up in seventh place, 32 games out of first. The Braves also fell further behind the Ted Williams led Red Sox in fan popularity in Boston and the New England area in general. In 1952 the Braves drew a little over 200,000 fans, a decline of one million since the 1948 pennant-winning year. The Braves' days in Boston were numbered and their owner, Lou Perini, was

2—The End of the Whiz Kids

ready to pull up stakes for the lucrative Midwest market of Milwaukee. During spring training 1953 the Braves surprised everyone by moving to Milwaukee, the first franchise shift since professional baseball became stabilized in 1903.[2]

Quinn had started retooling the Braves once it became clear that the 1948 team was a one-year wonder. He spent Perini's money lavishly on bonus babies, for example, paying $75,000 for a high school pitching phenom named Johnny Antonelli who would go on to have a solid career with the Braves and the San Francisco Giants. He also integrated the Braves a decade before the Red Sox added an African American player. Quinn bought Negro League star outfielder Sam Jethroe from the Dodgers in 1950 for $100,000, a huge sum to pay for an unproven player in those days. Jethroe was the first of a long line of African American players Quinn brought into the Braves organization. Jethroe hit well for two seasons and led the National League in stolen bases in his first two years in the majors. But he was 32 when he reached the majors and developed eye problems in 1952 that eventually ended his career.

The fact that Quinn was willing to take a chance on Jethroe says a great deal about his approach to baseball. He wanted to win and wasn't afraid to do something unusual. Old fashioned in many ways, always attired in a conservative suit and tie and very tight with the owner's money, Quinn didn't suffer from racial prejudice. He valued players for their ability, not the color of their skin. It didn't hurt that many of the players from the Negro Leagues came cheap. They were eager to play in the major leagues.

While phasing out veterans like Holmes and trading established players like Johnny Sain, Quinn gradually transformed the Braves. The 1952 team finished 25 games under .500 at 64–89 but it included the nucleus of a new Braves dynasty. Twenty-one-year-old Eddie Matthews took over at third base; Johnny Logan became the regular shortstop that year and a young Lou Burdette came over from the Yankees in the Sain deal to join Warren Spahn on the mound. Always a shrewd trader, Quinn made one of his best deals when he got Joe Adcock from Cincinnati for a journeyman infielder Rocky Bridges. Adcock would hold down first base for the Braves for ten years.

In 1953 with the Braves now in Milwaukee, Quinn's new team shocked the baseball world by winning 92 games and finished in second place. They would never finish lower than third or win fewer than 85 games during the rest of his tenure as GM.

The Braves farm system steadily produced key players such as pitcher Bob Buhl and outfielders Wes Covington and Bill Bruton and Hank Aaron, while Quinn filled gaps in the team by trades. Along with the Adcock deal with Cincinnati, he got Red Schoendienst from the Giants and outfielder Andy Pafko from the Dodgers. All three filled gaps that the Braves had and by the mid-1950s enabled them to overtake the Dodgers as the best team in the National League. The Pafko deal also was designed to placate the large Slavic population in and around Milwaukee. Pafko was among the most popular players on the Braves in the mid-1950s and a hero to the Slavic community.

In 1957 Quinn's Braves won the pennant and beat the Yankees in the World Series with ex-Yankee Burdette winning three games. The Braves became the first non–New York team to win the National League pennant since the Whiz Kids in 1950. They won the pennant again the next season only to lose the World Series when the Yankees overcame a 3–1 deficit to win a narrow victory in game seven. Quinn's work with the Braves in the mid-1950s is the reason Carpenter wanted him for the Phillies.

Carpenter knew what he was getting in Quinn — a thoroughly professional baseball man. He also knew what to expect, a thorough housecleaning of the Phillies, including those Whiz Kids who Carpenter was so fond of. Quinn was honest with the press after his hiring. He told them that trades alone couldn't remake the Phillies. "The real basis of a team," he said, "comes from its farms." And yet trade he did. Between 1959 and the beginning of the 1964 season he made a total of 41 trades, in most cases sending veterans for younger players. The transformation of the Phillies took a long time to pay off.[3]

The Phillies team Quinn took over was in a free fall. It had finished in the cellar in 1958 for the first time since 1945 although they had one of the highest percentages of any cellar team in National League history. The Whiz Kids simply were old and worn out. Hamey had done a decent job in keeping the farm system afloat. In 1959 seven of the eight Phillies farm teams finished in the first division in their leagues and three won their pennants, something which boded well for the future (*Sporting News Official Guide*, 1960, p. 191).[4] The farm system had begun producing new blood in the mid-1950s, but it had not proven enough to revive the team. Players like Harry Anderson, Ed Bouchee, and Don Cardwell who showed promise failed to develop. Bouchee who had been Rookie of the Year in 1957 was arrested shortly after the season on a morals charge. He missed part of the 1958 season, and when he returned he failed to achieve the greatness predicted for him. Cardwell was a baffling case. He possessed a powerful arm and a great fastball but something was missing in his makeup. He never became a consistent winner in the big leagues. Later, Gene Mauch would use one of his more wounding phrases to describe Cardwell "as a Southern gentleman and a losing pitcher."

There wasn't much Quinn could do about the 1959 season. The Phillies that year finished in last place with their lowest winning percentage since 1947. They were last in the National League in runs scored, next to last in homers and last in fielding. Not a single regular hit .300. Bouchee led the team in batting with a .285 average, while Wally Post, who the Phillies had gotten from the Reds for pitcher Harvey Haddix, hit 22 homers and drove in 94 runs while hitting just .254. No Phillie ranked in the top five in any offensive category.

The pitching staff was awful. Only Gene Conley, who Quinn had rescued from the Braves, finished with a better than .500 record. Roberts won 15 games but lost 17, while rookie Jim Owens showed some potential splitting 24 decisions. Ray Semproch, who had won 13 games for the Phillies in 1958, was completely ineffective and dropped to 3–10, while Gomez finished with a 3–8 record and an ERA of 6.10. The bullpen ranked last in the National League in saves largely because Dick Farrell had a terrible year winning just one game while saving six.

Harry Anderson, after hitting .300 in 1958, saw his batting average drop by 60 points, while Ashburn, the batting champion in 1958, was even worse — his average declined from .350 to .266. In 654 times at bat he drove in 20 runs. Anderson never again recaptured the form he had displayed in 1958. A one-dimensional player only interested in hitting, manager Sawyer warned him that if he ever stopped hitting he would be out of baseball in no time. That is exactly what happened. After the Phillies traded him to the Reds in 1961, Anderson was back in the minors a year later.

'Sparky' Anderson, brought in from the Dodger organization in a trade for Rip Repulski to play second base, hit just .218 in his only major league season. Some idea of his futility can be gauged from the fact that in 152 games Anderson had only 12 extra base hits. The Phillies' collapse in 1959 was a genuine team effort.

Midway through the season, Quinn started unloading the remaining Whiz Kids. Willie Jones and Granny Hamner were sent to the Cleveland Indians for little more than cash. At the end of spring training, Quinn made his first major trade, sending Stan Lopata, who was finished as a regular catcher, to the Milwaukee Braves for a handful of players including pitcher Gene Conley.

In December 1959 Quinn traded Richie Ashburn, one of the most popular of the Whiz Kids and something of an icon in Philadelphia, to the Chicago Cubs for pitcher John Buzhardt and infielders Jim Woods and Al Dark. It was clear that there were no untouchables on the Phillies now save perhaps Robin Roberts. Roberts was Bob Carpenter's favorite player and the greatest pitcher in Phillies history since Grover Cleveland Alexander. Carpenter couldn't bear to part with him. Roberts was the symbol of the Whiz Kids' greatness to Carpenter as well as a reminder of what he and Pennock had accomplished. Roberts' achievement of 15 victories was a remarkable performance for a team that played as poorly as the Phillies did that season. But since his last 20 victory season in 1955, Roberts had lost 11 more games than he had won. His days in Philadelphia were numbered.

After the 1959 season Quinn began the wholesale revamping of the Phillies. Following the Ashburn trade, Quinn sent the best player on the 1959 team, third baseman Gene Freese, to the Chicago White Sox for a young, untested outfielder, John Callison. Freese had led the Phillies in homers with 23 in only 400 times at bat and had hit five pinch homers, one shy of the National League record. Among his 23 homers were three grand slams. He was, however, a terrible fielder and led the league in errors, most of them on throws that wound up in the stands behind first base.

Callison who was just 20 was a highly regarded minor league player, often compared to the young Mickey Mantle, but he had only played a handful of games at the major league level. The trade that was unpopular at the time in Philadelphia was another sign that Quinn was not afraid to take dramatic action.

The Phillies team that went to spring training in 1960 bore little relation to the 1959 squad. Only Bouchee among the 1959 regulars made the 1960 team, a remarkable turnover in one year and a sign of how low the Phillies had sunk. And Bouchee's stock had fallen since his rookie year and his trouble with the law. The Phillies brought a large number of new players to camp including their highly regarded hitting prospect, first baseman Frank "Pancho" Herrara. Outfield candidates included Callison and newcomers Tony Curry, Ken Walters, Bobby Del Greco and B.G. Smith. The days of Wally Post and Harry Anderson were numbered. Del Greco, Walters and Smith had failed in previous major league trials but the Phillies were desperate and hoping to strike gold with one of them. Alvin Dark was supposed to play third, while newcomer Ruben Amaro, acquired from the Cardinals for outfielder Chuck Essegian, was slated to take over at shortstop. "Sparky" Anderson was released and failed to catch on with any other team — a sign of how highly his baseball skills were regarded. Sawyer, lacking a second baseman, started the ungazelle-like 6'3" 230-pound Herrara there. He looked like an elephant roaming the infield. Playing Herrara at second base should have been a warning that Sawyer had lost interest in managing. The move made no sense.

Only the pitching staff bore any resemblance to the 1959 team. The starters would be Roberts, newcomer Buzhardt, and 12 game winners Jim Owens and Gene Conley. Owens, nicknamed "the Bear," was a highly regarded product of the Phillies farm system. Unfortunately he was something of a hard head with a flair for the fast life. He never fulfilled the promise he showed in 1959 and never won more than five games in any season after 1959. He arrived in spring training out of shape and struggled throughout the 1960 season.

Conley also could be difficult to deal with. A fine professional basketball player, the 6'9" Conley was also a talented pitcher whose inconsistency drove managers mad. He would pitch well one season and then lose intensity the next. In a career that spanned 11 seasons, he won in double figures five times while having three years where he lost in double figures. Eventually he would clash with the Phillies management and demand a trade after the 1960 season. Buzhardt never developed into the pitcher that the Phillies expected although he did win 13 games for the Chicago White Sox in 1965. Overall, the 1960 Phillies were a blend of rookies, re-treads, has beens and never weres.

Quinn had inherited Eddie Sawyer who Carpenter had brought back in July 1958 in a desperate effort to revive the Whiz Kid image. The players liked Sawyer who was quiet and always trying to find something positive to say about them and their play. Quinn became convinced that he had lost interest in managing. He appeared to be going through the motions in 1959 and Quinn soon began looking for a replacement.

When the 1960 season opened, the Phillies lost to the Cincinnati Reds by a 9–4 score. The Phillies looked outclassed in every phase of the game. The next day Sawyer quit as manager saying, "I am 49 years old and want to live to see 50."

Gene Mauch

Quinn was ready. He had already decided on Sawyer's replacement — Gene Mauch, manager of the Minneapolis Millers of the American

Association. For Mauch, just 34 years old, the job of major league manager was what he wanted ever since he realized that he lacked the skills of a major league player.[5]

Mauch was born in Salinas, Kansas in November 1925 but moved to California when his family's bakery business failed during the Depression. A good athlete, he was signed by the Dodgers during World War II as Branch Rickey stocked his roster with potential talent for the postwar era. Mauch made his major league debut in 1944 as an 18-year-old shortstop. Never a regular, he was in and out of the majors from 1944 to 1957, amassing a grand total of 737 plate appearances with six different teams: the Dodgers, Cubs, Cardinals, Pirates, Braves and Red Sox. He also was traded five times. Like so many marginal players, Mauch became a keen student of the game. He would sit on the bench beside the manager and study his tactics, bombarding him constantly with questions: why did you do that, why make that move?

Among those who influenced him was Dodger manager Leo Durocher. For years Mauch wore number 2 in homage to his idol. His managerial style, however, was different from Durocher, a notorious hunch player. Mauch preferred "little ball" emphasizing the bunt, the hit and run while playing for one run. He believed that if you play for one run you sometimes end up with more. Mauch also learned a great deal from other managers, in particular Billy Southworth of the Braves. Southworth warned him that one fatal mistake a manager can make is to fall in love with his players. Mauch largely avoided that in his first seasons with the Phillies but in 1964 he fell into that trap with terrible consequences for the Phillies and for himself.

In 1953 at the tender age of 27 Mauch was named manager of the Atlanta Crackers on the recommendation of John Quinn. But Mauch failed miserably, engaging in constant battles with the umpires and often losing control of himself. He realized that he wasn't mature enough for managing. "I expected everybody to play with as much dedication as I had.... I was impatient. I ranted and raved. I fought umpires. I fought opponents. I fought my own players. I determined that my ideas were sound, but I wasn't prepared to put them into execution at the age of twenty-seven."[6] As he later admitted "the best thing that ever happened to me was that of managing Atlanta. It took that to teach me how much I didn't know about baseball."[7]

During his second job as manager with the Minneapolis Millers in 1958, Mauch finally mastered self-control. He won the Junior World Series in 1958 and the American Association pennant the next year. Both seasons he was voted the League's Manager of the Year. He lost the Junior World Series in 1959 to a fine Havana team from the International League. The games in Havana drew huge crowds for minor league baseball including Cuban dictator Fidel Castro and many of his sub-machine gun carrying soldiers. By this time Mauch was regarded as potential major league managerial material.

Quinn wanted a young manager, a knowledgeable baseball man, who would help him turn the Phillies into a contender. When Mauch took over he told the press that he only had one ambition: "to become the best manager in baseball." He made few changes at first saying "I wanted to see for myself what was necessary and what wasn't, see what kind of fellows these guys were."[8] For about a month he stood in the dugout — Mauch never sat on the bench in his managerial career — incessantly smoking and observing the material he was given to manage. He wasn't impressed with what he saw.

Mauch's first move was to get Herrara off second base before he killed himself or some unfortunate base runner. On May 13 at Mauch's urging Quinn sent first baseman Bouchee and pitcher Don Cardwell to the Cubs for second baseman Tony Taylor and backup catcher, Cal Neeman. Mauch now had a real second baseman.

The 24-year-old Cuban born Taylor was in his third year in the majors and had shown flashes of brilliance especially in the field. He wasn't bad with the bat either, hitting .280 and scoring 96 runs in 1959. But he had gotten fat and complacent. Mauch saw something in the flashy Cuban and gradually convinced him to take off weight and play to his potential. As Quinn noted: Mauch somehow got Taylor "to get rid of the chorus girl's waistline."[9] Taylor went on to become the Phillies regular second baseman for 11 years as well as one of the most popular players in the team history. It was typical of Quinn and Mauch's lack of racial prejudice that they traded two white players for a black Cuban.

The trade of Bouchee enabled Mauch to move Herrara to first where, despite his size, he proved a surprisingly graceful fielder. He went on to lead the Phillies in 1960 in homers and RBIs.

Neeman also proved a valuable addition. He stabilized a Phillies' catching situation that was chaotic. The three regular catchers from the 1959 team — Carl Sawatski, Valmy Thomas and Joe Lonnett — had been released. Mauch had inherited two rookies, Clay Dalrymple and Jim Coker. Both were raw, and Coker never developed into an everyday backstop. Mauch saw something in Dalrymple and began working with him on his catching, eventually helping him become a fine defensive backstop. The Mauch-Dalyrmple relationship was a rocky one. Mauch rode Dalyrmple hard, demanding that he become a take-charge backstop. Dalrymple resented Mauch's interference at first but then came to realize that it was a sign that he wanted him to be a team leader on the field. Dalyrmple hit .272 in 1960 and went on to become the Phillies regular catcher for the next seven years.

During the 1960 season Mauch tested the players he had inherited, trying to find who had major league ability. Some, like outfielder Tony Curry, could hit but were a defensive liability. Others, like Bobby Del Greco and Ken Walters, could catch the ball but couldn't hit. Midway through the 1960 season the Phillies brought Ruben Amaro up from the minors, and he and Taylor stabilized the middle of the infield. Amaro proved to be a brilliant defensive shortstop, a smooth fielder who seemed to glide to the ball. For the first time since the glory days of Granny Hamner, the Phillies had a solid defensive shortstop. Along with Herrara at first, the Phillies now had three quarters of the infield in decent shape.

Third base was a constant problem. Originally Quinn believed that Al Dark would hold down third until the Phillies developed a replacement. But at age 37 Dark was finished as an everyday player and was traded on June 23 to the Braves for a rookie third baseman, Joe Morgan, who later went on to manage the Red Sox. Morgan was installed at third but he also flopped badly, hitting just .133. Jim Woods, who the Phillies had gotten from Cubs in the Ashburn trade, also was tried at third but he too didn't pan out. All told, the Phillies would use eight different players at third base in 1960, none would play more than a third of the team's games. The hot corner would remain a problem area for the Phillies until Mauch installed Richie Allen there before the 1964 season.

Quinn and Mauch tinkered more successfully with the outfield. They both liked the potential of Callison who showed flashes of ability both at bat and in the field. The Phillies started by playing him in left, but in 1961 Mauch would move him to right field to take advantage of his powerful throwing arm. Callison would become one of the best right fielders in a league rich in talent at that position — Frank Robinson, Hank Aaron, Roberto Clemente, to mention just a few. Callison would lead the National League in assists for four consecutive years 1962–65, no mean feat in a league in which Willie Mays was in his prime. Callison also developed into a fine hitter. In 1962 he hit .300, and he would remain the team's top power threat for four years until a mysterious slump saw his offensive numbers fade.

2—The End of the Whiz Kids

On June 15 Quinn traded Harry Anderson and Wally Post to the Cincinnati Reds for 23-year-old outfielder Tony Gonzalez, a young black Cuban who was a better than average fielder. Gonzalez had shown signs of offensive talent — he batted lefthanded but had surprising power to the opposite field. In 1962 when he hit 20 homers, 17 of them went to left field. Mauch knew him from the 1959 Junior World Series and liked his style of play. Gonzalez started in right field but Mauch eventually moved him to center. By mid-season the Phillies now had two thirds of a decent outfield in Callison and Gonzalez.

The pitching staff was a disaster area. Robin Roberts at 34 led the staff with 12 victories but lost 16 games with a high ERA. He and Mauch never hit if off. In an oft-quoted remark Mauch grumbled that Roberts threw like Betsy Ross. Perhaps Mauch felt threatened by Roberts, the last of the Whiz Kids and a favorite of Carpenter and the Philadelphia fans. "Turk" Farrell bounced back from his terrible 1959 season and had a good year winning 10, saving a handful of others. But Farrell had a serious flaw. He and his pitching pals, Jack Meyer, Jim "Bear" Owens, and Seth Morehead, caused Mauch no end of headaches in 1960. Known as the "Dalton Gang" they caroused their way through the National League, tearing up bars and hotel rooms. Meyer trashed his hotel room one night after a drinking bout, injured his back seriously and was fined $1,200 by Quinn. The fine constituted 9 percent of Meyer's yearly salary and was the highest in baseball history.[10] Other than Farrell, none of the "Dalton Gang" amounted to much. Mauch was unable to harness the potential of Owens, a pitcher of considerable talent. Eventually the entire gang was traded away.

Aside from Farrell and Roberts no Phillies pitcher won in double figures. A couple showed flashes of brilliance, especially left-hander Chris Short and the Phillies prized pitching prospect, right-hander Art Mahaffey. Short was young, just 23 years old, and very immature but possessed a powerful arm. Mauch nurtured him carefully, trying to discover whether he was better suited to starting or relieving. Mahaffey, just 22, came up to the Phillies midway through the 1960 season and won seven games with a low 2.31 ERA. He threw a moving fastball and had one of the best pickoff moves in baseball. In his first game against the Cardinals, the first two batters, Curt Flood and Bill White, got on and Mahaffey picked them both off first base. Mahaffey was something of a paradox. He had a strong arm and immense potential but had a tendency to doubt himself. In his first three years with the Phillies he won 37 games, the same number as his almost exact contemporary, Juan

Marichal. Thereafter Mahaffey, plagued by arm miseries, won just 22 more games, while Marichal won 206 more and went on to the Hall of Fame. Mahaffey's failure to develop was a source of conflict between him and Mauch.

To get some idea of how bad the Phillies pitching was, consider that the combined record of the team's starters was 36–63. Other than Jim Owens, who had a terrible ERA of 5.04, the starters at the least kept the Phillies in the game. But weak offense and shaky defense meant that the Phillies lost most close games.

The Phillies started out decently in 1960. They split their first ten games and reached the first division on April 24 for their highest position for the year. After finishing the month of April in sixth place, the Phillies slowly sank toward the cellar. They were in and out of seventh place until the end of August when they permanently settled into the basement. Their problem was typical of a young team — inconsistency. They had too many losing streaks, including one of six games and one seven gamer. They made rookie blunders and suffered from weak offense all year, finishing dead last in hitting with an average of .239 and only 99 home runs. You had to go back to 1942 to find a Phillies team that hit for a lower average than the 1960 squad.

The weak offense helps explain why the Phillies were shut out 20 times. Twice they were shut out in three consecutive games. The most embarrassing of these streaks came in early May when the Phillies lost back-to-back-to-back 1–0 games. Sam Jones of the Giants shut them out on May 11. Jack Sanford duplicated that feat the next night, beating Roberts while Jim O'Toole of the Reds beat Buzhardt in the next game. The three 1–0 whitewashings tied a major league record for offensive futility. The Phillies also managed to lose seven doubleheaders during the season.

There were no highlights for the Phillies in 1960. The entire season was a grim trek to oblivion. Perhaps the team's best moment came early in May. On Sunday, May 14, while playing the Reds in a doubleheader, the Phillies built up a commanding lead in the first game behind Conley. In the top of the eighth inning, Reds pitcher Raul Sanchez hit three of the first four batters he faced including Conley. Mauch charged the mound, hit Sanchez with a roundhouse right and set off one of the biggest brawls in Phillies' history. In a matter of seconds the infield was covered by players, rolling on the ground, punching each other. The best match of the day was staged by Conley and Reds second baseman, Billy Martin. While the 5'11" Martin tried to slug Conley, the 6'9" Conley held

2—The End of the Whiz Kids

him at arm's length while pummeling him with overhand rights. Martin lost a unanimous decision. Roberts and Frank Robinson also brawled, with Roberts winding up with his uniform in shreds.

It was clearly a ploy by Mauch to unite a young team that lacked any sense of identity, and it seemed to work for a time as the Phillies won seven of their next 11 games. Reality soon took over. The Phillies lost 10 of 11 games after their brief spurt, finishing the month of May with a 9–18 record.

They righted themselves briefly and played almost .500 baseball until the All-Star break when their record was 34–47. In July they lost three more shutouts but managed to stay just ahead of the struggling Cubs until a five game losing streak and a four gamer dropped them in the cellar for good on August 20th when Bob Buhl of the Braves shut them out in yet another 1–0 game. From that point they won just 14 games and lost 26 to finish with 59–95 for the team's worst record since 1945.

The 1960 team finished in the cellar for the third consecutive year with six fewer victories than in 1959. Yet by some standards, the 1960 team was an improvement. The 1959 squad had no future; the 1960 team did although it would take another difficult season before this would become apparent.

While the Phillies were struggling, football became the hot sport in the city. The Eagles, after almost a decade of incompetence, suddenly began to develop under the guidance of their shrewd coach, Earl "Greasy" Neale. In 1960 with veteran quarterback Norm Van Brocklin leading the way, the Eagles shocked the football world by winning the National Football League Championship. They beat future Hall of Fame coach Vince Lombardi's Green Bay Packers, 17–13, at Franklin Field in Philadelphia. It was the first major professional sports victory in the city since the Whiz Kids in 1950.

With the Phillies struggling the Eagles seemed destined to hold the sports limelight in the city for the foreseeable future. It didn't happen. Van Brocklin had expected to take over as coach in 1961. When the job instead went to assistant coach Nick Skorich, Van Brocklin left in a huff. His loss hurt the team in a number of ways. He was popular with the press and public and respected by his teammates. Skorich was a competent assistant but lacked the overall skills of a head coach. Moreover, he was a dour individual who never clicked with the difficult and demanding Philadelphia fans or media. After one more winning season the Eagles faded rapidly until, by the mid-1960s, they were one of the worst franchises in the NFL. Pro football would remain an orphan sport in Philadelphia until the arrival of Dick Vermeil in the late 1970s when it would surge to the front as the city's premier sport, a position it has held ever since.

Going into the 1961 season Quinn made few changes in the Phillies' roster. He and Mauch were counting on Mahaffey, Buzhardt and Short to continue to develop and Roberts to have one good year left in him. Quinn traded a disgruntled Gene Conley, who couldn't get along with Mauch, to the Red Sox for Frank Sullivan. Sullivan, a former number one starter for the Red Sox, was coming off two poor seasons in a row in which he won 15 games versus 27 defeats, figures that fit in nicely with the Phillies' starters. But Sullivan was only 31, kept himself in shape and had strung together five consecutive winning seasons in the late 1950s. Quinn and Mauch hoped a change of scenery would help him. It didn't. In two seasons with the Phillies, Sullivan, who once described himself as in the twilight of a mediocre career, compiled a terrible record of 9 wins versus 32 losses.

The Phillies also were hoping that everyday players such as Callison, Gonzalez, Herrara, Dalyrmple, Taylor and Amaro would continue to mature. Some of the team's obvious flops in 1960 were released or sent back to the minors, including pitchers Ruben Gomez, Hank Mason, and Taylor Phillips and infielder Ted Lepcio, whom Sawyer had called the worst looking major leaguer he had ever seen. The Phillies promoted no one from their minor league system in 1961, a sure sign that their farms were not ready to begin restocking the major league roster. No rookie made the 1961 team. For most of the year, Quinn had a revolving door as veterans were brought in, found wanting and let go. Among them were Elmer Valo (former A's great), the Phillies' former shortstop Joe Koppe and the legendary catcher Clarence "Choo Choo" Coleman, who pounded the ball that year at .128 average. In all, 38 players, most of them forgettable also rans, wore a Phillies uniform in 1961.

Early in the 1961 campaign, Quinn sent Tony Curry back to the minors for polishing. He never played for the Phillies again although he got a brief trial with Cleveland in 1966. In May Quinn traded reliever Dick Farrell to the Dodgers and got two regulars in return: outfielder Don Demeter and third baseman Charlie Smith. Smith became the regular third baseman and drove in 50 runs for them, the most by any Phillies third baseman since Willie Jones in 1957. Still it was clear that Smith had limitations both defensively and offensively. The Phillies traded him after just one season.

Demeter proved a valuable addition. He took over in center field, thus freeing Gonzalez to move to left field while Callison was settling in right field. Demeter led the Phillies in 1961 in homers with 21 and RBIs with 70.

Both Gonzalez and Callison showed signs of improvement. Gonzalez played a decent center field and hit .277 with 12 homers and 58 RBIS. Callison hit just .266 but showed signs of developing power with 11 triples. Mauch made him a special project because he saw the enormous potential that Callison possessed.

On July 2 Quinn traded Bobby Del Greco to Kansas City for outfielder Wes Covington. For the second time Del Greco had shown that while a superb outfielder, he couldn't hit major league pitching with any consistency. Covington was coming off two down years with the Chicago White Sox and Kansas City but had given Quinn two great years in 1957 and 1958 when the Braves last won pennants. Many people in baseball believed that Covington was finished, but Quinn thought at 29 he still had some good baseball in him. Mauch began platooning Covington in the outfield against right-handed pitchers and using him as the Phillies' most important pinch hitter. Covington rebounded for the Phillies, hitting .303 with seven homers in just 57 games.

Despite these moves nothing went right for the Phillies in 1961. Tony Taylor was injured and missed 48 games, weakening the infield. Herrara suffered from a bad case of the sophomore jinx, hitting just .258 with only 13 homers and 51 RBIs, all figures significantly lower than his rookie year.

Roberts lost his first seven decisions and never got untracked. He wound up with one win versus ten defeats, the worst one-year record of any pitcher who ever reached the Hall of Fame. He pitched just 117 innings and compiled a 5.85 ERA before Mauch removed him from the starting rotation late in the season. Mauch was convinced that Roberts was finished and saw his failure holding back the progress of the younger arms on the team. Mauch was wrong. He later admitted that he had mishandled Roberts. "I failed my first big test when I was incapable of saying the right thing to help Roberts make the transition he ultimately made on his own."[11]

After the 1961 season the Phillies sold Roberts to the New York Yankees for $25,000. Bob Carpenter wanted Roberts to go to a possible pennant-winning team. Eventually Roberts wound up with the Baltimore Orioles where he won 42 games in three and a half seasons but missed out on the World Series, which the Orioles won in 1966. He was traded to Houston in 1965 and finished his career with the Cubs the next year. The Phillies could have used him between 1962 and 1964.

Sullivan was equally useless, going 3–16. Buzhardt, of whom much was expected, was 6–18 although he pitched commendably at times. Mahaffey in his first full season showed signs of greatness. He shut out the Cubs on April 23 in a game in which he tied Dizzy Dean's National League record for most strikeouts, 17, by a right-handed pitcher in a nine inning game.

There were long stretches during the season when Mahaffey couldn't win. He ended the season 11–19 but led the Phillies' staff in virtually every pitching category: strikeouts, innings pitched and complete games. Mauch tried to spot him carefully so as to build his confidence. Mahaffey was 5–10 against first division teams and 6–9 against the rest. Mauch didn't start him after his last victory on September 17 so that he wouldn't lose 20 games for the season.

Chris Short was erratic, going 6–12 but continuing to show flashes of brilliance. Owens, who had struggled mightily in 1960, wound up with a 5–10 record, fighting Mauch and himself. The overall record of the Phillies' top starters was an astonishing bad 36 wins versus 73 defeats. Mauch made a discovery in reliever Jack Baldschun, who Quinn had drafted out of the Reds' minor league system. Baldschun led the National League in games pitched and had the only winning record on the team, 5–3, and did this with a decent ERA of 3.87.

The outfield stabilized after the addition of Demeter who hit 20 of his homers and drove in 68 of his runs for the Phillies. He was the first Phillies player to reach the 20 home run mark since Gene Freese and Wally Post in 1959. Callison and Gonzalez continued to show signs of progress. Along with Covington's reemergence as a solid hitter, this gave the Phillies some grounds for optimism about their outfield in the future.

The Phillies started poorly in 1961, losing three of their first four games including the first of 14 shutouts the team would endure that season. After being shut out by Mike McCormick 2–0 on April 14, the Phillies behind Dallas Green beat future Hall of Famer Juan Marichal also by a 2–0 score. Eight days later the Phillies reached what was probably the highlight of an otherwise grim season. They swept a Sunday doubleheader in Shibe Park against the Cubs, winning both games by shutouts. Frank Sullivan won a gutty 1–0 game while Art Mahaffey had his greatest game in the majors, a 17 strike out affair that he won 6–0. These victories lifted the Phillies to sixth place, the team's highest position in 1961.

In early May the tempo of the season was set when the Phillies lost ten consecutive games, four on the road and six at home. During this ten-game streak, the Phillies scored 13 runs, exposing the team's offensive weaknesses.

From mid-May the Phillies were in and out of the cellar and never higher than seventh place. They settled in the cellar for good on June 16 when they lost their ninth consecutive game to the Reds. The Reds would go on to beat the Phillies during their pennant-winning season 19 of 22 times. For the last three months of the season, the Phillies played at a .287 rate, winning just 29 games out of 101 played.

Just how bad were the Phillies? Between June 15th and July 13th they experienced an eight-game losing streak and two seven-game ones. They won just five games in a month and a total of ten games over a two-month period. Major league baseball hadn't seen anything as bad as this since the terrible Phillies teams of the 1930s and early 1940s. Only the first year expansion Mets would top the Phillies for sheer futility.

The Phillies hit bottom in late July. After beating the Cubs 6–5 on July 22, the Phillies stumbled through 23 loses in a row to set a major league record. Seventeen of the losses were on the road while eight were one-run defeats. The losing streak was truly a team effort. Owens lost four times during the 23 games while four other Phillies starters lost three times, including Mahaffey, Short, Sullivan and Buzhardt. During those 23 games the Phillies were outscored 123 to 54. They finally ended this ghastly stretch of baseball in the second game of a doubleheader against the Braves on August 20th as Buzhardt beat Carlton Willey 7–4. Interestingly Buzhardt had won the last Phillies victory back on July 28th.

After the win over the Braves, the Phillies flew home to Philadelphia. When they arrived at Philadelphia International Airport late that Sunday night, there was a large crowd of screaming fans waiting for them. The Phillies players were bewildered, not knowing what to expect. Frank Sullivan captured the situation perfectly: "They're selling rocks at $5 a bucket," he said. "Leave at five yard intervals, men, so they don't get us with one burst."[12]

Mauch always believed the losing streak, in a strange way, was the making of the Phillies. He and Quinn had known that the 1960 and 1961 Phillies couldn't compete against the good teams in the National League, but they hadn't expected anything as dramatic as losing 23 consecutive games.[13]

Mauch argued that the ultimate development of the Phillies in later years could be traced to the impact of the losing streak. "A feeling of unity came out of that whole rotten mess. They didn't like the insults that went along with that streak and they did not like to be identified as playing for a ball club that set a league record for losses in a row."[14] The losing streak, Mauch believed, turned a bunch of individuals into a team. A point that supports Mauch's view was the team's 17–20 record, or a .460 percentage, after they ended their losing streak. The Phillies scored almost as many runs in the remaining 37 games as their opponents: 145 versus 154.

The 1961 Phillies finished at 47–107, a record comparable to some of their awful teams of the 1930s and 1940s. They were 46 games behind the first place Cincinnati Reds, the worst performance by a last place team since a young Pirates team finished 55 games out of first in 1953. It seemed as though the Phillies had retrogressed under Quinn and Mauch's stewardship. Certainly the Phillies fans were disillusioned by a fourth consecutive cellar finish. Attendance declined by 272,000 from 1960 to 590,000, the lowest figure in the National League and the Phillies' poorest gate since the last year of World War II. The Phillies desperately needed a boost or they were in danger of becoming a permanent laughingstock of baseball, a team like the St. Louis Browns or Washington Senators. Fortunately, 1962 brought better things.

3

The Little General

Expansion

The 1962 season would prove to be a turning point in the revival of the Phillies. The Phillies' performance in 1961 certainly didn't generate much optimism for the future. With the National League committed to expansion in 1962 to bring them in line with the ten team Junior Circuit which had expanded the previous year, Quinn and Mauch knew that they would be judged harshly if the Phillies finished behind either of the new teams, the Houston Colts or New York Mets.

That the Phillies would finish ninth was the consensus of many baseball people going into 1962. The popular baseball magazine *Street and Smith's Yearbook*, for example, picked the Phillies to finish ahead of the Colts but behind the Mets.[1] This was quite a commentary given the quality of the team the Mets drafted from the expansion pool. The pitchers who made the Mets roster in 1962 had a combined record of 16–20 in 1961. The Mets starting line up had no .300 hitters and only one batter who had 20 or more homers, Frank Thomas with 27 homers to go along with 73 RBIs.

The Mets, guided by longtime Yankee general manager George Weiss, had decided to stock the team with veterans like Gil Hodges, Richie Ashburn, Gus Bell and Don Zimmer in hopes of winning the loyalty of the baseball wise New York fans. It didn't work. Before the season was over most of the vets were released. The biggest plus the Mets possessed was their manager Casey Stengel, whose flair for publicity helped ease the team's acceptance in New York.

Houston took a different route under the leadership of longtime American League general manager Paul Richards. Although they were a consensus pick for the National League basement, Richards decided to draft younger players. He didn't feel any special need to appeal to the fans in Texas who would be witnessing major league caliber baseball for the first time. Richards' choices for the team, named the Colt 45s, were designed to produce a better balanced team than the Mets. He picked pitchers like Bob Bruce and Dick Farrell and regulars such as Norm Larker, Bob Aspromonte and Roman Meijas. As a result the Colts fielded a decent team in their first year in the majors and went on to win 64 games. They finished 24 games ahead of the Mets and beat out the Cubs for eighth place.

Mauch wasn't impressed by either the Mets' or the Colts' roster. He asked a simple question of anyone who questioned him about the comparison of the Phillies with the Colts or Mets: "Would you exchange my 25 players for theirs?" Mauch knew neither of the expansion teams had any players to compare with the emerging young talents such as Gonzalez, Callison, Taylor, Mahaffey or Demeter, to mention just a few of the Phillies. Still the awful Phillies' performance of 1961 hung like a cloud over the team as a new season began.

Quinn made only a few moves going into 1962. He and Mauch were aware of how poorly the Phillies had done in one-run games. Their record of 19–35 reflected the lack of consistent clutch hitting. To rectify that, Quinn traded third sacker Charlie Smith and pitcher John Buzhardt to the White Sox for 35-year-old slugging first baseman Roy Sievers. Quinn told the Philadelphia baseball writers that, "one big hitter can turn these one run losses into victories."[2] Quinn proved to be a prophet. The 1962 Phillies reversed their poor record in one-run games, winning 26 of 40 decisions.

Mauch wanted Sievers for another reason. He believed that Sievers would stabilize the middle of the lineup and give young players like Gonzalez, Callison and Demeter someone to look up to and try to emulate.

The Sievers trade also had a downside. It was the first of a series of moves that would characterize Mauch's tenure with the Phillies. A mediocre player himself, he hero-worshipped the established veterans often at the expense of the younger players. For awhile Mauch controlled this tendency as he developed the young players he had inherited, but after the team's collapse in 1964 he would increasingly turn to vets as the missing piece that would put the Phillies back into pennant contention. Beginning in 1965 he and Quinn would begin a search for that one player that would put the Phillies over the top. A string of veterans, most of them over the hill, came to the Phillies after 1964: Dick Groat, Bill White, Bob Buhl, Larry Jackson, and Ray Herbert, to mention but a few. The Phillies got one good year out of White and Groat and three decent seasons out of Jackson. White tore his Achilles tendon after the 1966 season and was effectively finished as an everyday player. Groat had one season with the Phillies in 1966 and then retired after the 1967 season. Buhl and Herbert were clearly finished by the time the Phillies got them.

The cost to the Phillies wasn't too high save in one case, the trade that brought Jackson and Buhl to the Phillies early in 1966. Quinn and Mauch gave up two highly regarded rookies to get them: outfielder Adolpho Phillips and pitcher Ferguson Jenkins. At the time

The Little General — Gene Mauch. The winningest manager in modern Phillies history with 645 victories, Mauch built the team that almost stole the pennant. Among themselves, his fellow managers regarded Mauch as the most brilliant student of the game. (Courtesy Philadelphia Phillies.)

Mauch commented that the Phillies had gotten what they needed, two starting pitchers that would help make them contenders. The cost was slight in Mauch's words: "two bags of garbage." One of the bags of garbage, Jenkins, went on to win 284 games and earn a place in the Hall of Fame. The Jenkins trade would come back and haunt the Phillies for years and ranks as perhaps one of the worst in team history.

Sievers arrived in Philadelphia after two solid seasons with the White Sox. He had hit .295 in both years with 28 and 27 homers as well as 92 and 93 RBIs. Mauch was pleased during spring training when Sievers took batting practice, noticing the other Phillies hitters stopped and watched. Everyone admired Sievers' sweet swing. A 13-year vet and former home run champion in the American League, Sievers became a powerful positive influence on the Phillies' young hitters. Unfortunately Sievers faded badly in his two plus seasons with the Phillies. His batting average dropped by 30 points in 1962 and then took another 20 point decline in his last full-time season, 1963. His power numbers also were down, hitting 21 homers in 1962 and 19 the next season. Injuries ended his career with the Phillies in July 1964 just when the team desperately needed his right-handed bat.

From their farm system Quinn made two promotions in 1962, the first sign that Phillies' minor league teams were about to contribute to the parent club. One was the team's top hitting prospect, a 25-year-old African American outfielder, Ted Savage. Savage was coming off a great year in the International League that saw him lead the league in batting, runs scored, hits, and stolen bases while clubbing 24 homers. For this performance he was named the league MVP. He was called the most exciting player to come out of the International League since Jackie Robinson in 1946 — pretty fast company for any rookie.

Savage possessed tremendous raw talent, but something kept him from developing his full abilities. He was gone from the Phillies after one inconsistent season, beginning a process where he would change teams frequently. In a nine-year career in the majors, he would play for six different teams and would never equal the number of times at bat he had with the Phillies in his rookie year.

The other addition from the minor league system was pitcher Jack Hamilton, a burly 6' 200-pound right-handed fire-baller who impressed everyone during spring training. The 23 year old was coming off a 9–9 season as both a starter and a reliever at Williamsport in the Eastern League, but his record was deceptive. He gave up only 88 hits in 102 innings while compiling a decent 3.71 ERA. Mauch penciled him in as a third or fourth starter.

Although the Phillies seemed overstocked with outfielders, Mauch wanted to ease Savage's way in the pitching-strong National League. He would platoon him in left field with Wes Covington, leaving center field to Gonzalez with Callison in right. Mauch had a special plan for Demeter. Since the Phillies had traded Charley Smith and had been unsuccessful in finding a decent third baseman, Mauch had fastened on the deceptively agile Demeter as a possible fill-in at the hot corner. Mauch knew that Demeter had played third in the Dodgers' minor league system. At the very least if Demter could do a decent job at third, it would enable the Phillies to keep his powerful right-handed bat in the lineup. Mauch worked Demeter out at third in spring training, trying to boost his confidence in a new position. By the opening of the season, Demeter admitted that Mauch "convinced me that I could play third base."[3]

The only other surprise of note as the 1962 season began took place toward the end of spring training. The Phillies had been trying to negotiate a trade with the White Sox for former Yankee infielder, Andy Carey, in case Demeter couldn't handle third base. Carey adamantly refused to accept a trade with the Phillies, saying he didn't want to finish his career with a last place team like the Phillies. To replace Carey, the White Sox substituted Calvin Coolidge Julius Caesar Tuskahoma McLish, a 36-year-old journeyman pitcher who was coming off his second poor year in a row. He had gone 4–14 for the Reds in 1960 and then was traded to the White Sox where he finished with a 10 and 13 record. Mauch hoped that McLish would rebound to something approaching the 19–8 record he had in 1959. He also believed that McLish's experience would rub off on the Phillies' young pitching staff. On a personal level McLish was another veteran who Mauch first met during their rookie days with the Dodgers.

The Phillies clearly got the best of this exchange. McLish surprised everyone by starting 24 games, relieving in 8 others, and winning 11 against 5 losses. Carey wound up with the Dodgers in 1962 hitting .234 with 2 homers and 13 RBIs. The McLish deal was the first sign that the Phillies luck was beginning to change.

The Phillies started the 1962 season better than the past two campaigns. Using essentially just three starters, Art Mahaffey, Jack Hamilton and Cal McLish with Jim Owens an occasional fill in, the Phillies finished April just one game under the .500 mark. A five-game winning streak in early May saw them reach fourth place with a 13–11 mark when they beat the Cubs 12–2 on May 11 as Hamilton won his third victory of the season. Fourth place would be the team's high water mark for the year.

From this victory over the Cubs, the Phillies went into a tailspin reminiscent of the nightmare season of 1961. They won just 4 of their next 23 games, suffering two 4 game losing streaks as well as a 7 gamer. They hit bottom on June 1st when they were defeated twice in a doubleheader at home by the Dodgers. Don Drysdale beat the Phillies for the 13th consecutive time in the second game of the doubleheader. The Phillies turned the tables on him thereafter, defeating him nine straight times.

It looked as if all this brave talk of improvement was just that, talk. Quinn and Mauch's work was at stake. Another poor season might have cost both of them their jobs. Interestingly, this time the Phillies losing streak was different than the nightmare the team had experienced so often in 1961. The Phillies were in most of the games they lost, losing two one-run games, one two-run game while suffering five three-run defeats. A little better pitching and a slight improvement in offense and the Phillies could have turned those games around, something not true in 1961.

On June 2nd the Phillies began the slow process of righting their season. Behind their highly regarded minor league prospect, left-hander Dennis Bennett, they shut out the Dodgers 7–0. Bennett stopped a Dodger 13-game winning streak while gaining his first victory in the majors. He would go on to be one of the keys to the Phillies' success in the latter half of the 1962 season and give promise of being one of the National League's best young left-handers.

Mauch was experimenting with his starters, looking for a combination that would give Phillies' offense a chance to win. He gradually moved Owens, who pitched poorly as a starter in April and May, out of the starting rotation and replaced him with Bennett. The Phillies' four starters from June on — Mahaffey, McLish, Hamilton, and Bennett with an occasional appearance by Chris Short — gave the team a chance to win.

After their doubleheader loss to the Dodgers, the Phillies suddenly began to play better baseball, going 64–50 the rest of the season. They put together three out of four winning months the rest of the season. In their only losing month, July, they still were only two games under .500 at 15–17.

The Phillies did this despite a couple of bad stretches when they suffered through eight game losing streaks, one in early July and one in early August. But unlike in past seasons, they rebounded with winning streaks of their own, including two streaks of six consecutive victories as well as two five-game winning streaks.

The Phillies' improvement was across the board. They were 45–34 at home and won 19 of their last 26 games to finish 81–80 for their first winning season since 1953. The reasons for the Phillies' turn around were varied. Sievers began to hit in the clutch after a cold start, getting most of his 21 homers and 80 RBIs in the second half of the season. But the real offense came from the outfielders Gonzalez, Callison and Covington as well as from Demeter at third. Callison and Gonzalez got hot and were over .300 most of the season. Gonzalez wound up hitting .302 with 20 homers, many of them left field home runs, something unusual in Shibe Park. Gonzalez also compiled one of the longest hitting streaks in the National League, 17 games in a row. Callison finished at .300 when he asked Mauch to rest him on the last day of the season to protect his average. Later he regretted that he hadn't played — he thought it somehow detracted from his fine season.[4] Callison also hit 23 homers, tying him with Harry Anderson for the most of any left-handed Phillies batter since the team moved to Shibe Park in mid-1938. He also led the National League in triples while driving in 83 runs and scoring 107. He was the first Phillies player to score 100 runs since Richie Ashburn did it in 1954.

Demeter, although playing a strange position, third base, began to put up power numbers for the Phillies not seen since the days of Del Ennis. He batted .307 and finished the season with 29 homers, the most by any Phillie since Stan Lopata hit 32 in 1956 and 107 RBIs. No Phillie had topped the 100 mark in RBIs since Ennis did it in 1955. In 105 games at third, Demeter did an adequate job.

The platoon of Covington and Savage in left field put up decent numbers also, combing for 16 home runs and 83 RBIs and 90 runs scored. Savage struggled at the plate and in the field. He hit just .266 and failed to progress the way the Phillies hoped. In his part-time role Covington hit nine homers and drove in 44 runs. He also hit .300 as a pinch hitter.

Catcher Clay Dalrymple had his best year in the majors, batting a career high .276 with 11 homers and 54 RBIs. Among regular catchers, only Smoky Burgess had a higher batting average. Dalrymple also improved behind the plate, making only nine errors in over 700 chances.

The second base-shortstop combination was adequate. Tony Taylor hit just .259 but scored 87 runs and stole 20 bases. Mauch platooned at shortstop with Amaro and rookie Bobby Wine. Both were brilliant defensively but neither hit very much: Amaro finished at .243, Wine .244. Wine was a highly regarded right-handed hitter in the Phillies minor league system. But after being beaned in his third year in the minors he never recovered his offensive stroke. He wasn't as smooth a fielder as Amaro but had a much more powerful arm, in fact one of the best throwing arms of any shortstop in the majors.

Overall the Phillies improved in almost every offensive category compared to 1961. Their total of 142 home runs was the most for any Phillies team since 1929 when Chuck Klein and Lefty O'Doul reigned supreme. The 1962 team scored 121 more runs than the previous year and its batting average increased an amazing 17 points, from .243 to .260, a remarkable performance given that the league batting average actually dipped by one point between 1961 and 1962.

The Phillies offense gained a measure of respect throughout the National League. Fred Hutchison, the highly regarded manager of the Cincinnati Reds summed up the view of many around the league about

Second baseman Tony Taylor watches as Bobby Wine turns a double play against the Pirates. After catching the flip from Taylor, Wine avoids the runner and fires to first, completing the twin killing. The Phillies' superb defensive combination would finish the 1964 season ranked third in double plays. (Urban Archives, Temple University, Philadelphia Pennsylvania.)

the hitting prowess of the Phillies. "Every time you look at the line up," said Hutchinson, "the Phils got another hitter coming up at the plate who can hit. It didn't use to be that way."[5]

Another factor in the Phillies improvement was the blossoming of the pitching staff. The addition of Bennett strengthened the starting pitching. Bennett combined a blazing fastball and wide sweeping curve with unusual control for a 22-year-old rookie. He went 9–9 for the season but pitched much better than that. In 174 innings he struck out 149 while giving up just 144 hits. His hits to innings pitched ratio was third best in the National League behind two future Hall of Famers, Sandy Koufax and Bob Gibson. Pretty good company for a rookie.

What impressed Mauch about Bennett was his utter fearlessness. He pitched as if he wasn't afraid of any hitter. The Phillies brass believed that they had a potential 20 game winner in Bennett. It was not to be, as his career was shortened by arm problems.

Chris Short also came into his own in 1962 after showing flashes of talent in the past two seasons. He went 6–5 as a starter and 5–4 in relief for a combined 11–9 record. At times he was unhittable, beating good teams like the Dodgers and Cardinals while hurling low hit games. The Phillies knew they had a keeper in Short.

Art Mahaffey had his greatest season in 1962 and was a major contributor to the Phillies' success. He won 19 games against 14 losses, struck out 177 batters while completing 20 games, the second highest total in the league. Mauch continued to spot him carefully, hoping to boost his confidence for the future. Mahaffey was a worrier and something of a perfectionist as well as a fierce competitor. He would get down on himself when he didn't do well, and Mauch sought to channel his huge potential. In time Mahaffey would come to hate Mauch and blame him for his arm problems. But Mauch helped make Mahaffey a success in 1962. Being used carefully, Mahaffey went 12–2 against second division teams and 7–12 against those in the first division. He won his 19th game on September 16th but lost his last three starts trying to become the Phillies' first 20 game winner since Roberts in 1955. Interestingly, the last game was a 4–0 loss at the hands of the Reds' John Tsitouris. He and Mahaffey would have a more fateful match up two years later.

Another big reason for the Phillies' success in 1962 was the emergence of Jack Baldschun as an outstanding relief pitcher. He won 12 games, more than any relief pitcher in the National League, and finished the year second in games pitched, fifth in saves while compiling a superb 2.96 ERA. He drove Mauch crazy by constantly pitching deep into the count but had such faith in his fastball and screwball that he never seemed to worry.

By the end of the season, the starting rotation of Mahaffey (19–14), Bennett (9–9), McLish (11–5), Short (11–9) and Jack Hamilton (9–12), a combined 59–49, gave the Phillies something they had lacked since the mid-1950s: five pitchers with a chance to win every time out. The bullpen beyond Baldschun was shaky and needed propping up in the future, a fact that Quinn and Mauch recognized.

Overall the team's ERA was high at 4.28, a reflection of the rise in offense that came with expansion and the dilution of pitching talent in the league. There were over 400 more homers hit in 1962 than the previous season, a sure sign that the pitching quality was down.

Despite that, the Phillies staff made a vast improvement over their 1961 performance. The team ERA dropped by about ⅓ a run per game. Still, pitching was one area where there was room for improvement.

For his role in guiding the Phillies to a seventh place finish and a plus .500 record, 81–80, Mauch was named National League Manager of the Year. He deserved the honor even if some of his critics noted that the Phillies' improvement came largely at the expense of two poor teams, the Colts and Mets. The Phillies were 17–1 against Houston and 14–4 versus the Mets. Mauch noted everyone else had to play them so the Phillies had no special advantage.

Overall the Phillies were competitive with every team in the National League except for the Dodgers and Giants who beat them badly. The Phillies reversed their terrible 1961 3–19 record against the Reds and beat them 10 of 18 times.

A sign that the Phillies had finally gained respectability was the fact that three of their players, Demeter, Callison and Mahaffey, had actually gotten votes for the Most Valuable Player Award. The last time a Phillies player had received any consideration for an MVP award was 1958 when Richie Ashburn had won the batting title.

Mauch had impressed the baseball establishment with some of his innovations. He was always thinking, looking for an edge. Not for nothing had he tutored under Leo Durocher. Shortly after he became manager of the Phillies, he moved their bullpen from the left field corner to right field, in sight of the Phillies dugout. His reasoning was interesting: "most of the balls hit to left field in our park are straight away and will be caught or else go for home runs. Right field is different. It's tough to tell if a ball will be caught or if it will hit the wall. Let's say we get runners on second and third and somebody hits a ball to right. Somebody in the bullpen will wave to the base coaches and they can start to spin the runners around. On defense the guys in the bullpen can direct the outfielder and warn him about the fence and tell what base to throw to."[6]

Mauch also was one of the first managers to make extensive use of the double-switch, an idea he may have gotten from the *Philadelphia Evening Bulletin*'s Ray Kelly, the dean of Philadelphia baseball writers.[7] When changing pitchers Mauch would make two moves, with a regular taking the pitcher's spot in the batting order. In that way he wouldn't have to use a pinch hitter for the pitcher.

Mauch often replaced Sievers at first base for defensive purposes when the Phillies had a lead late in the game. In 1962 he used Frank Torre, a fine fielding first baseman, in his only season with the Phillies. Later instead of using another first baseman, Mauch would put his slick fielding shortstop Ruben Amaro on first. When he did this the first time during the 1963 season, reporters questioned the move. Mauch simply said if you can play short you could play any infield position. What play would you experience at first, he noted, that a shortstop couldn't deal with — a throw, a groundball a short hop?

Philadelphia fans reacted enthusiastically to the improved Phillies. Attendance, which had reached a 16-year low in 1961, increased by 272,000, the largest one-year increase in team history since the Whiz Kids pennant-winning year. The Phillies were quickly becoming the most popular sports team in the city.

They Played the Best Ball in the National League

The Phillies' strong finish in 1962 generated optimism about the team's future. It seemed to many that the Phillies finally had found a sense of direction. They were picked to move up two notches in the National League by *Street and Smith 1963 Baseball Yearbook*.

Quinn and Mauch confidently expected the Phillies' maturing process to continue in 1963. Their optimism was built around the obvious improvement of Callison and Gonzalez offensively as well as the progress of the pitching staff where Mahaffey, McLish, Bennett, Baldschun and Short constituted the nucleus of a solid staff.

Quinn made two trades going into the 1963 season. The first seemed a minor one but would have a major impact on the Phillies in the near future. He exchanged Jim Owens who had worn out his welcome in Philadelphia to Cincinnati for reserve infielder Cookie Rojas. When pressed to justify giving up a pitcher of Owens' potential for an untried player like Rojas, Mauch gave a classic answer: "Sometimes you add by subtraction." Contrary to what most baseball people thought, the Phillies got the best of the deal. Owens went 18–20 after leaving the Phillies, while Rojas turned into one of the most versatile players in baseball. For the Phillies he played second, shortstop, outfield and even caught a couple of times. He also turned into a decent hitter, twice batting .300 and finishing his career with over 1,600 hits. He was also a fan favorite in Philadelphia and later Kansas City because of his joyful brand of play.

Quinn's major deal came in November 1962. He traded Savage and Pancho Herrera to the Pirates for third baseman Don Hoak. This deal caused some consternation in Philadelphia. The Phillies were giving up on one of the prizes of their minor league system. Mauch's justification was simple: the trade strengthened the Phillies in two ways. First, it enabled Mauch to move Demeter back to his natural position in the out field where he was more comfortable than playing third base. Second, the Phillies felt they had to fill the glaring void at third where they had tried 18 different players since Mauch took over as manager. Mauch was ecstatic. In Hoak he had another of the hard-nosed veterans whom he admired. In a statement that is revealing of Mauch he said of Hoak: "he's the kind of a player I always wanted to be myself." Hoak's nickname was "Tiger"—an appellation that reflected the forceful way he played the game. Mauch argued that the Phillies were now better than in 1962 because "we feel we now have an established performer at every position."[8] There was a potential problem. Hoak was 35 and coming off the worst year of his career as a regular. In 1962 he hit just .241 with only five homers and 48 RBIs in 121 games.

Some of the Phillies' optimism was dissipated when Dennis Bennett broke his ankle in a serious car accident in Puerto Rico while playing winter baseball. The injury would keep him from pitching until well into the season. As it turned out he didn't make his first appearance with the Phillies until June 25th and only won his first game three weeks later on July 17th. Bennett did not make his first start until July 21 with the season more than half over.

Bennett's injury created a hole in the Phillies pitching staff and forced them to take a closer look at one of their young prospects, a hard throwing right-hander from Texas, Ray Culp. Culp, 21 years old, had quietly moved through the Phillies' minor league system without causing much interest. Then in 1962 he had his breakthrough season with Williamsport of the tough Eastern League. He won 13 games while losing 8 but struck out 183 batters in 200 innings. Culp normally would have opened the season at the Phillies Triple A affiliate of Little Rock, Arkansas of the International League but Bennett's injury made the Phillies brass take a close look at him in spring training. Mauch decided to keep Culp on the roster when the season began. Mauch first used him in relief where he got his first major league win over the Reds. In late April he was moved into the starting rotation where he blossomed. He won 10 games by early July and was named as the Phillies' sole representative at the All-Star Game. He pitched two scoreless innings in the mid-summer classic.

Despite Mauch's hope that the Phillies would take up where they left off in the last part of the 1962 season, the loss of Bennett and another slow start by Sievers saw the Phillies stumble out of the gate. By the end of June the Phillies were in eighth place, 10 games out of first, with a 35–41 record.

Mahaffey had opened the season, beating Cincinnati 2–1 on a brutally cold April night. He didn't pitch again for 15 days and struggled throughout the first half of the season with a series of arm problems. On July 30 just as he was showing signs of recapturing his 1962 form, Mahaffey suffered a freak accident. In a game in San Francisco, he caught his spikes on the pitching mound and severely tore the tendons in his ankle. He was effectively lost for the rest of the season although he came back in the last week and beat the Dodgers in the final game of the year. He wound up 7–10, a huge drop off from his 19-victory season the year before. More importantly, 1963 saw the beginning of Mahaffey's decline. Perhaps because he was favoring his ankle, he developed arm problems that plagued him for the rest of his career.

For the first three months of the season, the Phillies drifted around the second division. With Bennett out, Mauch was forced to improvise with his starting pitching. Because of bad weather in April, Mahaffey, McLish and Chris Short started 11 of the team's first 15 games. After his victory on opening night, Mahaffey was erratic, finishing April with just two victories. McLish and Short along with an occasional start by rookie Paul Brown got the Phillies through April with an 8–10 record.

To replace the injured Bennett, Mauch first experimented with a 19-year-old left-hander from the Phillies farm system, Marcelino Lopez. Lopez picked up a victory over the Cardinals, but it was clear that he needed more seasoning and was shipped back to Arkansas.

The Phillies struggled through May and early June until they hit their low point with a doubleheader loss to the Mets on June 23. The Phillies managed just one run against the awful Mets pitching staff. The Phillies' humiliation was made worse when Jimmy Piersall hit the 100th homer of his career in game one against Dallas Green and ran around the bases backwards.

At that point the Phillies were 31–40 in eighth place 10½ games out of first. Aside from Culp, who was 10–5 by the beginning of July, hardly any of the Phillies' regulars, either pitchers or position players, were performing to their potential.

After Bennett returned, the Phillies suddenly turned their season around. The hitters, especially Gonzalez, Sievers and Callison, finally started to hit. Cal McLish began winning consistently as did Short. During the second half of the season, Sievers got hot as did Callison.

With Bennett, Short and McLish anchoring the starting rotation in July the Phillies jelled. They reeled off winning streaks of seven and eight games between July 16 and August 19 to pull themselves into third place, the team's highest point in the standings that late in the season since 1950. From their low point in late June, the Phillies went 56 and 35. Only the pennant-winning Dodgers had a better record than the Phillies in the second half of the season.

The Phillies finished with a record of 87–75 in fourth place just one game behind the third place Giants. It was their best performance since the Whiz Kids won the pennant 13 years earlier. Buzzy Bavasi half-seriously half-jokingly summed up the attitude of many baseball people in 1963. He said that the Phillies should represent the National League in the World Series: "they played the best ball in the league the last two months."[9]

Part of the reason for the Phillies' success, according to Sievers, was that the team finally came together and found a way to win the close games. He credited this to Mauch. "Even the guys who couldn't stand him," Sievers noted, "they knew Mauch was better than whoever the other manager was at figuring out a way to win."[10]

The Phillies' improvement in 1963 was mainly based on pitching, despite all their assorted mound woes. For example, they won more shutouts, 12, than they lost, 11—a far cry from the whitewashings the team took in the past three seasons. 1963 was the year that the strike zone was widened and the pitching mounds around the league were raised as high as 15 inches. It was the beginning of a cycle of pitching domination that would culminate in the disaster of 1968 when league ERAs would reach dead ball levels. The Phillies' pitchers benefited greatly from these changes. Three starters, Short, Culp and Bennett, plus two relievers finished with ERAs under 3.00. Johnny Klippstein, who the Phillies had purchased from the Reds, compiled a stunning ERA of 1.93. The team ERA was 3.09, third lowest in the National League behind the pitching great Dodgers and the surprising Cubs staff, and the lowest of any Phillies team since 1917. The league earned run average of 3.29 was the lowest since 1920, the beginning of the long ball era in baseball.

Culp, after starting fast at 10–5, won four and lost six after July. Because he threw so many curves, he suffered from elbow miseries the last half of the season. He still finished with 176 strikeouts, an excellent 2.97 ERA and five shutouts. He and Pete Rose were regarded as the best rookies of 1963. Each won Rookie of the Year Awards with Culp being named the outstanding rookie by the *Sporting News* while the Baseball Writers' Association picked Rose for that honor.

Bennett went 9–5 after his return from the disabled list and compiled a fine 2.65 ERA. McLish was 13–11. He gained his 13th victory on

Labor Day but developed a sore arm and didn't win a game thereafter. In fact, his arm problems persisted and he never won another game in his career. In July 1964 after trying to rehabilitate his arm, the Phillies gave him his unconditional release.

Chris Short had a strange year. He began by going 0–8 and then went 9–4 for the last half of the season. He had a low ERA of 2.95 and pitched more innings, 198, than any other season in his career up to that point. Among his wins were three shutouts, and he struck out 160 batters. Part of his problem was bad luck. The Phillies didn't seem to score runs when he was on the mound. He lost two 2–1 games and a 3–2 game.

Jack Baldschun had another great year out of the bullpen. He won 11 games and saved 12 others while compiling a low 2.30 ERA. Among National League relievers he ranked third, behind Lindy McDaniel and Ron Perranoski. The Phillies bullpen performed brilliantly, winning 26 games to go along with 21 saves, the team's best record in years.

Offensively the 1963 Phillies did not match the performance of the 1962 team, but then no one in the league did. The widening of the strike zone along with a raised mound saw pitching dominate through the National League. The league ERA declined by three-quarters of a run, one of the biggest drops in baseball history. The Phillies offense actually held up better than most teams in the league. Their batting average declined by seven points and home runs dipped from 142 to 126, but considering that the league batting average declined by 16 points, this was a commendable performance. The Phillies' team average of .252 placed them third in the league.

For the Phillies only Tony Gonzalez topped the .300 mark although his home run total dropped from 20 to 4 due to a back problem. Covington hit .303 but without sufficient official times at bat to qualify among the league leaders. He did smash 17 homers in a part-time role including two pinch-hit homers. Callison's batting average declined by 16 points, Sievers by 22, and Demeter went from .307 to .258. Demeter's home run total dropped by 7 from 29 to 22 and his RBIs declined by 24.

Roy Sievers had started slowly and was hitting under .200 by mid-June. In the second half of the season, he got hot and hit 15 homers while driving in 54 runs. Only Tony Taylor had a better season in 1963 than he had the year before. He raised his batting average from .259 to .281. Callison led the Phillies in homers with 26, breaking his own mark for Phillies left-handed hitters in Shibe Park with its high right field wall.

Clay Dalrymple saw his batting average slip from his fine 1962 season. He hit .251 with 10 homers but only drove in 40 runs. Defensively he was superb, catching more games than any catcher in the National League other than Johnny Edwards of the Reds. Dalrymple also led all major league catchers in assists with 90.

Don Hoak proved to be a flop. He hit .231 with only 24 RBIs, and it was clear that he was finished as an everyday player.

In some ways Mauch did a better job in 1963 than he did in 1962 when he was recognized as Manager of the Year. Unlike 1962, the 1963 Phillies had numerous injuries that forced Mauch to improvise. The loss of Bennett until June and of Mahaffey for all but the last week of the second half of the year and sore arms to Culp and McLish led Mauch to scramble to put together a decent starting rotation. Only two Phillies pitchers, McLish and Culp, hurled 200 innings. Mauch finessed the pitching staff brilliantly, which was unusual for him, given his reputation for being impatient with pitchers. At one point he was forced to use as starters second line pitchers like Dallas Green, Ryne Duren and rookie John Boozer. He also had to dip into his bullpen more than he had planned but the relievers performed brilliantly. Aside from Baldschun who appeared in 65 games, Johnny Klippstein made 49 appearances out of the bullpen, Green and Duren 26.

Mauch's last contribution to the 1963 Phillies came as the pennant race wound down. The season ended for the Phillies with a three-game road trip to Houston and six games against the west coast teams. The Phillies had a real opportunity to finish in fourth place which would have been their best record in a decade. Also a first division finish would mean a World Series share for the players. Mauch calculated that four wins in the nine games would guarantee fourth place.

The Phillies lost the first game in Houston 3–2 when Ken Johnson beat Dennis Bennett. The Phillies won the next night in another close game, 4–3. In the last game of the series Chris Short and Hal "Skinny" Brown hooked up in a great pitchers' duel. Houston won in the bottom of the ninth when rookie Joe Morgan got his first major league hit.

Mauch was furious, believing that the Phillies had lost their sense of purpose. He entered the clubhouse screaming about being beaten by a Little Leaguer when he saw a table with a post game spread of food. Erupting in anger at the Phillies for their lackadaisical play, he threw over the table scattering chicken and spare ribs around the clubhouse. Tony Gonzalez's and Wes Covington's suits were splattered with spare rib sauce. Mauch stomped off into his office. Later he apologized to the team and bought new suits for Gonzalez and Covington.

When reporters kidded Mauch about his blow up, he laughed the whole thing off, saying that Fred Hutchinson of the Reds did these things much better: "Hutch threw whole rooms."[11]

Mauch's explosion worked. He woke the Phillies from their sluggish play. They won five of their last six games including victories over Juan Marichal, Johnny Podres and Don Drysdale, three impressive pitchers.

The Phillies fans continued their growing love affair with the team. They came out in increasing numbers especially in the second half when the team played the most exciting baseball in the National League. Attendance improved by 145,000 to push the Phillies over the 900,000 mark for the first time in five years.

The Phillies were easily the most popular sports franchise in Philadelphia. The Philadelphia Warriors professional basketball team had decamped for California leaving the city temporarily without a basketball franchise. The Eagles hit rock bottom that fall winning just two games versus ten defeats to finish next to last in the NFC East. As a result the Phillies had the professional sports scene to themselves.

Given the Phillies' improvement over the last two seasons, optimism about the future prevailed in Philadelphia. There was even talk of the Phillies having a real shot at the pennant in the near future although this was dismissed as unrealistic.

4

A Phillies Surprise

A Dark Horse

Despite their strong finish in 1963, the Phillies were a consensus pick to finish no better than fourth or fifth going into the 1964 season. The *Sporting News* polled 232 members of the Baseball Writers Association, and by a narrow margin they picked the Giants to nose out the Dodgers for the pennant. Just ten writers picked the Phillies to win the pennant, while three actually predicted a ninth place finish. The Cardinals were a consensus choice for third with the Reds and Phillies to follow.[1] The odds makers made the Phillies no better than a 8–1 bet to win the pennant.

Sports Illustrated in its *Baseball Annual* also picked the Phillies to finish fourth behind the Dodgers, Cardinals and Giants in that order. They believed that the Phillies were a young and up-and-coming team with good pitching, solid defense and enough hitting to make them dangerous. The magazine predicted that Art Mahaffey and Dennis Bennett, who won just 16 games between them in 1963, would win 35 games. In fact, they went 24–23. *Sports Illustrated* was taken with Bennett in particular. They loved his cockiness. He told them that there was "no way to stop me from winning 20 games and I might add three more to match my uniform number."[2]

Even the local press, famous for its skepticism about the Phillies, did not see them as a serious pennant threat. For instance, Allen Lewis, baseball beat writer for the *Inquirer*, believed that fourth place was a realistic estimate of where the Phillies would finish. (3)

At the annual Philadelphia Sports Writers banquet in January, the Phillies got an endorsement from a surprising source. Sandy Koufax, coming off his first Cy Young Award winning season (25–7, a 1.88 ERA

4—A Phillies Surprise

and 306 strikeouts) told the assembled scribes that he regarded the Phillies as a dark horse for the pennant. He was especially impressed by the Phillies starting eight: "they got guys who can swing the bat." Like *Sports Illustrated*, he believed that if Dennis Bennett and Art Mahaffey were healthy the Phillies staff "would be tough."[4]

Mauch agreed with this assessment although he tried to play down the pennant talk. He told Sandy Grady of the *Bulletin* that the Phillies were one of five or six teams in the Senior Circuit capable of winning 95 games. Mauch believed the Phillies were that good for two reasons. First, he said, he had the best 1 through 7 pitchers in the National League: Bennett, Mahaffey, Cal McLish, Jack Baldschun, Chris Short, Ray Culp and newly acquired Jim Bunning. Mauch also said he expected that Bunning would be the Koufax type staff leader the Phillies had long needed. A second reason for Mauch's optimism was that the Phillies players had finally come to believe in themselves. 1963 changed the team's attitude; he said: they now "conduct themselves like a winning club."[5]

Despite this brave talk the Phillies still lagged behind their major competitors. The Giants had won the pennant in 1962 and finished third in 1963 with 88 victories, one more than the Phillies. The Dodgers won both the pennant and World Series in 1963 while reeling off 99 victories. Both were great teams with unique strengths and no glaring weaknesses. Even the Cardinals had to be taken seriously. They had been the surprise team of the 1963 season, winning 93 games, the most of any Cardinal team since 1949.

Offensively the Giants were one of the powerhouses of the National League, if not all baseball. They hit 197 homers in 1963, 58 more than any other National League team. Five Giants, led by Willie McCovey with 44, Willie Mays with 38 and Orlando Cepeda with 34, hit more than 20 homers. The Giants had a balanced attack with solid hitters one through eight. They also had a prize rookie in third baseman Jim Ray Hart. Hart had just been called up in July 1963 when he broke his collarbone and missed most of the season. A weak defensive player, he was slated to take over third base in 1964 with his defensive backup being the sure-handed Jim Davenport.

Defensively, despite the presence of Willie Mays, the Giants had been a poor team in 1963, a factor that contributed to the team's pitching woes. They ranked next to last in double plays and had the fifth highest total of errors in the league.

What sank the Giants in 1963, however, was the failure of their pitchers to duplicate their success in 1962. Only Juan Marichal in his breakthrough season with a 25–8 record topped his 1962 stats. Jack Sanford and Billy Pierce, who combined for 40 victories in 1962, slipped to 19 in 1963. The writers who picked the Giants to win the pennant were counting on the pitching staff to return to 1962 levels.

What made the Dodgers a strong contender in the eyes of the baseball writers was their overall performance in 1963. Their 99 wins was second only to the Yankees' 104. The Dodgers' strong suit was its pitching staff. Led by Sandy Koufax and Don Drysdale, who combined for 44 victories, the Dodgers had the only ERA in the majors below 3.00 — they were at 2.85. They also led the majors in shutouts with 24 with Koufax accounting for 11 by himself. The Dodgers' bullpen was the best in the National League. Ron Perranoski, their ace reliever, won an incredible 16 games in relief, saved 21 others and had one of the lowest relief ERAs in recent baseball history, 1.67. Dodger hitting was feeble. Only Tommy Davis and Maury Wills topped the .300 mark. What the Dodgers did do well was run the bases. With Wills and Willie Davis setting the pace, the Dodgers easily led the National League in stolen bases. When combined with good pitching and decent defense, the Dodgers had enough offense to win most games. The Dodgers scored 90 more runs than their pitching staff allowed. Only the Cardinals had a better spread.

The Cardinals had surprised everyone in 1963 by challenging the Dodgers for the pennant. At one point in late August–early September, the Cardinals reeled off 19 victories in 20 games to get within three games of first place only to lose a crucial three-game set against the Dodgers. The Cardinals were the best-balanced club in the National League. They led the league with a .271 batting average. Their infield of Bill White at first, Julian Javier at second, Dick Groat at shortstop and Ken Boyer at third base was the best in the National League. Their young catcher Tim McCarver had come into his own in 1963, hitting .289. White and Boyer drove in 100 runs, the only infielders in the National League to do so. Groat, White and outfielder Curt Flood also reached the 200 hit plateau. The Cards also had four solid starters in Bob Gibson, Curt Simmons, Ernie Broglio and Ray Sadecki who combined for a 61–36 record for a winning percentage of .629. No other pitching staff, not even the Dodgers' with Koufax, Drysdale and Johnny Podres, could match that record.

The Reds also were picked to finish ahead of the Phillies because they had a stronger pitching staff. Led by their four starters Jim Maloney with 23 victories, Jim O'Toole with 17 and Joe Nuxhall with 15 to go along with John Tsitouris' 12, the Reds had won 67 games among them compared to the Phillies top four with 45 wins. On the other hand the Reds offensive hadn't been impressive in 1963. Only outfielder Vada Pinson had an outstanding season, hitting .313, with 22 homers and driving in 106 runs. Frank Robinson had an off year, hitting just 21 homers with 91 RBIs while batting a career low .259. The Reds were counting on sophomore Tommy Harper, veteran Bob Skinner who came over from the Pirates and highly touted rookie outfielder/first baseman, Deron Johnson to pick up the offensive slack. Despite their offensive problems in 1963, the Reds finished just one game behind the Phillies.

Interestingly all four teams were among the most integrated in the National League, having recognized the value of African American players early. The Phillies, laggards in this respect, didn't make that mistake under Quinn and Mauch, both of whom were color-blind when it came to baseball skills. Starting in 1960 the Phillies began to seriously pursue African American players. That year no less than nine Black or Black Latins appeared on the Phillies roster. Thereafter the Phillies always had an African American presence on their teams. The 1964 squad would contain no less than six Black or Black Latin players, including four regulars— Taylor, Allen, Gonzalez and Covington. Jack Baldschun said that if there was one thing true about the 1964 squad, it was that there was no racial tension on the team and rumors to that effect were in his word "crap."[6] For comparison the Cards had four African American or Black Latins on their roster, the Dodgers six, the Giants seven and the Reds five.

Going into the 1964 season, the Phillies made only two major moves, but they were the most significant of the Quinn-Mauch era. On December 4, 1963 Quinn somehow talked the Detroit Tigers into trading Jim Bunning and catcher Gus Triandos for outfielder Don Demeter and pitcher Jack Hamilton. The Tigers had grown disenchanted with Bunning who they labeled a "briefcase pitcher" because of his job as stockbroker in the off-season.[7] A possible trade of Bunning for outfielder, Felipe Alou, had fallen through before the Phillies' deal because Giants owner, Horace Stoneham, had rejected it. "Who needs Bunning," he said. "He's washed up."[8] Stoneham would come to regret that remark.

The right-handed hitting Triandos was needed to take pressure off Clay Dalrymple who had caught 265 games over the past two seasons. In 106 games in 1963, Triandos hit 14 homers and drove in 41 runs while batting .239. His home run and RBI totals were better than Dalrymple's in 1963. Triandos was old and slow but was better than any backup Dalrymple had during his four years with the Phillies. The Phillies had some catching depth at the minor league level. Twenty-three-year-old Pat Corrales was a defensive standout and slated for some fine-tuning at Triple A Little Rock in 1964. Veteran Bob Oldis, who the Phillies got from the Pirates, also was available if necessary.

Jim Bunning, however, was the key to the trade. He had become available because the Tigers were downsizing and were willing to unload him in order to save some salary. Quinn and Mauch were looking for someone to anchor the Phillies' staff. They had hoped that Art Mahaffey would grow into that role, but he had retrogressed since his 19-victory season in 1962. He was also becoming disgruntled, believing that Mauch had lost faith in him. He was right. Dalrymple, who had caught Mahaffey throughout his career, thought that the big right-hander's problems were "more mental than physical." Mahaffey had "more of a tender head ... than a tender arm," according to Dalrymple.[9]

In fact, Mahaffey's arm problems dated from early in the 1963 season. He had won the opening day assignment that year and beat the Reds on a brutally cold April night, but he struggled the rest of the season until he broke his ankle in July. During spring training in 1964, Mahaffey admitted to Sandy Grady of the *Evening Bulletin* that there were times that year when he "couldn't lift my arm enough to comb my hair." He felt good during spring training in 1964 and was actually hoping to become the Phillies' opening day pitcher again.[10] There was little realistic chance of this happening now that Bunning had joined the Phillies. It was a good sign that the often-fretting Mahaffey was optimistic about the coming season.

Bunning was coming off a losing season, having gone 12–13 in 1963. But he was only 32 and had won 19 games the year before. His career numbers were outstanding, 118 wins versus just 87 defeats. He was a hard worker, always in shape and one of the toughest competitors in baseball, having led the American League in hit batsmen for six of the last seven years. Bunning was a classic intimidator much in the mold of Bob Gibson and Don Drysdale. Never afraid to pitch close to hitters, Bunning is the only pitcher that made Mickey Mantle ever charge the mound after being hit by a pitch.

Bunning's 1963 losing record was deceptive. That year the Tigers were a mediocre team with a losing record of 79–83 and a big payroll. Bunning's numbers were not that bad. He had hurled 248 innings and struck out 196 batters, the second highest total in the American League. No Phillies pitcher in 1963 could match either of those figures. There were rumors that Bunning had trouble getting left-handers out, but

Quinn and Mauch noted that he averaged less than a hit per inning and had a decent ERA of 3.88. They believed that Bunning would bring a degree of maturity to an otherwise young cadre of starters. The Tigers were happy to part with him, his salary and his reputation as a "briefcase ball player." The Phillies were happy to get him.

The cost for Bunning and Triandos wasn't too high although the loss of the right-handed hitting Demeter unbalanced the Phillies lineup, leaving them vulnerable to left-handed pitching. The Phillies' best hitters: Callison, Gonzalez, Covington and Dalrymple were all left-handed. Only the 37-year-old Sievers was a threat from the right side, and his numbers had declined sharply in 1963. Without Demeter the Phillies would see more left-handed pitching than they had in 1963 when their record against them was a less than impressive 23–31. Left-handers Dick Ellsworth, Warren Spahn and Sandy Koufax each had beaten the Phillies three times, while Curt Simmons and Billy O'Dell had taken three of four decisions from them. Sandy Grady wrote that unless the Phillies get another right-handed bat the team would be "patsies to the league's good left-handed pitching."[11] Grady's insight would be borne out once the season started. Every team in the National League dipped into their farm system to throw left-handers at the Phillies.

Quinn and Mauch recognized this flaw in the Phillies' makeup. They tried to swing a deal during spring training for a veteran right-handed hitter. There was talk of a Mahaffey for Orlando Cepada trade, but that deal never got beyond the probing stage. It was also known that Quinn had offered the Mets a batch of young prospects for Frank Thomas and pitcher Al Jackson.[12] The Mets were tempted, but the deal was put on hold when Thomas suffered a series of minor injuries.

Either deal would have made sense for the Phillies. Cepada was one of the premier right-handed hitters in the National League and the Giants could afford to give him up because they had Willie McCovey to play first. As good as the Cepada deal would have been, the Mets trade in the long run would have helped the Phillies more. Thomas could play first base or left field, in both cases filling a Phillies need: platooning with Covington and serving as insurance in case Sievers broke down. Al Jackson would have been a great addition to the Phillies staff. The little lefty was a crafty pitcher with a rubber arm, and he could have helped out as either a starter or reliever. In his two seasons with the awful Mets, he had averaged 228 innings with an ERA of just over 4.00—an impressive performance considering the Mets lost 231 games in those years.

To solve their lack of a right-handed hitter, the Phillies had an acc in the hole. They were counting on their prize hitting prospect, Dick "Don't Call Me Richie" Allen, to fill the gap left by Demeter. Allen, a 5'11" 185 pounder, was just 22 years old. He had been signed out of high school in western Pennsylvania to a $70,000 bonus and had put up impressive offensive numbers at every minor league level.

Allen was the greatest pure talent the Phillies' organization had produced since Chuck Klein. He was also the first great African American player they had ever signed. He came into his own in 1962. At Williamsport in the pitching tough Eastern League, Allen hit .329, drove in 109 runs while alternating between second base and the outfield. In 1963 playing with Little Rock of the International League, he hit .289 and led the league in triples, homers and RBIs for which he was named the League's Most Valuable Player. Considering that Allen's first year in Arkansas coincided with the emergence of the bitter struggle for civil rights in the South he handled himself well despite all kinds of racial taunts. At one point in the season Allen had asked John Ogden, the scout who signed him, to get the Phillies to move him to a more congenial location. But when they refused Allen settled down and conducted himself as a thorough professional and even won the respect of the Arkansas fans.

In a brief September appearance in 1963, he hit well enough to convince the Phillies that he was ready for the majors. Mauch was awed by Allen's hitting skills and fearless attitude and couldn't wait to install him in the Phillies' everyday lineup. He also had a surprise in store for everyone. He decided to move Allen to third base where Hoak had flopped in 1963. This would solve the single biggest gap in the Phillies' lineup.

Allen had started as a shortstop and then alternated between second base and the outfield in the minors. This convinced Mauch that he would be able to handle third base. Mauch claimed that Allen's pure athleticism would enable him to handle the position better than Demeter had. Just in case Allen needed any help when the season started, Mauch told the Phillies' ground crew to keep the grass in front of third base high to slow down ground balls.[13]

Allen's move to third base would also end the Phillies' search for someone to take over the hot corner. Over 20 players had failed at that position since Willie Jones was traded away in 1959. Mauch's move was a daring experiment with serious implications for the team and for Allen. Mauch believed that he could handle the pressure because he was one of those special talents that come along rarely in baseball — a true natural. His faith in Allen would be more than borne out in 1964.

4—A Phillies Surprise

During spring training Mauch carefully tried to put together a squad that balanced youth and experience. To back up the aging Sievers, Mauch decided to keep the rookie left-handed outfielder/first baseman, John Herrnstein. Herrnstein, a 6'2" 210-pound former college football player, had been signed out of college by one of the Phillies' best scouts, Tony Lucadello. Herrnstein had hit with power throughout his minor league career, smashing 23 homers in 1962 and 22 the next season. Initially an outfielder, the Phillies had begun remaking him into a first baseman so that he would be ready to become Sievers' replacement in the near future. A favorite of Bob Carpenter, the quiet, intelligent Herrnstein never panned out for the Phillies.

Richie Allen was the greatest offensive player the Phillies had produced since Chuck Klein. Rookie of the Year in 1964, he led the National League in runs scored, triples and total bases, all while playing a new position at third base. (Courtesy Philadelphia Phillies.)

Mauch also decided to add Danny Cater, another versatile infielder/outfielder, to the roster. Cater's minor league stats also were impressive. He had hit for average if not for power at every minor league level. In 1961 at Williamsport, Cater had hit .343 while playing third base. Although he lacked raw power, Cater was regarded by the Phillies as a valuable reserve. At Triple A Buffalo and Arkansas in 1962–63, he had played the outfield, second, third and first base while batting close to .300. Mauch always liked to have players who were versatile, and Cater's flexibility appealed to him — he could even play third base in an emergency. He made it easy for Mauch to keep him by having a good spring training.

During the 1964 season both men would prove their value. Herrnstein would alternate between first base and the outfield, playing 69 games in the outfield and 68 at first base. Cater, who was injured during the season, was in left field most of the time, 39 games, but he filled in at first in seven games and even took over third base one time.

Top: Jim Bunning, his uniform soaked with sweat, tells Phillies trainer Joe Liscio that he is fine. Mauch, catcher Gus Triandos, Ruben Amaro, Tony Taylor and John Herrnstein look on. *Bottom:* Rookie Johnny Briggs steals second against the Mets, as second baseman Ron Hunt loses the ball. (Urban Archies, Temple University, Philadelphia Pennsylvania.)

Along with these three newcomers, the Phillies were forced to carry two other rookies, Rick Wise and Johnny Briggs, or risk losing them under the first year bonus rule then in effect. Both Wise and Briggs had played at Bakersfield in the fast paced California League. Wise was an 18-year-old pitcher with great potential, while Briggs was 20, and in his first season in professional baseball had hit 20 homers while batting .297. It was typical of Mauch that instead of just sitting them on the bench he managed to get some use out of them during a pennant race.

Briggs got into 61 games, most of them as a left-handed pinch hitter or defensive replacement, while Wise went 5–3 in 25 games including eight appearances as a spot starter. He pitched the second game of the doubleheader against the Mets in which Jim Bunning threw his perfect game. Wise didn't give up a hit himself until the fifth inning of that game. Wise says he spent the year in a fog, just happy to be in the majors. He was in awe of Mauch and gladly did whatever was asked of him, either starting or relieving.[14]

By keeping five rookies Mauch belied his reputation for preferring veterans and distrusting younger players: "valuing pedigree over performance" in the words of *Daily News* baseball writer, Bill Conlin.[15] He had nurtured Gonzalez, Taylor, Short, Dalrymple, and especially Callison who was regarded as his pet, through difficult times and watched them grow into solid major leaguers. When he first came to the Phillies, Herrnstein thought that Mauch did not fully trust rookies but Allen's success and the professionalism the first-year players showed gradually won Mauch's respect as the season wore on.[16]

The Phillies had a set lineup by the end of the spring training. The infield would consist of Sievers at first, Taylor at second, Wine and Amaro sharing shortstop and Allen at third base. Dalrymple, backed by Triandos, would handle the catching. The outfield would be Callison in right and Gonzalez in center. Covington in left field would alternate with various right-handed hitters. Danny Cater was Mauch's first choice to platoon with Covington off his fine spring training. The infield and outfield reserves would be Cater, Herrnstein, Briggs and Cookie Rojas. Mauch planned to use Rojas as both the backup to Taylor and as a possible infield-outfield replacement, especially if Cater faltered.

Rojas emerged as one of the most pleasant surprises of the 1964 team. While hitting a tough .291, in 109 games Rojas played wherever Mauch needed him: 70 games in the outfield, mostly in difficult center field, 20 at second base and 18 at shortstop. He gave Mauch the kind of flexibility he loved as a manager. Along with Callison, Allen, Short and Bunning, Rojas was one of the most valuable players on the 1964 squad.

Mauch tried various combinations of the batting order all spring as he searched for the proper mix. He finally settled on just the top four: Taylor would lead off followed by some combination of Allen, Callison and Gonzalez batting second or third with Sievers hitting cleanup. As it turned out Mauch had to improvise constantly during the season while he sought to keep a hot bat in the top of the lineup. Other than Callison and Allen who Mauch relied on heavily, he juggled the lineup throughout the season. In effect, the Phillies never had a set batting order in 1964.

The starting pitchers would be Bunning, Bennett, Mahaffey and Culp with Chris Short as a swingman between the bullpen and the starting rotation. Baldschun headed the relief corps, although Quinn and Mauch were worried about their bullpen depth. They had used Johnny Klippstein there in 1963 and he had performed admirably, saving eight games while compiling a team best 1.93 ERA. However, Klippstein was 36 and the Phillies' brass was looking for someone younger to take the pressure off Baldschun. Dallas Green had been used as both a starter and reliever in 1963, winning seven games. But he was suspect in Mauch's eyes. Green had never recovered from the arm problems he developed in the minors and was a journeyman at best. He struggled badly in spring training and probably was kept by the Phillies because Bob Carpenter admired his fellow Delawarian. The other bullpen specialist in 1963, former Yankee fireballer Ryne Duren, had won six games that year but he had a long history of alcohol problems which shook the Phillies' faith in him.

During the season Quinn would tamper with the pitching staff as he searched for more depth. Two weeks into the season, he bought Ed Roebuck from the Washington Senators to give the bullpen another strong right arm. Roebuck would pay great dividends, especially early in the season. The rest of the bullpen was let go early in the 1964 season. Green was sent back to the minors although he would finish the season with the parent club. Duren and Kippstein were sold to other major league teams, a move that turned out to be a mistake as the Phillies would be shorthanded in the bullpen by the end of the season as Mauch overworked Baldschun and Roebuck.

The Phillies went 12–14 in their Grapefruit League games. Allen astonished everyone with his power, hitting long homers while playing third adequately. He finished with nine homers in spring training, the most of any major leaguer and a portent of things to come. The Phillies team that broke camp in April 1964 looked like a thoroughly professional team and ready to pick up where they left off in 1963. A few of the players even believed that they had an outside chance to win the pennant if everything broke their way. Still a lot of questions remained. Could a team that was carrying five rookies compete with the top clubs in the National League? Did Sievers have another year in him? Would Allen be as good as he seemed? What about Mahaffey? Could he make a comeback from his ankle and arm problems? How about Bennett? Would he finally be healthy for a full season?

Herrnstein, a rookie trying to secure a place for himself, didn't believe the Phillies were a pennant contender at first. He thought that the team's momentum from the previous season was "a plus. But winning the league was not a hot topic of conversation at the beginning of the season."[17] Bob Oldis, a backup catcher struggling to make the team, agreed. He also didn't think the Phillies had a realistic shot at winning the pennant.[18] Roy Sievers, on the other hand, was impressed by the team's attitude and positive outlook going into the 1964 campaign. He based his optimism on the fact that the Phillies had played well in 1963 and way "everyone showed up with a desire to win" in spring training.[19]

The only unusual aspect of the 1964 spring training was a typical Mauch gambit. He didn't pitch Bunning against any National League team, instead carefully spotting him against the American League opponents. This led to speculation that Mauch was afraid to expose Bunning to the National League's tough left-handed hitters. Mauch's reasoning was different. Always looking for an edge, he believed that National League hitters would have a harder time adjusting to Bunning then the reverse. "The biggest adjustment," Mauch argued, "between pitchers and hitters who haven't seen each other is on the side of the hitter."[20] He told Bunning "when the National League hitters see you, they will be seeing you for the first time and only when it counts."[21]

Only in his last start in spring training against the Pirates did Mauch allow Bunning to face National League hitters. He was bombed, giving up 8 hits and 11 runs in just 3⅔ innings. The Philadelphia writers were concerned but they didn't know that Mauch had told Bunning to just loosen up for his first start of the season. "Don't show them anything," Mauch told Bunning, "just get yourself loose. To hell with the game."[22]

Mauch was right — there was nothing to worry about. Bunning began the season 10–2 and didn't lose a game at home until July 11th.

A Fast Start

There was tremendous excitement in Philadelphia as the 1964 season began. The Phillies had built up a loyal following since the early 1960s and attendance had risen the last two seasons to over 900,000 in 1963 with predictions it easily would surpass the million mark in 1964. Things looked good going into the new season. The Phillies announced that ticket sales had increased by 50 percent. While the most expensive box seats in the ballpark, selling for $3.25, were becoming more difficult to come by, there still were plenty of general admission tickets available at $1.25. Just before the season began it was announced that Mauch had been named winner of the prestigious Wanamaker Award, given to the coach or manager who reflected the greatest credit on the city of Philadelphia. Past winners had included Eagles linebacker Chuck Bednarik, and among future winners would be the Philadelphia novelist, John Wideman, of the University of Pennsylvania.

Philadelphia in 1964 was in the midst of one of the city's biggest boom periods of prosperity in its history. Industry continued to grow, unemployment was low and there was a tremendous degree of optimism in the city not only about its favorite sports team but also about the city's future itself. The Kennedy assassination had thrown a pall over the city where the ex-president had been extremely popular. He had carried Philadelphia in 1960 by over 331,000 votes—the largest majority in the city's electoral history, greater than anything that Franklin Delano Roosevelt had been able to command. The new president, Lyndon Johnson, had cultivated the local Democratic powers that be as he prepared for his election in the fall. Viet Nam was a minor cloud on the horizon, as yet hardly mentioned in the city's three major papers. In a sense 1964 was the high watermark of Philadelphia's post–World War II expansion. In the next few years, bitter racial divisions in the city and the growing cloud of war in Viet Nam combined to put the city into a funk it never really recovered from until the boom decade of the late 1990s.

As opening day approached Philadelphia didn't show much interest in the coming presidential election. The city, with its large Irish and Catholic population, had been enamored with John Kennedy and showed little enthusiasm for either his successor Lyndon Johnson or the Republican front-runner, Barry Goldwater. Goldwater all but wrote off Philadelphia and the state of Pennsylvania, which seemed safely in Democrats' hands come November.

Johnson eventually poured on the pressure to capture the city and state by big margins. Just before the election he toured Philadelphia and drew huge crowds. In the election he won the city by over 400,000 votes, the largest margin in the city's history, and easily carried Pennsylvania by almost a million and a half votes.

At the local level the mayor James H.J. Tate had been elected to a full term in 1963 but by the smallest margin since the reform movement had taken power in the city in the late 1940s. The biggest problem for Tate and the seemingly all-powerful Democratic machine was an investigation launched by the Republican attorney general of the state into corruption in the judicial system, specifically payoffs and bribes in the Magistrates Court. Appointed to run the investigation was an aggressive and ambitious lawyer Arlen Specter. Specter would secure indictments leading to the abolition of the Magistrate Court system and begin his career as a major political force in Philadelphia and Pennsylvania politics.

The investigation into the Democratic machine made Tate uncomfortable and looking for a way to enhance his image. In mid-summer he finally convinced City Council to put a $25 million bond issue for a new multipurpose stadium on the November ballot. It passed in the Johnson landslide, and the city took the first step toward building a new ballpark as the 1964 season drew to a close.

Tate as mayor did not enjoy the tradition of throwing out the first ball of the season because of the fans booing. The booing wasn't personal but instead was the fans' way of saying "lets get this game started." Tate's predecessor, Richardson Dilworth, had laughed off the booing, waving back at the fans, but the insecure Tate took it personally.

Just before opening day the local newspapers and their baseball writers, Stan Hochman of the *Daily News*, Allen Lewis of the *Inquirer* and Ray Kelly of the *Bulletin*, were upbeat in their predictions about the Phillies and gave them an outside chance at the pennant although they thought that third place seemed a more realistic possibility. They agreed that if Bennett and Mahaffey were healthy, and Bunning could win in a new league and, most importantly, if Allen could handle third base, the Phillies would be tough. Mauch had told the press that he believed 95 games would win the pennant and he believed the Phillies were capable of adding eight more victories to the 87 they won in 1963. As it turned out he wasn't off by much: 93 victories won the pennant.

There were some clouds on the horizon for the Phillies as the season began: Cal McLish was still suffering from the arm problems that plagued him during the last month of the 1963 season. Mauch hoped that McLish would round into shape in spring training, but the Phillies started the season with him on the disabled list. The Phillies now were counting on him to be ready to pitch by June or July. Of equal concern Roy Sievers suddenly looked old. At 37 it was hard to believe that he could match his hitting feats for the Phillies during the last two seasons. Ray Culp was slow to recover from the sore elbow he developed in the second half of 1963. As to the Allen issue, Mauch pointed out that third base was easier to master than second base or shortstop, positions Allen had played in the minors. What Mauch didn't mention was that Allen was a poor defensive second baseman or shortstop, the reason the Phillies brass had moved him to the outfield.

Mauch remained cautiously optimistic as the season began. He and Quinn had decided to cut down on the number of doubleheaders the Phillies were scheduled to play from 13 in 1963 to 7. Mauch believed that doubleheaders put too much strain on the pitching staff and in particular wore out the bullpen. He and Quinn were also optimistic because the Phillies had been one of the best second-half teams in both 1962 and 1963.

Clay Dalrymple, who was becoming the closest thing to an on the field general, told Allen Lewis of the *Inquirer* that he believed the Phillies could win with the players they started the season with. "I don't think we really need any more than everybody have a good year."[23]

The Phillies started off fast. To the surprise of a lot of people, Mauch named Bennett as his opening day pitcher against the New York Mets instead of Bunning. Mauch wanted Bennett to keep the confidence he had gained after coming back from his ankle injury and pitching well in the second half of 1963. Before a crowd of 21,000 on a cold, rainy April night, the Phillies won their opening game 5–3. Roy Sievers hit a three-run homer in the first inning off Al Jackson, raising hopes that his spring training woes were a fluke and he was going to have a good year.

Bennett struggled and was removed after four innings. The victory went to Johnny Klippstein working out of the bullpen. The Phillies' defense, often underrated, made two spectacular double plays to bail them out of potential big innings and kill Met rallies.

Bunning handily won game two, 4–1, giving up just 1 run and 7 hits while striking out 11 in his first National League start. He set the tone for his season by striking out the first three batters he faced and closed out the game by striking out the side in the ninth inning. Tony Gonzalez won the game with a three-run homer in the eighth inning.

Mahaffey started the third game of the season against the Cubs in

Chicago, but he wasn't around at the end. Again the bullpen, in the person of Johnny Klippstein, saved the day as the Phillies won 11–8 when Sievers hit his second homer in three days. This was a source of optimism for the Phillies as Sievers did not hit his second homer in 1963 until May 26th. Sievers' early success soon faded as he was beset with injuries which eventually ended his season with the Phillies and shortened his career.

The next day, Culp in his first start of the season, suffered the team's first defeat 7–0 at the hands of a notorious Phillie killer, Bob Buhl, who had beaten them 12 times dating back to 1959.

In their first four games, the Phillies' starters, other than Bunning, hadn't pitched particularly well, but the weather was terrible and the team didn't look comfortable as yet. The Phillies were winning with good defense and some timely home run hitting. In their 11–8 triumph over the Cubs, the Phillies hit three home runs in one inning.

Over the next two and a half weeks, Mauch alternated the same four starters. In fact, they started the first 20 games of the Phillies' schedule. After Culp's loss to the Cubs, the Phillies went on to finish April with six victories in seven games for a 9–2 record, including a five and one record at home, the teams best start in over 30 years. Phillies' fans, always difficult to please, were starting a love affair with the home team. There was a definite growing sense that something positive might be happening. Suddenly "Go Phillies Go" signs began to appear all over the city. After losing to Buhl, the Phillies dropped one more game, a 4–1 setback to Larry Jackson of the Cubs. All the Phillies starters except for Mahaffey had contributed victories in April.

In early May after having won four straight, the Phillies suffered through their first losing streak, four games on the road to the Braves and the Cardinals. On May 6th this left them in third place, the lowest point they would reach during the season. Neither Mahaffey nor Culp were pitching well although Mahaffey's loss to the Braves was by a 1–0 score. A journeymen right-hander Hank Fischer, who always seemed to crank up a good game against the Phillies, beat him.

Culp with a 1–1 record was a major concern. His elbow was still tender and probably made worse by the unseasonably cold weather in April and early May. He lost the first game of the Phillies' four-game losing streak when the Braves bombed him 11–2. While Mahaffey and Culp struggled, Chris Short was virtually unhittable working out of the bullpen. Mauch was using him in long relief and he was simply overpowering. He relieved Mahaffey on April 28th in the eighth inning of a

Early in the season, first baseman Roy Sievers stretches for a throw to double a Braves' runner off first. (Urban Archives, Temple University, Philadelphia Pennsylvania.)

game against the hard-hitting Reds and retired all six batters he faced, five of them by strikeouts. Eventually Mauch pulled Culp from the starting rotation and put Short in his place. Short made his first start of the season on May 10th against the Reds and lost a tough 2–0 decision to Joe Nuxhall, another Phillie killer who took great pleasure in beating Mauch. Mauch, a notorious bench jockey, took special pleasure in taunting the 35-year-old veteran who was in his second tour of duty with the Reds. Nuxhall reciprocated the ill feelings. He disliked Mauch and would go on to beat the Phillies three out of four times in 1964. After his performance against the Reds, Short became a regular starter and blossomed into one of the best left-handed pitchers in the National League.

Short was just 26 and had been a part of the Phillies' staff since 1960. He had shown signs of impressive talent in the past — his fastball ranked with the best in the league — but he was inconsistent like so many young left-handers. Mauch stuck with him because of his live arm, and Short started to come around in 1962 and 1963 when he averaged 10 wins.

Short was a typical left-handed flake. His nickname was "Style" not because of his pitching delivery, which indeed was stylish, but because he was easily the worst dresser on the team. On some road trips he carried his clothes in a plastic bag. His teammates loved him because he was a genuine eccentric. What Mauch liked about him, other than his live arm, was his confidence and ability to pitch without a great deal of rest. Short believed he could get any hitter out, and in contrast with the equally gifted Mahaffey who was a constant worrier, Short just rolled along. Short went on to become the most successful Phillies left-hander until Steve Carlton came along. He won 132 games in his career with the Phillies, including a 20-victory season in 1966. He still holds the Phillies record for most strikeouts in a game, 18, in a 15-inning game against the Mets in 1965.

The Phillies' bats had finally come alive in late April. Allen got off to a torrid start, hitting .350, and was third in the league in RBIs on May 8 as well as leading the Phillies in every offensive category. Tony Taylor was over .300 and Wes Covington finally began to hit after a very slow start that saw his average dip to .160. Gonzalez was struggling around the .235 mark while Johnny Callison, Clay Dalrymple and Roy Sievers were all slumping. Sievers was in and out of the lineup with various complaints, the most serious a nagging calf injury that was not responding to treatment. He was largely reduced to pinch hitting assignments.

After their four-game losing streak in early May, the Phillies rebounded with four consecutive victories including three against a slug ging Braves team led by Hank Aaron, Eddie Mathews and Joe Torre. Ed Roebuck, who the Phillies bought from the Washington Senators on April 26th, won the first game against the Braves with two innings of brilliant relief work. He would eventually pitch 18⅔ innings before giving up his first run in a Phillies uniform. Covington got the game-winning hit, a two-run homer in the eighth inning. Culp was ineffective once again.

The next night, May 7th, the Phillies pummeled the Braves 9–6 behind Mahaffey as they got revenge against Fischer for his whitewashing of them four days earlier. Mahaffey pitched well, silencing the Braves' bats as the Phillies built up a seven run lead for him, 9–2. But then he was rocked for four runs and Mauch had to go to the bullpen once more. This time Jack Baldschun ended the Braves threat and saved the game for Mahaffey. Dalrymple was the big gun, breaking out of a terrible slump with his first hit in two weeks, a two-run homer.

Over the next two nights, the Phillies beat the Reds twice with Covington driving in five runs in the first game as Dennis Bennett surrendered just four hits while improving his record to 3–2. Bunning was battered the next night, but Dallas Green come on in relief to win the game as Tony Gonzalez drove in the winning run with a two out hit in the bottom of the eighth inning.

Chris Short was the greatest left-handed pitcher in Phillies history, until Hall-of-Famer Steve Carlton surpassed him. He came into his own in 1964, winning 17 games while compiling an excellent 2.20 ERA. Short would win 132 games for the Phillies over his 14-year career. (Courtesy Philadelphia Phillies.)

At this point the Phillies were 14–6 in second place. They were finally getting decent hitting but more importantly, the hitting was also spread throughout the lineup and not confined to just a couple of hitters. Allen, Taylor, Gonzalez, Covington, as well as rookies John Herrnstein and Danny Cater were all swinging the bats well.

4—A Phillies Surprise

Starting May 10 with Short's loss in his first start, the Phillies lost three consecutive games, all to left-handers. After Nuxhall beat Short, Ray Sadecki and Curt Simmons of the Cardinals beat the Phillies. For Simmons this brought his record against them to 13–2. He would defeat them three more times in 1964 including a crucial game during the September collapse. Like Nuxhall Simmons took a special pleasure in beating his old team for giving up on him in April 1960. Between 1960 and the end of the 1964 season Simmons would win 59 games, 14 of them against the Phillies. If it wasn't for his victories over the Phillies, Simmons would have been just a .500 pitcher.

The losses to Nuxhall, Sadecki and Simmons highlighted the Phillies' weakness against lefties. Aside from Allen and perhaps Taylor, the right-handed batters in the Phillies lineup didn't scare anyone, especially with Sievers all but useless.

Not everyone was worried about the Phillies' vulnerability to left-handed pitchers. Alvin Dark, manager of the Giants, thought the Phillies could overcome this weakness. He believed that only the top left-handers, the Koufaxs and Spahns, could dominate them. "The rinky dink lefties can't do it," he predicted.[24] It's funny that Dark mentioned Spahn among the top lefties because the Phillies beat him three times in 1964.

Dark's prediction didn't hold up. During one stretch of 17 games in July, the opposition started 11 left-handers against the Phillies. The Phillies won six of the games but were beaten by the likes of Wade Blasingame of the Braves, Gordon Richardson of the Cardinals and Larry Miller of the Dodgers—rinky dinks all.

The Phillies quickly rebounded from their brief three-game losing streak, something they would do throughout the season until the last two weeks. Until their late September collapse, the Phillies would never lose more than four consecutive games. In fact, consistency was a hallmark of the 1964 Phillies. Their longest winning streak was five, a figure they achieved twice, and their longest losing streak before the collapse was four. Throughout most of the season, the Phillies played steady .600 baseball.

After losing to Simmons, the next night, May 14th, Bunning raised his record to 4–1, beating the Cardinals with relief help from Roebuck. At this time the Phillies also made a major roster change. They released Don Hoak, signaling that there were no longer any doubts about Allen's ability to handle third base. They also sold Ryne Duren to Cincinnati. With the success of the Baldschun-Roebuck tandem, Mauch believed that Duren was expendable. The Phillies could have used him later.

On May 15th Dennis Bennett beat the Colts in Houston, shutting them out 4–0 as the Phillies began a 13-game road trip that included stops in Houston, San Francisco, Los Angeles and finishing in Pittsburgh. Overall the Phillies went 7–6 on this their longest road trip of the season. They began the trip in first place by percentage points and arrived home in second place, one game out of first — not bad, all things considered.

After Bennett beat the Colts, Ray Culp lost the next night, lowering his record to 1–4 as former Phillie Dick Farrell beat him. Mauch took Culp out of the starting rotation at this point and started to use him in long relief in hopes of both rebuilding his confidence and his arm strength. Culp would not start another game for almost three weeks and would not win another game for almost a month. His struggles along with Mahaffey's erratic efforts were the first chink in Mauch's pre-season boast about having the best first through seven pitching staff in the National League.

Short and Bunning threw back-to-back shutouts over the Colts in the last two games of the Houston series. It was Short's first victory of the season, a nine-strikeout gem. Bunning's performance was an overpowering one hitter with Jim Wynn singling in the fifth inning for the Colts' only hit. Bennett saw his record drop to 4–3 as he lost the first game of a three-game set to the Giants. Former Phillie Jack Sanford, who was struggling and would go on the disabled list in mid-July, hurled a four hitter.

The Phillies beat Juan Marichal 7–2 in the second game as Richie Allen hit his eighth homer of the season and Johnny Callison went 5–5 to break out of his sluggish streak of hitting. The Phillies' triumph ended a 12-game winning streak by Marichal. The victory went to Jack Baldschun in relief of Art Mahaffey who had pitched a decent game.

Eighteen-year-old Rick Wise made his first major league start in the next game but the Phillies lost 9–4. Johnny Klippstein took the loss. Giant lefty Bob Hendley was the winning pitcher.

The Phillies moved on to Los Angeles where they took two of three from the Dodgers. Short beat Don Drysdale with his second straight shutout. At this point Short had allowed just one earned run in 32 innings of pitching. The defeat for Drysdale was the fifth consecutive Phillies victory over him after he had beat them 13 straight times dating from 1958 to May 1963. They would saddle him with four more defeats before he beat them again.

Bennett won the second game, a 14-inning marathon, by a 4–3

score. Bennett pitched 13 innings in the game, including a stretch of ten shutout innings. At that time it wasn't unusual for pitchers to go that long in a game. Given Bennett's arm and shoulder problems later on in the season, one wonders if it might not have been wiser to limit his innings. In the last game of the three-game set, Bunning saw his record drop to 5–2 when rookie Joe Moeller shut out the Phillies, 3–0. The Phillies who had beaten the Dodgers seven in a row had a chance to win the game late, but Dodger manager Walter Alston brought Sandy Koufax in to save the game. It was his only relief appearance of the season. At this point on the western road trip, the Phillies had won six of ten games. Their record stood at 21-13 and they held on to first place by percentage points.

The Phillies ended the long road trip by losing two of three to the Pirates. Short was bombed for the first time and was knocked out of the box after just ⅔ of an inning in game one. Culp, in a relief appearance, gave up six hits and three runs in five innings. Mahaffey won the second game of the series with a 2–0 shutout over Bob Friend. It was the second of five victories he scored over the Pirates in 1964. For some reason he had the number of the hard hitting Pirates team. The Phillies lost the last game of the series 6–5 as Bennett was knocked out of the game and reliever Jack Baldschun gave up the winning run in the bottom of the ninth inning.

Perfection

All things considered, the Phillies were not doing badly as the team returned home on May 29th for the longest home stand of the season, 16 games. They had a 22-15 record good enough for second place behind the red-hot San Francisco Giants. They were getting good starting pitching from Bunning, Short and Bennett and effective work from the bullpen duo of Roebuck and Baldschun. The offense had finally picked up. Allen kept getting better and was among the league leaders in batting average, home runs and RBIs. Callison was showing signs of coming around, and the two rookies Herrnstein and Cater were doing their part. Cater was platooning in left with Covington, while Herrnstein had taken over at first for the slumping and injured Roy Sievers.

The Phillies by now were concerned about Sievers' future. His calf muscle injury had grown worse and he was now hemorrhaging around the ankle. Quinn and Mauch were coming to the belief that he would have to be replaced. Sievers was making an occasional start and pinch hitting, and he felt that the calf injury was slowly healing. He told Quinn not to give up on him, as he would be ready for a September stretch drive. Quinn and Mauch however were preparing to unload Sievers. Interestingly, in September with the woeful Washington Senators, Sievers would hit four home runs. He believes that he was just the kind of right-handed hitter the Phillies needed then.[25] He doesn't note that he batted just .172 for the Senators.

The Phillies' longest home stand would be against the west coast teams plus the Pirates and the Mets. They won their first three games over Houston to raise their record to 25–15 on June 1st. It was a vast improvement over the same point in 1963 when they were 18–22.

The first game of the home stand showed how the Phillies overcame adversity all season. Bunning started against Bob Bruce and had a no hitter with two out in the sixth inning. Then the roof caved in when Wes Covington, never known for his glove work, misplayed a fly ball to left. Bunning came unglued and not only lost his no hitter but also saw Houston score five unanswered runs, knocking him out of the game. Bennett came on and eventually won the game in relief, 7–6 on a pinch-hit double by Gus Triandos that tied the score and a triple by Cookie Rojas that drove in the winning run.

The game was typical of how the Phillies rallied all season. For some reason they often did their best hitting late in the game. They also were very tough in the clutch, especially Allen and Callison. The victory put the Phillies back in first place by percentage points again. This was their best record on that date in 50 years.

Rojas was proving a godsend for Mauch. He was playing everywhere, filling in at short when Mauch pinch hit for the light-hitting combo of Wine and Amaro. He also spelled Tony Taylor at second and was more than adequate in left or center field where he often played if a left-hander was pitching. At this point in the season, Rojas was hitting an astounding .528. In Rojas the Phillies had added a superb reserve, the forerunner of the great, versatile bench players of the future.

The Phillies began the home stand with five consecutive victories. In the first game Roebuck pitched brilliantly in relief, while Short improved his record to 3–2. Dennis Bennett upped his record to 7–3 the next night. In the last game of the Colts series, Mahaffey pitched a three hitter but with seven walks to win 4–1. Roebuck also saved the game, his fifth since the Phillies got him in late April. He was proving invaluable to Mauch, who was not afraid to go to his bullpen with the game on the line.

4—A Phillies Surprise

On June 3rd the Phillies beat Drysdale again in a tough 1–0, 11-inning game that saw the winning run score when Jim Gilliam failed to handle Tony Gonzalez's infield chopper with a runner on third. It seemed at times as if the Phillies were inventing new ways to win games.

The Phillies first loss in the home stand game on June 4th when Sandy Koufax hurled the third no hitter of his career, one which he labeled the "best of all."[26] It was almost a perfect game as Koufax was overpowering. Only four balls were hit to the outfield while Koufax struck out 12, including a clearly over-matched Bobby Wine, to end the game. Koufax faced 27 batters as he walked Richie Allen on a questionable call, but Allen was out trying to steal. Short was the losing pitcher, giving up just three runs with the big hit being a long home run to the roof of the left field stands by Frank Howard. The defeat left Short's record at 3–3.

The no hitter threw the Phillies into a slump as they lost the next three games to the Giants for their second four-game losing streak of the season. These games featured managerial duels between Mauch and Dark—old friends who each tried to outwit and out-maneuver the other. In one of the games, Dark put the winning run on base and got out of the inning. In another he ordered a walk with men on first and second to load the bases. He got out of that inning also.

Art Mahaffey started the first game of the series against Juan Marichal. Neither pitcher was around at the end as Jack Baldschun was tagged for two runs in the 11th inning. Mahaffey pitched well as he usually did against the Giants, allowing three runs on four hits but he was wild, walking seven batters. In the second game of the Giants series, Roebuck was beaten when Tom Haller hit a two-run homer, the first runs that Roebuck had allowed in 18⅔ innings or relief. In the series finale, the Giants won 4–3 in ten innings. Bunning pitched well for the Phillies, but Roebuck was the loser for the second consecutive game.

The Phillies rebounded and went 5–2 in the remaining games of the home stand. Mahaffey beat the Pirates for the third time in the first game. He was in command until Jerry Lynch hit a three-run homer to move the Pirates to within one run of the Phillies. Mauch brought in Roebuck to save the game despite his back-to-back losses, and he closed the door for Mahaffey. Culp, making his first start since May 16th, was beaten by rookie Steve Blass, giving up four runs and seven hits in just less than five innings. The Phillies won the last game of the Pirates series as Chris Short threw a four hitter and struck out eight batters.

The Mets arrived in Philadelphia on June 12th for a big weekend series. On Friday night Dennis Bennett was pounded for five runs in just 2⅔ innings as the Mets battered the Phillies 11–3. The Phillies swept the last three games of the home stand, including a doubleheader triumph on Sunday. Bunning won Saturday's game 8–2 although he was in and out of trouble the entire game. The Sunday doubleheader attracted 21,000 fans, and they saw the Mets take a 4–3 lead against Short and knock him out of the box in the first game. The Phillies rallied to win 9–5 as Culp came on to pitch five strong innings in relief. In the second game Mahaffey won 4–2 to raise his record to 6–2 for the season. In the last three games, Callison hit two homers to raise his total to six for the season. Allen hit an unbelievable 425-foot inside the park home run in the first game Sunday, a high towering drive that bounced off the light tower in right field. It was his 13th of the season and kept him among the league leaders in homers.

Mauch was encouraged by Culp's performance. He seemed to be coming around as he had pitched effectively in relief the last few times. Mauch decided to move him back into the starting rotation where he and Mahaffey alternated as the fourth starter behind Bunning, Short and Bennett.

Monday June 15th was the trade deadline in those days, and the Phillies had an off day before heading to Chicago for a two-city eight-game road trip. The Phillies were in first place with a 32–21 record as they remained right around the .600 mark. They now were clearly a serious contender for the pennant. Quinn, a master trader, made no moves, indicating he thought the Phillies were right where they wanted to be at this stage of the season. Talks with the Giants about reviving the Cepada for Mahaffey trade got nowhere when the Giants were in town, probably because of Mahaffey's inconsistency despite his deceptive 6–2 record.

The Phillies didn't make any trades, but that day one was made that would prove perhaps the decisive turning point of the season. The Cubs sent outfielder Lou Brock to the Cardinals for pitcher Ernie Broglio. Broglio was 3–5 at the time but had been a big winner in the past, having won 18 games in 1963 while Brock, still young at 25, had shown potential but was hitting just .251 with two homers at the time of the trade. The Cards were getting a youngster who in two seasons with the Cubs had yet to hit and who also was considered a poor outfielder. At the time the trade was considered a minor one. If anyone had the edge, the consensus was that it was the Cubs because Broglio had been a big winner in the past. As it turned out Broglio was damaged goods and had serious elbow problems, while the change of scenery was just what Brock needed.[27] He went on to hit .348 with the Cards and steal 33 bases in the process, giving them the final piece they needed to complete their outfield: Mike Shannon in right, Curt Flood in center and Brock in left. The Cardinals' trade launched Brock on the road to Cooperstown. Given their solid infield of Boyer, Groat, Javier and White plus a handful of quality starters—Bob Gibson, Curt Simmons, Ray Sadecki—the trade for Brock meant the Cardinals had the potential to be a truly good team. At the time the Cardinals got Brock, they were playing terrible baseball, having lost 17 of their last 23 games. He soon helped change that.

Following their long home stand, the Phillies arrived in Chicago for three day games—there were no lights in Wrigley Field—before heading to New York for a five-game set against the pathetic Mets. The Phillies were hoping to make headway against two of the weaker teams in the National League, something they successfully had done in the past two seasons.

The Phillies played exceptional baseball during the road trip, winning six of the eight games behind solid pitching. In the eight games, the Phillies staff allowed an average of 2.5 runs. Bennett and Short won their two starts against Larry Jackson and Dick Ellsworth, two of the Cubs' best pitchers. But Bob Buhl continued his mastery over the Phillies as he beat his longtime cousins for the second time that season. Bunning started the game for the Phillies but was knocked out by the Cubs although the loss went to Baldschun in relief.

When the Phillies arrived in New York June 19th for their five-game series, two doubleheaders plus a Saturday game, they remained in first place by percentage points over the Giants. Behind Mahaffey and Culp, who gave up just three runs between them, the Phillies easily swept the Friday twi-night doubleheader. Mahaffey saw his record improve to 7–2 as he won his third consecutive start. On Saturday Bennett started against the Mets right-hander Jack Fisher but was not around at the finish as the Mets won 7–3. Dallas Green was the losing pitcher although Jack Baldschun was hit hard, giving up five hits and three runs and turning a close game into a Met rout. The game was noteworthy for another reason. Roy Sievers hit his fourth and last home run of the season for the Phillies. He would play infrequently after this and eventually be sold to his old team, the Washington Senators, in mid-July. He never recovered from the calf injury he suffered early in the season.

The loss of Sievers' right-hand bat eventually created a major problem for the Phillies. They had no strong right-handed hitter to replace him although they tried Danny Cater at first. He did an adequate job, hitting for a high average, but he lacked power. Then he was injured in a collision at first base and was not a factor in the pennant race.

While Sievers struggled, John Herrnstein took over at first base against right-handed pitching but his average began to dip once the word got around the league that he had trouble with off-speed pitches. Pitchers avoided throwing him fastballs and served him a steady diet of breaking balls and change of pace offerings the last three months of the season. When Herrnstein faltered, the Phillies eventually tried nine players at first including one of their prized minor league prospects, Costen Shockley. Shockley, like Herrnstein a left-handed hitter, smacked a long homer against the Reds early in his stay with the Phillies, but it soon became clear he was overmatched by major league pitching. The Phillies continued to try various combinations at first until early August when John Quinn got Frank Thomas from the Mets to solve the first base problem.

None of these problems seemed to matter as the Phillies on Father's Day, Sunday, June 21st, swept a doubleheader against the Mets. In game one, Jim Bunning upped his record to 7–2 as he hurled a perfect game, the first in the majors since Don Larsen did so against the Dodgers in the 1956 World Series and the first to do so in a regular season game since 1922.

Jim Bunning won 19 games for the '64 Phillies, and served as the anchor of the pitching staff for four years. Besides striking out 219 batters over the season, he also pitched the first perfect game in the major leagues since 1956. Bunning lost three games during the ten-game losing streak. (Courtesy Philadelphia Phillies.)

In humid 91 degree weather, Bunning was overwhelming, striking out 10 while throwing 90 pitches, 69 of them strikes. His control was so good that he went to a three-ball count just twice and was behind two balls no strikes only two times. There was only one close play. In the fifth inning the Mets' catcher Jesse Gonder hit one of Bunning's few mistakes, a smash in the hole between first and second base. Tony Taylor dove for the ball, knocked it down and threw Gonder out.

Bunning knew he had something special going according to Mauch. Late in the game, Mauch said Bunning broke the cardinal rule of baseball and began to chatter about his no-hitter. He "came back to the dugout yelling, 'nine more to go ... six more ... three more. Do something out there — dive for the balls.'" Bunning's teammates were aghast and tried to avoid him on the bench.

Gus Triandos, the catcher for the game, said that Bunning was chirping away like a magpie. "With two outs to go," Triandos said, "he called me to the mound and said I should tell him a joke, just to give him a breather. I couldn't think of any jokes."[28] Bunning finished the game with a flair by striking out the last batter, pinch hitter John Stephenson.

Bob Carpenter, the Phillies' owner and someone who loved good pitching, called Bunning's masterpiece "one of the greatest thrills I ever had in baseball." For no hitting the Mets, Bunning was invited to appear on the highly rated Ed Sullivan television show that night. He got $1000 for appearing, quite a sum of money in those days of low salaries.[29]

In the second game of the doubleheader, Rick Wise won the first game of his career, giving up just three hits. The Mets didn't get their first base runner of the game until the third inning when Wise walked a batter.

Bunning's and Wise's wins moved the Phillies into a two-game lead over the Giants with a record of 38–23. A sense of expectation began to grow in the city of Philadelphia among the long-suffering Phillies fans. "Maybe this was the year." Everything was falling into place. Allen was a clear favorite to win the Rookie of the Year Award with his incredible hitting feats. Chris Short had arrived as a dominant left-handed pitcher. Dennis Bennett was headed toward a 20-win season. Johnny Callison had started to hit and drive in runs. It was becoming, in the words of Triandos, "the year of Blue Snow," when nothing could go wrong.

When the Phillies returned home for three games late in June, they were the talk of baseball. The National League pennant was theirs for the taking.

5

A Long Hot Summer

Everything They Do Is Right

The summer of 1964, especially the month of July, was an unusually hot one in Philadelphia, a city famous for its sweltering heat and humidity. Air conditioning was still rare outside of theaters, restaurants and bars. As the city sweltered in long periods of 90-degree weather — in 14 days during July temperatures were above that mark, hitting 99 on July 1st — baseball became a distraction as the city's love affair with the Phillies grew deeper. They had played solid baseball for the first two and a half months of the season, moving in and out of first place. But it was Bunning's perfect game that crystallized the romance between the Phillies and their victory starved fans.

Philadelphia's three major newspapers began to expand their coverage of the Phillies as they sensed that something special was happening. Attendance at the run-down old ballpark slowly rose, and it seemed likely that the Phillies would not just break, but would shatter, the single season attendance record set in 1950 when the Whiz Kids won the pennant.

Following Bunning's perfect game, the Phillies seemed to spin their wheels, and they went almost a month playing slightly better than .500 baseball. They alternated periods of brilliant games with stretches of poor play marked by frequent errors and sudden pitching collapses. July turned out to be the team's poorest month in 1964 until the collapse at the end of September. The Phillies' record that month was a so-so 16–14.

The team's mediocre play, especially its fielding lapses, was difficult to explain. Mauch's Phillies were an excellent defensive team. He had stressed basics from the day he took over the Phillies, and the team he put on the field in 1964 was fundamentally sound. Poor fielding was the exception not the rule. Aside from Allen at third who was learning the position and the slow, awkward Covington in left, the Phillies caught the ball and made all the plays. In fact, Allen often made brilliant stops on hard hit grounders, but as Callison noted "he'd throw it all over hell."[1] Wine and Amaro were among the best, if not the best, defensive shortstops in baseball. Both were Gold Glove winners, Wine for the 1963 season while Amaro would be given the award in 1964. With Taylor at second, Wine and Amaro at short, the sure-handed Tony Gonzalez in center and Dalrymple behind the plate, the Phillies were strong up the middle. Gonzalez, it is true, was not a natural centerfielder, but he was steady and made all the basic plays. Callison in right field was the equal of any outfielder in the National League including Aaron and Clemente.

Statistically the Phillies ranked among the best fielding teams in the National League. They made the fourth fewest errors, were third in double plays and fourth overall in fielding average. As a team they normally didn't beat themselves. Their shoddy defensive play in July was the exception not the rule for the 1964 Phillies.

The team's pitching had been strong since the beginning of the season as Bennett, Bunning, Short and occasionally Mahaffey gave the staff four solid starters. Only Culp had problems getting untracked from his elbow problems. The bullpen duo of Baldschun and Roebuck was superb. Roebuck alone saved five games in May and four in June, this at a time when saves were harder to come by than today.

Mauch's approach to his bullpen was to go with the hot hand. As a result he tended to use Roebuck rather than Baldschun in key situations. The danger in this was that Mauch was neglecting the rest of the bullpen. Dallas Green was being used mostly in mop up roles as Mauch had little faith in him. Johnny Klippstein, who had performed brilliantly in 1963, was largely forgotten. At this point, two and a half months into the season the bullpen's performance was superb. But the bullpen's depth was very thin.

When the Phillies arrived home on June 23 for a brief three-game home stand, their record stood at 38–23, which put them in first place, just percentage points ahead of the Giants who would remain their closest rivals throughout July and August. Almost one month later the Phillies were 52–37, having split 28 games. They remained in first only because neither the Giants nor any other team had been able to take advantage of this stretch of mediocre baseball by the Phillies. In fact, if either the Giants or the Phillies had gotten hot at this point, they might have sewn up the pennant as the Cardinals, Reds, Braves and Dodgers also were struggling.

The 1964 Giants were a puzzling team and could easily have won the pennant. They would go on to win 90 games and finish just three games out of first place. But they were riddled with dissension. Alvin Dark, their manager since 1961, had done a good job as skipper. Under him the Giants finished third, first and second, averaging 92 wins. But he had strange ideas about Latin players and even American blacks. He thought somehow they were not as focused as white American players. When he voiced these sentiments during the season in an interview with the writer Stan Isaacs, he courted trouble with a team filled with Latins such as Juan Marichal, Orlando Cepeda, and Matty Alou as well as American Blacks such as Willie Mays, Willie McCovey and Jim Ray Hart.[2] After Isaacs publicized Dark's remarks, Jackie Robinson came to his defense, saying he had known Dark for years and had always "found him to be a gentleman and above all unbiased."[3] Dark now was a marked man. The talk in baseball circles that summer was that Dark would be fired if the Giants didn't win the pennant. The scuttlebutt proved correct and Dark eventually was replaced by Herman Franks, a much more easygoing character.

Despite his baseball brilliance, the baseball establishment never took Alvin Dark seriously again. He continued to manage but was regarded as something of an oddball, especially as he became more outspoken in his religious beliefs. In those days to be branded a religious fanatic was poison. When Dark took over the Oakland A's in the mid-1970s, the egomaniacal owner Charles O. Finley constantly undercut his authority. Dark's Oakland A's team won the World Series in 1974 and the pennant in 1975. For that Finley fired him the next year. Dark never managed again.

The Giants would go on to lead the league in homers with 165 but bat only .246 as a team in 1964. Mays led the National League with 47 homers and drove in 111 runs, while Cepeda hit 34 homers to go along with 97 RBIs. Willie McCovey had a terrible year, batting just .220. But the Giants' real problem all season was pitching. The Giant staff had a decent ERA of 3.19 but only Marichal was a consistent winner — he was 21–8. Only two other Giants won in double figures: Gaylord Perry was 12–11, while Bob Hendley won 10 games versus 11 defeats. The rest of the staff was mediocre. Jack Sanford struggled all season and was effectively finished at age 36. Better starting pitching and more timely hitting could have won the 1964 pennant for the Giants.

5—A Long Hot Summer

The Phillies' three-game home stand against the Cubs began on June 23rd with a twi-night doubleheader which drew the largest crowd of the season, 35,500, as fans flocked to cheer Bunning and see their heroes in action. The Phillies lost the first game to lefty Dick Ellsworth who shut out Short 2–0. In the second game Culp duplicated Ellsworth's feat, hurling a 9–0 whitewash of the Cubs. Culp had a no hitter for 5⅔ innings until reserve outfielder/first baseman Len Gabrielson lined a single to right. It was the only hit off Culp, who pitched his best game of the season and perhaps his career. Culp was furious with himself for not putting the ball where Dalrymple had called for. It was a terrible pitch, which Gabrielson was able to sling into right field.

The Phillies banged out 17 hits including Covington's seventh homer of the season. Callison and Allen had both gotten hot at the same time. After a long struggle early in the season, Callison had now raised his average to the .280 mark, while Allen was fourth in the National League in home runs with 13.

The Phillies won the third game of the abbreviated home stand 9–8 behind the slugging of Allen, who hit a three-run homer, and John Herrnstein, who had one of his best games as a Phillie, going 4–4 including his fourth home run of the season. Allen's three-run homer came in the first inning but Mahaffey couldn't make it stand up. He lasted just 1⅔ innings, with Dallas Green getting the victory. Mahaffey's inconsistency was driving Mauch mad. He would pitch brilliantly in one outing and then suddenly couldn't get beyond the first couple of innings the next time he started. There even were times when Mahaffey had trouble warming up.

Beginning on Friday June 26th, the Phillies embarked on an 11-game road trip to St. Louis, Houston, Los Angeles and San Francisco before the All Star break. They split four games against the Cardinals, who seemed to be going nowhere but played the Phillies tougher than any other team in the league. Bunning was ineffective and Ed Roebuck won the first game 6–5 when Clay Dalrymple hit a two-run homer in the ninth inning. Curt Simmons continued to mystify his former team, raising his record against them to 14–2 with a 9–4 victory. Dennis Bennett pitched poorly, getting knocked out in the first inning, giving up four runs and four hits. His record was now 8–4 but he had pitched poorly in his last two starts. After the game Bennett said he felt fine "but there had to be something wrong when left-handed hitters start ripping you."[4] There was talk that he had a sore arm but Bennett denied that.

At this point Mauch had two reliable starters, Short and Bunning, with Culp, Mahaffey and Bennett being consistently inconsistent. The record of the latter three looked good on paper. They were 19–12 but none of them gave Mauch great confidence when they took the mound.

The Phillies split a Sunday doubleheader with Chris Short hurling a 5–0 shutout in the first. He raised his record to 6–4 while giving up just five hits to a tough Cardinal lineup. In the second game Ray Sadecki beat Culp 8–2 as the Phillies uncharacteristically made six errors. This loss dropped them to second place a game and a half behind the Giants.

The Phillies split two games against their cousins the Houston Colts as Mahaffey was out pitched in game one by Houston's best starter, Bob Bruce. Bunning evened the series and raised his record to 8–3 while allowing only five hits in the second game as the Phillies won handily 8–1. They were still a game and a half behind the Giants in second place.

The Phillies finished the road trip with five games on the west coast, starting with two in Los Angeles. Bennett finally pitched a good game but lost to a better lefty as Sandy Koufax allowed the Phillies five hits, one of them a homer by Callison, struck out 10 and won the game 3–2. The next night Callison hit another homer, his 12th of the season, while Allen hit number 15 as Short beat the Dodgers by the same score 3–2. The Phillies remained in second, still a game and a half out of first place because the Giants couldn't put together a winning streak.

When the Phillies arrived in the City by the Bay on July 2nd for a crucial three-game series with the Giants before All Star break, first place was at stake. At this point the Phillies had split the first eight games of their road trip. A Giant sweep would have sent the Phillies the message that they were not for real despite their fine play so far. As it turned out it was the Phillies who did the sending. They won all three games, two in dramatic fashion to seize first place by one and a half games.

In game one Culp threw a six hitter and held the Giants to one run as Allen went three for three including his team leading 16th home run. The red-hot rookie was now fourth in the National League in homers. Culp raised his record to 5–6, not too bad considering at one point he was 1–5. The next day Jim Bunning went 11 innings as the Phillies beat Gaylord Perry 5–2. In the top of the 11th, Allen tripled home the tie-breaking run and Covington followed with a long home run to ice the game for Bunning. Bunning pitched all 11 innings and retired 17 of the last 18 Giants batters he faced.

The last game of the series was a nail biter. Bennett out dueled Marichal 2–1, as he held a hard-hitting Giants lineup that included such tough right-handed hitters as Willie Mays, Orlando Cepada and Jim Ray

Hart to just six hits. This game raised Bennett's record to 9–4 and may have been the best game he pitched all season but it would be his last victory for almost two months as the mysterious arm problem resurfaced.

The Phillies had taken over first place and in the process wiped out a Giant lead of a game and a half. The National League standings at this point showed that seven teams were within 10½ games of first place.

The Phillies 47–28 entered the All Star break in first place having proven their mettle against their major competitors. At this point Cincinnati was six games back in third place, while Pittsburgh at seven games back rounded out the first division. The eventual pennant winners, the St. Louis Cardinals were a game below .500 at 39–40 and 10 games out of first place. Los Angeles was also 10 games back while the Braves and Cubs were 10½ games out.

Some baseball people had already begun writing off teams that had started slowly, with the consensus being that the Phillies, Reds and Giants would battle for the pennant the rest of the season. Pittsburgh, the Braves, Cubs and Dodgers all had problems that made it unlikely that they could compete for the pennant. The Cards were also being written off as rumors swirled that the volatile owner of the Cardinals, Gussie Busch, was so disgusted by his team's play that he was planning to get rid of the manager, Johnny Keane and replace him with Dodger coach, Leo Durocher.

A close look at the standings shows how the Phillies took advantage of the weaker teams in the league. They were an incredible 24–8, a .750 percentage against the League also rans, the Cubs, Colts and Mets. Against the rest of the league, they were barely better than .500 at 23–20. The Phillies were following a traditional scenario for winning the pennant: beat the also rans and play .500 baseball against the good teams. The only team in the National League with a winning record against the Phillies at this point was the eventual pennant-winning Cardinals.

The Phillies' success was built around the skilled maneuvering of Mauch and the superb play of a half dozen players. Allen and Rojas were hitting better than .300, while Callison had raised his average, after a slow start, to .285. Allen had 16 homers, Callison 12 and both were among the league leaders in RBIs with 44 and 43, respectively. No one else was hitting much although Covington had some good days. Herrnstein, after a fast start, was fading rapidly. Sievers was still hurt and being used infrequently. The Phillies had just about given up on him. Triandos was hurting, which left virtually all of the catching to Dalrymple who had lifted his average to the .230 range after a very slow start. Tony Taylor was doing most of the leading off, but he was not hitting as well as he had in 1963 when he had batted .281. This season he was struggling to keep his average in the .250 range. Neither Amaro nor Wine was hitting well. Both were around the .240 mark but were driving in an occasional run and giving the Phillies superior defense at shortstop. Tony Gonzalez was also having a poorer than average season for him. After hitting better than .300 for two straight seasons, he was down in the .270s where he remained for the next two months.

Among the pitchers, the five starters were a combined 35–20 with Short leading all National League hurlers with a brilliant ERA of 1.58. Bunning was not far behind at 2.16. Dennis Bennett had won nine games by this point and on paper at least gave the Phillies the best one, two, three pitchers in the National League. Baldschun and Roebuck constituted one of the National League's best bullpens. The remaining starters, Mahaffey and Culp combined for a winning record, but both were a puzzle to Mauch.

Any doubt that 1964 was the Phillies' year was removed by Callison's dramatic performance in the All-Star Game, held in Shea Stadium on July 7th before the largest crowd, over 50,000, to witness a mid-summer classic since 1959. Callison was a reserve and not expected to play with right fielders like Hank Aaron and Roberto Clemente ahead of him. Bunning and Short also were picked for the game — the first time the Phillies had three representatives on the All-Star squad since 1955 and a sure sign that the Phillies had arrived as a serious pennant contender.

Bunning performed well, hurling two shutout innings, but Short was roughed up. He gave up two runs when Willie Mays just missed a shoestring catch on a line drive that went for a triple.

Callison pinch-hit for Bunning in the fifth, popping to short right. He was surprised to be left in the game. In the seventh he hit a long 400-foot drive to deep center but Mickey Mantle ran it down. With the National League behind 4–3 going into the bottom of the ninth and the great closer, Dick "The Monster" Radatz, on the mound Callison didn't expect to get another at bat. But Mays led off the ninth with a single, stole second base and came home on a single by Orlando Cepada to tie the score. Two outs later with two runners on, Callison came up using a bat borrowed from Cubs outfielder, Billy Williams. Radatz threw a blazing fastball and Callison drilled it deep into the upper deck in right for a three run game-winning homer.

Callison says that all he can remember now about the homer is "floating around the bases." Even today he is constantly reminded of it when fans meet him. He says he feels like Bill Murray in the movie *Groundhog Day*. "I've seen the movie and can relate to it a lot. Every day someone tells me about it. Good thing, too, because at my age, I'm having trouble remembering what really happened."[5]

Callison's home run was just the third walk-off homer in All-Star Game history—the other two were by future Hall of Famers, Ted Williams and Stan Musial. Callison was in pretty good company.

A perfect no hitter and a game-winning home run in the All-Star Game, all within two weeks—it seemed as if the baseball gods were smiling on the Phillies. Earlier in the season Dick Groat remarked that the Phillies reminded him of the

Johnny Callison was well on his way to winning the Most Valuable Player Award in 1964, thanks to his clutch hitting, when the Phillies collapsed. He led the team in homers and RBIs and was one of the few regulars to hit well during the losing streak. After another strong year in '65, Callison faded into mediocrity. At only 27 years of age, his best days were behind him. (Courtesy Philadelphia Phillies.)

1960 Pirates: they may not be the best team in the league but "every thing they do is right."[6] Philadelphia the city of losers, love affair with the Phillies deepened. The local papers were filled with serious talk of a pennant for the first time since 1950.

Spinning Their Wheels

Philadelphia's baseball fans may have been inspired by Bunning's and Callison's feats but the team hardly acted that way. As was the case after Bunning's no hitter, after a dramatic performance by a Phillies player, the team played flat baseball. They came home for a brief home stand before going on the road for 11 games and proceeded to lose 6 out of 8 games. Also for the first time in 1964, the Phillies had a losing home stand.

In their first game after the All-Star break on July 9th the Phillies beat the Reds and pitcher John Tsitouris 4–3 behind Ray Culp. The victory, Culp's sixth, finally got him to the .500 mark. Callison continued his heroics by throwing out the tying run at home in the ninth inning. Callison's recent play gave rise to talk among baseball people that, should the Phillies win the pennant, he would be the logical choice for league's Most Valuable Player Award.

Starting the next night the Phillies proceeded to lose four consecutive games, their longest losing streak at home until the fateful collapse at the end of the season. Jim O'Toole beat Bennett in a slugfest 9–6. Bennett lasted only three innings and lost his third straight game. With the temperature in the sweltering 90s, Joe Nuxhall outpitched Bunning 3–1 the next night. Bunning was cruising along with a shutout when the Reds got to him for three runs. It was just Bunning's third loss against 10 wins and the first time he had been beaten at home. The Phillies as usual could do nothing against Nuxhall who enjoyed beating and exasperating Mauch.

The next day, a Sunday doubleheader against the Braves, saw Short lose to a 20-year-old rookie, Wade Blasingame, 4–3 despite Callison's 13th homer. In game two Mahaffey was hit hard. Journeyman lefty Billy Hoeft came out of the bullpen to pitch seven strong innings and stifle the Phillies' hitters. The Braves won easily 7–2.

The four consecutive losses dramatically exposed the Phillies' weakness against left-handed pitching. All four games were won by lefties of whom only O'Toole was a dominant pitcher. Blasingame was a rookie; Nuxhall, at 35, was nearing the end of a long career as was Hoeft, once a big winner but now pitching middle relief. Without Sievers in the lineup and with no right-handed hitter able to pick up the slack, the Phillies were easy pickings for almost any southpaw. Something would have to be done or every team would start digging into its minor league system for a left-hander to throw at the Phillies. Talk of a trade for a right-handed hitter that first surfaced in spring training revived with Frank Thomas of the Mets again the leading target.

The Phillies temporarily got back on track in the last game of the Braves series as Culp won for the second straight time, pushing his record over the .500 mark for the first time all season. He beat Warren Spahn 3–2. Mauch was so desperate to end the brief losing streak that he brought Bunning into the game in the ninth with two runners on and no one out. Bunning got the final outs and saved the game for Culp.

The season had reached the midpoint and the Phillies with a 49–32

5—A Long Hot Summer

record found themselves in second place, two games behind the Giants who had picked up ground due to the sluggish play of the Phillies since they swept San Franciso just before the All-Star break. Mauch was not discouraged. Despite all their problems scoring runs since the All-Star break, the Phillies were within breathing distance of first place. Culp had won his last two starts and showed signs of getting untracked. If Culp pitched the way he did in the first half of 1963, the Phillies would be able to deal with the struggles of Bennett and Mahaffey.

As the Phillies began an 11 game road trip on July 14th Mauch took a chance. Against the Pirates he started Cal McLish for the first time since September 1963 when he hurt his arm. Mauch had kept McLish around in hopes that his arm and shoulder problems would go away. To make room for McLish on the roster, the Phillies sold Johnny Klippstein to Minnesota, a move that would come back to haunt the Phillies when they would need bullpen help in September.

Mauch was hoping that the crafty McLish could pitch now and then giving the rest of the staff a needed breather. It wasn't to be. McLish lasted just ⅓ of an inning, giving up two runs and two hits. Bennett pitched five strong innings in relief as Mauch tried to get him untracked, but it didn't matter as Bob Veale won the game 4–3. Again the Phillies were beaten by a lefty, although this time by one of the best in the National League. All five of the Phillies' recent losses had been by lefthanders. A week later on July 21, McLish was given his unconditional release. He never appeared in another game in the majors.

On July 15 Bunning suffered his fourth loss despite pitching well when Jerry Lynch hit a three-run homer in the fourth inning. Bob Friend of the Pirates quieted the Phillies' bats and threw a shutout.

During this string the Phillies lost six of seven games as their bats were silent. They averaged just 1.8 runs per game. It wasn't time to panic, as the Phillies remained in second place two games behind the Giants who also were struggling.

The Phillies won the last game of the four-game series with the Pirates 7–5. Mahaffey improved his record to 8–4 and beat the Pirates for the fourth time. Cookie Rojas was the hitting star, starting two rallies while playing centerfield in place of the struggling Gonzalez. So far this season Rojas had played second base, shortstop, left field and right field. He was proving to be not only versatile but a solid clutch hitter with a batting average near or over .300 all season.

The Phillies continued to play inconsistent baseball during a five-game series against their next opponent, the Reds. They won the first game with Short outlasting Joey Jay 7–5. That day, July 16th, the Phillies finally gave up on Sievers, selling him to his old team, the Washington Senators, for the waiver price of $20,000. Sievers never recovered from his leg problems. He managed to get into 33 games with Washington, hit four homers in September but batted just .172 for them. He retired 12 games into the 1965 season. To replace him the Phillies called up one of their top prospects, Costen Shockley, from their Triple A farm team in Little Rock. He was tearing up the Pacific Coast League where Little Rock had moved in 1964 and would eventually lead the league in homers and RBIs. Unfortunately, he was yet another left-handed hitter when the Phillies desperately were searching for right-handed power.

Short's victory over the Reds, his eighth, put the Phillies into first place by percentage points as the Giants went on a brief losing streak. Despite all their recent problems, the Phillies would hold onto first for the next 73 days, gradually building their lead to a seemingly insurmountable 6½ games by September 20th.

In the last four games with the Reds, the Phillies lost three. Culp was bombed 14–4 as he lasted just 1⅔ innings. Shockley, in his first game with the Phillies, hit a homer into the right field bleachers. The teams split a Sunday doubleheader as Bunning blew a 4–0 lead in game one. Left-hander Billy McCool was the winner 7–4. Mauch started rookie John Boozer, just up from Arkansas, in the second game. Boozer got the win pitching eight strong innings when John Callison hit a two-run homer in the top of the ninth inning to turn a 3–2 Reds lead into a 4–3 Phillies victory.

In the series' last game, Joe Nuxhall continued to taunt the Phillies, winning an easy 6–2 victory. Bennett was the losing pitcher as he suffered his sixth loss in his first start in 10 days as his arm problems continued. Bennett came to believe that his arm and shoulder problems could be traced to the car accident he suffered in Puerto Rico in December 1962. "Crack a shoulder blade and the calcium builds up," he said. He was fine until he began to experience pain about half way through the season. "I was 9–4. The next thing I knew I was 9–12."[7] At the time people suspected it was just a temporary slump, something all players, not just hitters, go through. In fact, it was the beginning of the end for Bennett as a winning pitcher. From the time he was 9–4 with the Phillies midway through 1964 until he retired from baseball, his pitching record was 16–29.

Together with Culp's and Mahaffey's inconsistencies in the second half of the season, it can be seen that Bennett's ineffectiveness had a rippling effect on the pitching staff. Looking back on the 1964 season 10 years later, Peanuts Lowery, the Phillies coach, believed that the injury to Bennett was the one thing that cost them the pennant by dramatically weakening the pitching staff.[8]

Going into the final three games of the road trip, the Phillies had been 5–9 since the All-Star break, hardly a pennant-winning record. They were barely holding on to first place. But at this point the Phillies began to play their best baseball of the 1964 season. From July 21st until the beginning of the 10-game collapse exactly two months later, the Phillies would play at .623 rate. They did this despite the pitching woes of three of their starters. Bennett, Culp and Mahaffey during this two-month span would win just eight games. The Phillies hoped for a rebound from these three, and Mauch continued to send them to the mound but with decreasing optimism as the season wore on.

Bunning, Short and the bullpen carried the Phillies from late July to mid-September. Between them Bunning and Short accounted for 17 of the team's 38 victories during this two-month period. The problem that would eventually force Mauch to use Short and Bunning on limited rest in the team's collapse in September already existed in July. All things considered Mauch did a masterful job maneuvering his players in and out of the lineup while getting the maximum from his reserves.

As they had throughout the season, the Phillies rebounded from their 14-game stretch of poor play. Against the Braves Mahaffey won his ninth victory, 6–3, although he needed help from Baldschun in the eighth inning. Baldschun got Hank Aaron and Joe Torre out with the game on the line. The next night, July 22, Culp won his eighth victory 4–1 as light hitting Bobby Wine smacked a two-run homer to beat Warren Spahn. This proved to be Culp's last win in 1964. He now began to complain of arm and elbow problems. After a couple of shaky starts, Mauch ceased using Culp, saying he didn't want the ball, something Culp vehemently denied.

The problem was that Culp and Mauch did not see eye to eye. Mauch thought Culp was soft. According to Dalrymple, Mauch believed that part of Culp's problems related to his being overweight. "But instead of saying it softly, he said, 'you big fat SOB lose some weight.'"[9] Culp bristled and fought Mauch all the way. This was an example of one of Mauch's major flaws according to Dalrymple. He didn't understand pitchers and what is worse, at times he positively disliked them.[10] Mauch, who could turn on the charm when he needed to, lost patience with Culp and in the process lost him for the rest of the season just when the Phillies needed another solid starter.

Clay Dalrymple tags out a Cincinnati Reds' runner, as Pete Rose and catcher Johnny Edwards look on. (Urban Archives, Temple University, Philadelphia Pennsylvania.)

    The loss of Culp combined with Bennett's continuing ineffectiveness and Mahaffey's inconsistency eventually put a terrible strain on the Phillies' staff. It made a mockery of Mauch's boast in spring training of having the best pitching staff one through seven. That looked hollow now.
    The Phillies hoped that Boozer, who had once won 19 games in the minors, would pick up the slack. It didn't happen. A tall 6'3" country boy from South Carolina with a strange sense of humor, Boozer had great stuff but never reached his potential. He was content to be in the majors. He pitched some good games for the Phillies in 1964, especially in long relief, but never panned out as a reliable starter.
    The Phillies closed out the 11-game road trip on July 23rd in a wild game that they won 13–10 over the Braves. In one of Bunning's worst performances, he was knocked out after just two innings giving up five hits and five runs. Baldschun won the game in relief as Rojas doubled in the winning runs in the 10th inning off Braves reliever Bob Tiefenauer.
    At this point the Phillies had taken a two-game lead over the slowly

fading Giants. Just nine games separated the first seven teams in the National League. The standings on the morning of July 24th were:

Phillies	55–37	.598	
Giants	55–41	.573	2 games back
Reds	52–43	.547	4½ games back
Pitts	48–42	.533	6 games back
Braves	47–46	.505	8½ games back
Cubs	47–46	.505	8½ games back
Cards	47–47	.500	9 games back

The Phillies returned home on July 24th to begin their longest home stand of the season, 16 games against the Cards, Giants, Dodgers, Colts and Mets—three tough challengers and two teams the Phillies beat with regularity. Over the next three weeks, the Phillies would widen their lead over the Giants to 4 games by winning 12 of 17 games.

Phillies catcher Gus Triandos tags St. Louis' Bill White out at home as umpire Al Forman calls the play. In this July 26 Saturday game played at Shibe Park, the Phillies trailed 10–2 going into the bottom of the ninth inning. They rallied for seven runs before losing 10–9.

In the first game of the home stand, Short easily beat Bob Gibson 9–1, in the process striking out eight and improving his record to 9–5. The Phillies then lost the next three games, raising the Cardinals' record against them to 9–4. The second game of the series, a Saturday afternoon game when the Phillies for some strange reason played badly, was the kind that can haunt a team. With Curt Simmons on the mound continuing his sway over his former mates, the Cardinals built a commanding 10–2 lead going into the bottom of the ninth. Suddenly the Phillies rallied, pushing across seven runs with no outs and knocking Simmons out of the box in the process. Alex Johnson, in his first game since being called up from Little Rock, was on first having driven in the last of the seven runs. Herrnstein hit a long drive to deep center that Curt Flood ran down. Johnson tried to tag up and go to second but was out on a perfect throw from Flood. The next batter, Gus Triandos, made the third out as the Cardinals held on to win a squeaker, 10–9.

Johnson's play was a reckless one, especially with no outs, and a typical overly aggressive rookie mistake. But it revealed a side of Johnson that became apparent as he finished the year with the Phillies.

Johnson possessed awesome talent. Just 21, he had never hit less than .300 in any league. In his second year in baseball, he had led the Pioneer League in homers and RBIs while batting .329. He could hit for both average and with power. At the same time he had a halfback's speed. Unfortunately no one could get through to him. He was virtually unreachable, at times moody and sullen. In the words of one anonymous Phillie, Johnson "didn't listen to anybody."[11] This flaw would eventually shorten his career. After two years with the Phillies, he was traded to the Cardinals who quickly gave up on him, sending him to the Reds. After two .300 seasons with Cincinnati, they too got rid of him, sending him to the California Angels. Johnson won a batting title with the Angels in 1970, but he was uncontrollable and his career ended when he suffered emotional problems. He was another of the "what if" crowd of the 1964 Phillies.

Following Saturday's heart breaking loss, the Cardinals swept a doubleheader behind two left-handers, Ray Sadecki and Gordon Richardson. Sadecki, a quality left-hander who would go on to win 20 games in 1964, beat Mahaffey 4–1. Richardson outdueled John Boozer 6–1. Richardson was one of those minor "rinky-dink" lefties Alvin Dark said the Phillies would have no trouble with. He was precisely the kind of pitcher teams threw at the Phillies all season.

Richardson went on to have less than a sparkling career — his record was six wins and six losses in three years in the majors. The Cardinals thought so much of him that they traded him to the Mets after the 1964 season. No matter, in 1964 he was another Phillie killer.

The Phillies held on to first but they had lost a game and a half off their lead. They led Giants who would be their next opponents by a game and a half. With first place at stake, as they had so often, the Phillies showed an amazing ability to bounce back from tough defeats. In the first game of the Giants' series, Bunning rebounded from his poor start against the Braves to shut the Giants out 4–0 behind Gus Triandos' three-run homer. It was the big Greek's first homer in three months as he had been suffering from a finger injury that occurred early in the season. Bunning was overpowering and held the powerful Giant lineup to no hits for 5⅔ innings.

The next night before a large crowd of 28,000, Juan Marichal went all 10 innings as the Giants won, breaking a 3–3 tie against Jack Baldschun. Bennett pitched well against the overwhelming right-handed hitting Giant lineup, giving up three runs in 5⅓ innings. The Phillies managed just four hits, two of them homers: Richie Allen's 18th and Ruben Amaro's second.

The next night, Thursday, again before a crowd of 28,000 was another example of why the Phillies could be so tough in 1964. Culp went the first 8⅓ innings, giving up nine hits, two runs while striking out eight for his best start in a long time. The Giants broke a 2–2 tie in the top of the 10th against Mahaffey making a rare relief appearance. In the bottom of the 10th the Phillies loaded the bases with two out. Mauch had run out of pinch hitters and had to send 20-year-old left-handed hitting Johnny Briggs to bat against crafty veteran Billy Pierce. Briggs hit a Pierce pitch high off the right field wall driving in the tying and winning run.

The win boosted the Phillies' lead over the Giants to two and a half games with the Dodgers coming to town for a big weekend series beginning July 31st. Short easily got his 10th victory in the first game before a crowd of 24,000. Callison gave Short a lead in the first inning by hitting a two-run homer off rookie Joe Moeller. Dalrymple iced the game later with a two-run single.

On Saturday, with an almost full house of 32,000 in the ball park, the Phillies beat Don Drysdale for the eighth consecutive time. Herrnstein hit a homer, his fifth, and Tony Gonzalez, who always hit Drysdale, drove in a key run. The Dodgers managed to knock Bunning out of the box, scoring four runs against him in two innings but the Phillies pounded Drysdale and the Dodger bullpen for 10 runs. Rick Wise got the win with 4⅓ innings of relief.

The Phillies moved to a three and a half game lead over the Giants. The Reds had taken over third place, and at 4½ games back were closing in on the Giants. The eventual pennant-winning Cardinals were in fifth place but had gone over .500 at 53–50. They were eight games out of first place. Over the next two months, the Cardinals would win 40 of their remaining 59 games, while the Phillies would barely be better than .500.

The Phillies hope for a series sweep of the Dodgers failed to materialize as yet another minor league lefty, Larry Miller, beat John Boozer 6–1. Miller, like the Cardinals' Richardson who earlier beat the Phillies, was a mediocre left-hander whose career lasted less than three years. The Phillies' difficulties with left-handers were no longer a joke, and Mauch pressed Quinn to make a deal for a right-handed hitter.

The fourth game of the Dodger series was called off because of threatening weather. By game time the skies were clear and the rain had passed. Many of the city's baseball writers believed the real reason was Sandy Koufax was scheduled to start. If this is so then the Phillies' cancellation proved a costly one. The game was rescheduled for the next Dodger visit early in September, which turned out to be the game in which Frank Thomas fractured his thumb.[12] By trying to be clever and avoid Koufax, the Phillies' brass may have outsmarted themselves.

At this point the Phillies were getting virtually no offense out of their first basemen. Herrnstein was playing most of the time, but his average was dropping into the .250s. He had just five homers with over 100 games played, hardly what you wanted from a power position.

After a day off and a rainout, the Colts arrived in town for three games beginning with a twi-night doubleheader on Wednesday night August 5th. The Phillies swept both ends of the double bill before another large crowd of 27,300 as they continued to draw fans at a record pace. Eventually the 1964 Phillies would set a Philadelphia attendance record of 1.4 million that would last until they moved into Veterans Stadium in 1971. Philadelphia fans in those days loved doubleheaders especially twi-night affairs. Two games for the price of one appealed to the basically working class Phillies fans.

Bunning won the first game 4–1, raising his record to 11–4, allowing just five hits and one run in seven innings of work. The Phillies won a typical Mauch game — the key runs were the result of two sacrifice flies and a squeeze bunt. Allen won the second game with a walk-off ninth inning homer, his 19th of the season against Houston's top reliever, lefty Hal Woodeschick. Ed Roebuck got the win in relief of Ray Culp who pitched effectively: six innings allowing just four hits and one run. The two victories raised the Phillies' record to 62–41, a better than .600 winning percentage and a 2½ lead over the Giants.

Turk Farrell, another ex-Phillie, stymied his former mates in the third game of the series. Farrell was coming off six consecutive defeats and was hardly overpowering, giving up six runs, but Short had one of his rare bad outings as the Phillies lost 10–6. An interesting sidelight to this game was Mauch's use of Dennis Bennett in relief for the second straight game. Mauch was trying to get Bennett untracked and he seemed to be fine, giving up one hit and no runs in four innings of relief work over two nights.

The Big Donkey

With the Mets coming to town to conclude the home stand, Quinn finally swung a deal for a right-handed hitter that he and Mauch believed was needed to clinch the pennant. It had long been obvious that the Phillies were vulnerable to left-handed pitching. The team's record over the last 22 games against left-handers was just 7 wins versus 15 defeats. Something drastic had to be done.

The Phillies got Frank Thomas, who they had coveted since spring training, for two rookies, pitcher Gary Kroll and infielder-outfielder Wayne Graham. Kroll was the key to the deal for the pitching starved Mets. A 6'6" right-handed flame-thrower, he had once struck out 300 batters in the minors. Kroll never panned out, staying with the Mets through 1965 and winning and losing six games. Graham at 27 was a career minor leaguer who in 20 games with the Mets hit a resounding .091.

For Thomas the trade was a godsend. Nicknamed "The Big Donkey" because of insensitivity and stubbornness, he was 37 at the end of a career that started auspiciously in Pittsburgh but then saw him traded from team to team. Thomas was thrilled to be going to a team with a good chance to win the pennant. He told the press that he was "sure he could help the Phils. I'll give them all the hustle I can."[13] Clay Dalrymple says that the Thomas trade convinced him that the Phillies were going to win the pennant. "He was the shot in the arm we needed at exactly the right time."[14]

Thomas was as good as his word. In his first game in a Phillies' uniform, he helped beat his former mates by driving in two runs in a 9–4 victory over the Mets. Mahaffey started for the Phillies against a team he usually handled easily, but he wasn't around at the finish and the win went to Ed Roebuck in relief.

The Phillies swept the last two games of the series with Thomas driving in five more runs. Rick Wise won the second game 12–5 as the Phillies exploded for eight runs in the fifth inning aided by poor defense on the part of the Mets' second baseman Ron Hunt and first baseman, Ed Kranepool. Covington and Amaro homered as the Phillies topped their 1963 attendance. Bunning won the last game of the series, Sunday, August 9th, shutting out the Mets 6–0. He didn't allow a hit until two were out in the fifth inning when Joe Christopher beat out a bunt. At that point Bunning had retired 45 Mets in a row over a three-game span.

The Phillies finished the home stand with a 10–6 record and had increased their lead over the Giants to four games, their biggest margin of the season so far. The Giants had been the Phillies' most consistent challenger all season but they faded badly in August winning 14 and losing 15 games while the Phillies won 19 of 29. No other team in the league was closer than 6½ games. Now with Thomas backing up Richie Allen, the Phillies were no longer vulnerable to second line left-handers. From the time they got Thomas until he fractured his thumb sliding into second base one month later, the Phillies' record against lefties was 7–3, a dramatic reversal from past feebleness against southpaws. One wonders what the Phillies would have done if they had gotten Thomas in spring training and he had been with them all season. Perhaps they could have padded their lead. They certainly would not have been an easy mark for every left-hander in the National League.

Thomas continued his torrid hitting pace as the Phillies left for a short road trip to Chicago and New York. With Thomas hitting three doubles that drove in three runs plus Callison's grand slam, the Phillies clobbered the Cubs 13–5. The win went to Boozer in relief as Culp was shaky, lasting only 4⅓ innings while giving up seven hits and five runs.

The next day the Phillies won their fifth game in a row 4–1 as Covington hit a three-run homer to pave the way for Chris Short's victory, his 11th against six defeats. The last game of the series saw Ernie Broglio pitch his best game since coming to the Cubs for Lou Brock. Retiring the first 11 Phillies, he gave up just three hits and beat Dennis Bennett 3–1. It was Bennett's ninth loss and fifth in a row and saw his record

5—A Long Hot Summer 99

Johnny Callison slides into second base on a double against the Mets. (Urban Archives, Temple University, Philadelphia Pennsylvania.)

reach 9-9 after a 9-4 start. Bennett pitched well but the Phillies could do nothing with Broglio.

The Phillies went into New York August 14th for a four-game weekend series beginning with yet another doubleheader. Bunning easily won the first game 6-1 as the Phillies improved their record against the Mets to an astounding 14 wins versus just 2 losses. Bunning walked Ed Kranepool in the first inning, ending a string of 32 consecutive innings against the Mets without issuing a base on balls. In the second game Rick Wise raised his record to 4-1. Thomas hit a two-run homer in the seventh to ice a 6-4 Phillies win. Richie Allen had six hits in the doubleheader, including three consecutive doubles in the opener.

The Phillies were red-hot pounding out 26 hits, including 15 of them in the second game. Tony Taylor and Johnny Callison with number 20 joined Thomas in homering. The next night the Phillies scored six runs in the first inning, sending 10 men to the plate in an 8-1 romp. To make matters worse for the Mets, their normally sure-handed second baseman Ron Hunt had another bad defensive game, making three errors. The Phillies even pulled off their second triple play of the season. Boozer got the win with eight strong innings of relief when Culp again was ineffective and left the game after one inning. At least the

Mets got the satisfaction of knocking Culp out of the game. He had beaten them five consecutive times.

In the last game of the year between the two teams, the Mets got a measure of revenge. They routed Mahaffey and scored 12 runs as the Phillies played sloppy baseball, making five errors. Mauch brought Culp into the game to see if he could straighten out some of his problems, but in one inning he gave up three hits and three runs. Culp would be virtually useless the rest of the season.

The Phillies returned to Shibe Park on Monday August 17th where they were playing .618 baseball for eight games against the Cubs and Pirates. Short won victory number 12 as the Phillies got revenge against Ernie Broglio for his win over them a week before. With Callison hitting two triples and Short striking out nine batters, the Phillies won easily 8–1. Short, with an incredible ERA of 1.98, was now second in the National League to Sandy Koufax. The next night before a good crowd of 18,400, the Phillies lost a heartbreaker, a 5 hour 33 minute 16-inning marathon. Dennis Bennett gave his best performance in weeks, allowing just six hits and two runs in 7⅔ innings. The game remained tied until weak hitting Joey Amalfitano hit a two-run double in the top of the 16th inning with two out. What made it hard to take was a homer by Dalrymple in the bottom half of the inning that meant nothing but could have won the game. Boozer pitched the last four innings and was the losing pitcher. The Giants failed to gain any ground, losing 1–0 to the Reds.

The next night the Phillies opened a six-game lead over the Giants who were beat 7–1 by the Reds' Bob Purkey. The Phillies battered the Cubs 9–5 with a five-run eighth inning keyed by Covington's pinch double. Bunning started the game and recorded 11 strikeouts, but Baldschun got the win in relief. In an example of the versatility that Mauch loved, Cookie Rojas started the game in right field to give Callison a rest and then moved to left and finished at shortstop.

While this was happening an event took place in St. Louis that had a fateful effect on the pennant. On August 17th owner Gussie Busch fired Bing Devine, the Cardinals general manager and the architect of the team's revival over the past two seasons. Devine was caught in a power play by Branch Rickey who held the title of Senior adviser to Busch. At the press conference announcing the firing, Busch pointedly said nothing about Johnny Keane's future as manager. Keane was furious at the firing of Devine and heard rumors that he was to be replaced by Dodger third base coach Leo Durocher. The Cardinals players generally liked

Keane and did not look forward to playing for Durocher, a notoriously difficult man to deal with.[15] At this point the Cardinals were struggling in fifth place nine games behind the Phillies. From that point they turned their season around, winning 30 of their last 42 games or a .714 winning percentage.

The Pirates came to town the next night, August 20th, for a twi-nighter. Before the largest crowd of the season, 35,814, Art Mahaffey and Rick Wise led a sweep of the two games. For Mahaffey it was his 11th win and one of the best games of the season as he bested Bob Friend 2–0. Wise's victory improved his record to 5–1 and would prove to be his last win of the season. The Phillies won in an aggressive fashion that characterized their play all season. In the bottom of the eighth Tony Gonzalez scored from second base on a long sacrifice fly by Johnny Callison. The Phillies scored five runs along with just 13 hits in the doubleheader but they were tough in the clutch. Also Mahaffey, Wise and Roebuck in relief allowed the hard-hitting Pirate lineup just two runs in 18 innings.

At this point the Phillies' lead was the biggest it would be all season. They were 74–46 and led the Giants and Reds who were tied for second by 7½ games.

The Phillies won their fourth in a row the next night as Short shut out the Pirates and their best pitcher, lefty Bob Veale, 2–0. Short, whose record was now 13–6, gave up six hits and struck out 10. He and Bunning now were a combined 26–10, the best one two pitching duo in the National League.

The next game was yet another example of a mediocre left-hander beating the Phillies despite having Thomas' bat in the lineup. This time it was a Pirate farmhand named Frank Bork making his first start in the majors since being called up from Columbus of the International League in early August. He beat Bennett 9–4. For Bennett it was his sixth consecutive defeat. He had not won a game since July 5th. It was also the 17th consecutive time he had failed to complete a game. Bork would go on to win one more game in a career that lasted two months.

The Phillies finished the series by pounding out a 9–3 win over lefty Joe Gibbon before a decent Sunday crowd of 19,000. Bunning won victory number 14 against just four losses but wilted in the 91-degree heat and humidity and needed relief help. Richie Allen drove in four runs on two homers, numbers 22 and 23. Gus Triandos also homered and drove in three runs.

The win put the Phillies 29 games over .500. Mauch became fixated on getting to 30 games above the .500 mark. Psychologically for him it meant that the Phillies were a quality team. He was also experimenting with the lineup almost every day. He now had Rojas leading off and playing centerfield in place of the struggling Gonzalez. Tony Taylor's long struggle to get his batting average above .250 led to his being dropped to seventh or eighth place in the batting order. But no lineup remained in place long with Mauch. Soon he would restore Gonzalez to center and move Taylor back to the lead-off position. The constant juggling of the lineup didn't seem to bother the Phillies as long as Callison, Allen and Thomas were hitting.

The Phillies left town for a brief six-game road trip against the Braves and Pirates. They played sloppy baseball and won only two of the six games with three of their defeats coming at the hands of left-handers. In the first game Mahaffey continued to frustrate the Phillies. After his 2–0 whitewash of the Pirates, he reverted to bad form and lasted just ⅓ of an inning as the Braves won a wild game 12–9. The Phillies banged out 13 hits including a homer by Dalrymple, while Covington had one of his greatest games in the majors. He hit two homers along with two doubles that accounted for six runs. It wasn't enough to overcome a big Braves lead. Bennett in relief got the loss, his seventh in a row.

Wise lost the second game 7–5 which the Braves won behind Tony Cloninger who was cruising with a three hitter until Callison hit a three-run homer in the eighth inning. The other two Phillies runs also were the result of homers by Covington and Thomas. The back-to-back losses were the first the Phillies experienced since July 26th.

Short finished out the series with a six hitter for his 14th victory of the season. His ERA was now an amazing 1.70. The Phillies, who were on a long ball tear, hit four more homers in this game including two by Triandos.

The first game of a weekend series with the Pirates was one that the Phillies would look back on with regret. It was the kind of game that no team, especially one with its eye on a pennant, could afford to lose. Going into the bottom of the ninth inning, Bunning was leading 2–0, having given a tough Pirate lineup that included Roberto Clemente, Willie Stargell and Manny Mota just three hits and striking out 11. The game was seemingly in the bag when Bill Virdon singled to lead off the inning. Bunning got an out but then walked the dangerous Jerry Lynch to put the tying runs on base. Mauch decided to go to Roebuck—"he throws ground balls" as Mauch said—in hopes of getting a double play. Stargell singled in Virdon and Smoky Burgess then won the game with a homer into the right field stands for a 4–2 win. Two weeks later the Pirates sold Burgess to the Chicago White Sox. There were a handful of games like this that the Phillies would look back on with regret after the season.

The Phillies bounced back again to win the next night, 10–8. Mahaffey went seven innings but gave up three runs along with five walks before turning the game over to John Boozer. Boozer was pounded for five runs but the Phillies held on for a win when Baldschun shut the door on the Pirates. It was Mahaffey's fifth consecutive defeat of the Pirates and his 12th victory. As it turned out it, this was his last win in 1964. During the team's remaining 34 games, he would start just five more times without a win. Mauch had lost confidence in him. At a time when the Phillies needed another reliable starter, Mahaffey failed to deliver. The Phillies starting pitching was shaky. Culp did not start another game after August 15th, Mahaffey was ineffective and Bennett hadn't won since early July. This was not the way a team wanted to enter the last six weeks of a pennant race.

Allen was the hitting hero of Mahaffey's victory, belting his 24th homer and driving in four runs. Bob Veale finished off the Phillies easily on Sunday, winning 10–2 as Allen made two costly errors. Short was the loser with both Culp and Bennett pitching in relief and getting hit hard.

Despite Veale's win the Phillies' bats had come alive since early August. They were hitting home runs in bunches led by Callison, Allen and Thomas. Callison now had 22 homers and 79 RBIs, while Allen had 23 to go along with 68 runs knocked in. Whatever juggling he did with the batting order, Mauch made sure that Allen and Callison hit back to back usually second or third in the lineup. Mauch didn't worry as much about Callison facing left-handers as he was hitting more homers against them than right-handed pitchers. Mauch raved about Callison's skills. He told Arthur Daley of the New York Times around this time: "Callison is the most complete ballplayer to enter this league since Willie Mays. He can run, throw, field, hit with power. There's nothing he can't do well on a ball field."[16] High praise indeed considering that Hank Aaron, Roberto Clemente and Frank Robinson had entered the National League after Mays.

Along with Callison and Allen, Covington and Rojas also were swinging hot bats. Rojas was hitting .300 while Covington had raised his average to a season high .297. The addition of Thomas had made the middle of the Phillies lineup tough going for any pitcher, left or right.

On August 28th while the Phillies were in Pittsburgh, one of the worst riots in Philadelphia history broke out in the area just south of Shibe Park. America's "Long Hot Summer" had at last arrived in Philadelphia — late as usual as Philadelphia was always a step or two behind the times.

Shibe Park was located in an area called North Penn that was experiencing a slow but steady racial transformation. The neighborhoods to both the north and south of Shibe Park already had witnessed an influx of African Americans, mostly from the deteriorating neighborhoods south and west of the ballpark. Shibe Park and its immediate environs remained white for a time, but the riot marked a turning point for that area. Over the next couple of years, the neighborhoods surrounding Shibe Park would change racially from white to black, and the Phillies organization would be caught up in the uproar over racial protest in the city. Given the team's history of racial insensitivity, this change couldn't have come at a worse time.[17]

The riots saw stores burned down throughout the busy shopping center that was on Columbia Ave. just off Broad Street about a mile south of the ballpark. The mostly small businesses, almost all of which were white owned, were looted while police and fireman were injured by rocks thrown down on them from rooftops. Over 650 people were arrested. Mayor Tate, using a little known 1850 state law, imposed a 100-block curfew in the area surrounding the riots. This included the area where Shibe Park was located. State stores (Pennsylvania's name for state run liquor stores) and bars were closed, and 1,500 police flooded the area of north Philadelphia. Fifteen of the rioters got jail sentences of up to three years, while over 600 others sat in jail awaiting trial.

The 1964 riot spurred the racial polarization of the city that would grow with intensity over the next decade. The white flight that had begun in the mid-1950s increased in tempo, and Philadelphia's population began to decline in raw numbers as well as change racially. By the late 1960s the entire area around Shibe Park would be African American.

When the Phillies opened their last long home stand of 11 games on September 1st, security was tight around Shibe Park. Beer sales were banned at the game to cut down on potential trouble. With police patrolling around, Shibe Park attendance was down while fans attending the games were tense.

The home stand was something of a letdown. The Phillies, among the best home teams in the National League, went 6–5. More significantly, the home stand saw them lose Frank Thomas with a broken

Looters on Columbia Avenue during the August 28 riot, about a mile and a half southeast of Shibe Park. (Urban Archives, Temple University, Philadelphia Pennsylvania.)

thumb. He would attempt a comeback during the 10-game losing streak, but he couldn't hit with any authority.

The Phillies began the last month of the season ensconced in first place with a 5½ game lead over the Reds who had swept past the Giants to move into second place. Historically, teams in first place on September 1st win the pennant. 1964 would make a mockery of that tradition.

The Phillies' first opponent was one of their baseball "cousins," the Houston Colts. Before just 13,000 fans with others scared away by the riot, Bunning won his 15th victory, 4–3, as the Phillies got three homers in the seventh inning from Thomas, Callison and Allen. Allen's was spectacular—a drive that bounced off the 447 sign in deepest right center for an inside-the-park home run. The Colts threw a scare into the Phillies by scoring three runs in the top of the ninth. After the game Mauch said it was a typical Phillies effort. "If we don't beat 'em one way, we beat 'em another. We grind people up."[18]

Short easily won the second game of the series, 2–1, tying Bunning for the team lead with 15 victories. Short's win was a tidy four-hit 10-

strikeout effort even though he was pitching on just two days rest. He and Bunning now were a combined 30–13 for the season. With a chance for a sweep, Mauch sent Bennett to the mound for his first start in two weeks. The Colts, practically conceding the game, were pitching the nearly washed-up Don Larsen who would go 4–9 for the year.

Larsen won effortlessly, shutting out a listless Phillies team 6–0 on a four hitter. It was his first whitewash in 35 starts dating back to 1959. Bennett's record dropped to 9–12 as he lost his eighth decision in a row. An ominous sidelight of the game was the savage booing of Allen who failed to make two plays at third. Some people in the press box thought that there was a racial tinge to the booing, a kind of baseball backlash to the local riot. A couple of Colt players expressed shock at the booing, hinting that it was the kind of thing that could cost the Phillies the pennant.[19] Mauch also was upset by the fans' reaction. "I just don't understand it," he told the writers. "I guess when people have exceptional talent they are expected to be exceptional every minute of the day."[20]

The Giants, now in third place, came to town for a three-game weekend series hoping to force their way back into the pennant race. On Friday night before a huge crowd of 28,000 who braved the warnings about the neighborhood's dangers, Mahaffey gave Mauch a decent outing. He went 6⅔ innings and gave up just three runs on eight hits. He left the game behind 3–1, but the Phillies broke through for four runs in the bottom of the eighth to win.

Allen opened the eighth inning with a single, and then Frank Thomas tied the game with his ninth homer and sixth since he joined the Phillies. With one out, the Phillies won the game on a double by Triandos, a single by Callison who ultimately scored on a bunt by pitcher Jack Baldschun. The last run tickled Mauch — he loved the squeeze play. Baldschun got the win in relief of Mahaffey.

The next night before an even larger crowd, 31,600, Dark and Mauch engaged in a game of trying to outwit each other. Dark had lefty Bob Hendley warming up in the bullpen, which meant that Mauch would start his right-handed hitting unit. Then, just before the game began, Dark switched to righty Bob Bolin. Mauch stayed with his original lineup and the Phillies scored four runs in the first inning on their way to an easy 10–3 win. Thomas hit his tenth and last homer of the season, but it was Triandos' grand slam that broke the game open for winning pitcher Jim Bunning.

Juan Marichal won the final game of the series, 4–3, striking out 13 Phillies. The real hero of the game was Willie Mays. He scored the winning run in the ninth inning in typical Mays fashion. He was on first when Baldschun tried to pick him off and threw the ball past the first baseman, Thomas. Thomas retrieved the ball down the right field line and tried to get Mays going to third but his throw sailed past Allen, allowing Mays to score.

With the seventh place Dodgers playing under .500 baseball due in next, the Phillies maintained a 5½-game lead over the Reds with both the Giants and Cardinals 7½ back. In effect, despite playing mediocre baseball, the Phillies had not lost ground in a week.

The Dodgers and Phillies split a doubleheader on September 7th with Dennis Bennett gaining his first victory over 18 starts dating back two months. He allowed the Dodgers just five hits and one run and beat Larry Miller 5–1. Pete Richert, a young lefty who the Dodgers had recalled from Spokane of the Pacific Coast League three days earlier, edged Rick Wise 3–1 in the second game. Wise, in his worst outing of the season, gave up three runs without recording an out. Mauch now became reluctant to start Wise as the pennant race entered its last three weeks. Wise would make one more start as Mauch went with a four-man rotation of Bunning, Short, Bennett and Mahaffey.

The Dodger doubleheader saw the Phillies' attendance reach 1,224,172, 7000 more than in the Whiz Kids' pennant-winning season. With ten home games remaining, it seemed likely that the Phillies might top the one and a half million mark in attendance, an incredible figure for a ballpark that only had room for about 34,000 fans.

The last game of the series was revealing for a number of reasons. This was the makeup game for the August cancellation to avoid having to face Sandy Koufax. It was to prove a costly cancellation. The Dodgers gave 36-year-old reliever Jim Brewer his first start of the year. He won 3–2 as yet another lefty came out of the mothballs to beat the Phillies. Mahaffey had trouble warming up before the game and lasted just ⅔ of an inning, giving up two runs and taking the loss. In the Phillies' last two games, neither of their starters had gotten out of the first inning, a sure way to wear out the bullpen.

The major reason for the game's significance was the loss of Thomas. On a meaningless play, diving back into second base, Thomas broke his thumb. He stayed in the game and struck out in the ninth inning but was in obvious discomfort. Overnight his hand became swollen and when x-rays were taken, they revealed a break. He was seemingly lost to the Phillies for the duration of the season. In less than a month, he had hit seven homers for the Phillies, more than any other player, and driven in 26 runs while batting .294. With Thomas in the lineup, the Phillies were 21–12, a .636 record that was better than their overall winning percentage when they got him. Although his loss once again made the Phillies vulnerable to left-handers, it didn't seem to matter, as their grip on first place seemed secure. They had a six-game lead with 23 games remaining. Playing anywhere near .500 baseball would guarantee them the pennant.

The day after losing, Thomas Quinn purchased the contract of Vic Power from the Los Angeles Angels. The 32-year-old Power was an outstanding defensive first baseman and had once been a solid hitter. But in recent years he had slipped offensively and was only hitting .244 for the Angels when the Phillies got him. Quinn and Mauch hoped he had a month of pennant-winning baseball in him. He didn't.

Power was reluctant at first to change leagues: "I didn't like the idea of moving over to the National League," he told reporters. "But I got to thinking that almost every other Puerto Rican player had played in a World Series, and I said to myself, 'this is my chance.'"[21] Power was clearly optimistic about the Phillies winning the pennant—he took advantage of the player's right to buy World Series tickets and bought $90 worth for his family back in Minneapolis.

The day after losing Thomas, the Cardinals came to town for two games. The first game saw both starters, Curt Simmons and Jim Bunning, get knocked around. The Phillies banged out 10 hits against Simmons in 3⅓ innings and had the pleasure of knocking him out of the game. The Phillies led 5–3 going into the ninth inning, but the Cardinals rallied to tie the score. The Cardinals won the game, scoring five runs in the top of the 11th against Baldschun for a 10–5 win. It was the suddenly red-hot Cardinals' 13th win in 16 games. Short evened the series with a 5–1 six hitter. He struck out 12 Cardinals while raising his record to 16–7. In his first game with the Phillies, Power got one hit in four at bats along with an RBI and Callison hit his 26th homer of the season to tie his best mark in the majors. The Phillies' lead over the Cardinals was six games with 22 games remaining in the season; 15 on the road, seven at home. If they split those 22 games, there was no way they could lose the pennant. Instead they only won eight and lost everything, while the Cardinal's record in September was a stunning 21 victories versus 8 defeats.

On September 11 the Phillies embarked on their last long road trip, a tough ten-game affair in ten days, against the Western teams, the Colts, Giants and Dodgers. Bennett opened the three-game set against the Giants with his second consecutive victory, beating Juan Marichal 1–0.

The winning run was driven in on a double by the light hitting Ruben Amaro in the fifth inning. In the most dramatic moment of the game, Bennett struck out Willie Mays for the third time with the game on the line. It was a deceptive sign that the sore-armed lefty still possessed great stuff when his arm wasn't bothering him. In fact he was now pitching on sheer nerve.

Mahaffey lost the second game, this time going just two innings as the Giants pounded out three homers. The big blow was Cepada's grand slam homer off John Boozer in the third inning as the Giants won 9–1 behind the solid pitching of future Hall of Famer, Gaylord Perry. Bunning closed out the series, winning his 17th victory 4–1, going 10 innings for a complete game triumph. Callison gave the Phillies the lead in the top of the tenth with a single, and Allen followed with a homer, his 26th. The win kept the Phillies lead at six games over the second place Cardinals.

The Phillies went to Houston hoping for a sweep. They had handled the Colts easily all season and had a 11–4 record against them. On September 14th, Short won victory number 17, by a 4–1 score, giving up just four hits. This time it was Callison's homer, his 27th topping his best in 1963 by one, that won the game. With 18 games remaining in the season, Short would win no more games while making five starts. Bunning would manage just two more victories while also starting five times. Some idea of the state of the Phillies' pitching staff can be gauged by the fact that only Bennett among the other starters won a game the rest of the season.

The next night Bennett and Jack Baldschun combined for a 1–0 win. The winning run was the work of Allen and Callison. Allen led off the sixth inning with a double against the fence in left and Callison singled him home. By this time Bennett no longer had the sweeping curve and crisp fastball that had been his forte. He now was pitching with guile and was a shadow of the overpowering pitcher of the first three months of the season. His left shoulder was black and blue and hurt him constantly. Bennett had won his last game of the season and his last as a Phillies pitcher.

The final game of the Houston series proved controversial. Mauch, ever the gambler, rolled the dice and asked Bunning to start on two days rest instead of Mahaffey whose turn it was. Both Mahaffey and Bunning had dominated Houston in the past but Mauch was hoping to steal a win. Also by starting Bunning Mauch could bring him back against the Dodgers in the last game of that series. In that way Bunning would get two starts instead of one in the last five games of the road trip.

The Colts hit Bunning, the winner of eight consecutive games, hard.

He gave up four runs in the fifth inning, losing to journeyman right-hander, Don Nottebart, who wound up with a 6–11 record for the season. Larry Shenk, the Phillies' director of publicity, seeing that Bunning was pitching and had owned the Colts all season, went to bed without waiting for the final score. He was shocked when he awoke to discover the Phillies had lost.[22]

In light of what happened during the Phillies' collapse, Mauch's decision raised questions about his judgment. Why not give Bunning an extra day's rest? Mauch had tried to have Bunning pitch in every series the Phillies played, but having won the first two games of the Houston series it might have been worth the risk to start someone else and save Bunning for the Dodgers. Why didn't he start Mahaffey? Probably because in his last six starts, Mahaffey hadn't lasted through the first inning in three of them. If he had no faith in Mahaffey why not try someone else? Boozer? Wise? How about starting Bobby Shantz who the Phillies had picked up from the Cubs on August 15 and pitched well for them? Starting someone other than Bunning would also have given the tired Phillies staff another day's rest. In light of what happened at the end of the season, Mauch's handling of the pitching staff might have been the most fateful mistake he made.

The Phillies arrived in Los Angeles 30 games above .500 with a comfortable lead over the Cardinals, Reds and Giants. In game one, Mauch again bypassed Mahaffey, who never had much luck against the Dodgers, and started the 18-year-old Wise. Wise lasted only ⅓ of an inning, but the Phillies still pulled the game out as Shantz went 6⅔ innings in relief and won 4–3. Don Drysdale was the losing pitcher as the Phillies beat him for the fourth time in 1964.

The next two nights the Phillies lost heartbreakers. Short pitched a good game, giving up just three runs in seven innings, but the Phillies couldn't do much against left-hander Pete Richert or the Dodger bullpen. Baldschun took the loss, 4–3, when rookie Bart Shirley drove in the winning run in the bottom of the ninth inning for a 4–3 Dodger win. On Saturday night Bennett started against Larry Miller, as the Dodgers threw another left-hander at the Phillies. The game went into extra innings with neither team able to mount much of a threat.

In the bottom of the 16th, the baseball gods pulled the rug on the Phillies. With two out, Willie Davis slapped a hard grounder off first baseman John Herrnstein's chest — a play that the Gold Glove winning Power would have probably made easily — and beat Phillies pitcher Jack Baldschun to the bag. Mauch argued that Davis was out and that he had stepped on Baldschun's foot not the bag. He lost the argument. Davis wound up on third when Baldschun, perhaps favoring his foot, threw a wild pitch. Mauch ordered the dangerous Tommy Davis walked and called in rookie left-hander Morrie Stevens, who had just come up from Little Rock, to face the dangerous left-handed hitting Ron Fairly. Steevens fired two quick strikes past Fairly. Dodger third base coach, Leo Durocher, noticed that Steevens wasn't paying attention to the runner on third. He whispered to Davis "I know you can steal home. Go ahead."[23] On Steevens' third pitch Willie Davis stole home when Dalrymple couldn't get a firm grip on the ball to tag him out. Baldschun lost for the second night in a row.

After the game Willie Davis said that when you have a rookie on the mound you know he is nervous and try to take advantage of him: "You always try to do something to shake up a kid."[24]

Mauch was criticized for using the 23-year-old Steevens who had virtually no major league experience in such a crucial situation. In his defense, the Phillies staff was stretched thin.

Bunning found a silver lining despite the loss. The Reds beat the Cardinals in the first game of a doubleheader that day when Frank Robinson hit a three-run homer in the ninth inning off Bob Gibson. "That's another World Series share we've got to vote," Bunning joked when he heard of Robinson's blast. Mahaffey agreed. "It almost seems like the rest of the league is playing for us. 'We lose, they lose' That's why there's no pressure"— words that would come back to haunt the Phillies.[25]

Bunning closed out the road trip with a gutty 3–2 win. He struck out the dangerous John Roseboro with the game on the line in the bottom of the ninth. After two consecutive losses the Phillies once again had bounced back. They had gone 6–4 on this difficult trip, returning to Philadelphia for seven games with 6½-game lead. Their magic number was seven, a seemingly modest figure with 12 games remaining. After all, since moving into first place on July 16th the Phillies had played at a .600 level. All seemed well but the baseball gods were about to turn their backs on the Phillies.

Despite the shaky road trip, the Phillies had to feel confident. Walt Alston, the Dodger manager, thought they would win the pennant with ease. He told reporters that he believed that the Phillies would beat the Yankees in the World Series. If anything, he thought the Phillies were even better than the Dodger team that swept the Yankees in 1963. "We had an edge in pitching but Philadelphia appears to have better speed, better defense and more power."[26]

6

The Blue Snow Melts

The Magic Number

The Phillies arrived home early Monday morning from Los Angeles, September 21st, to be greeted at the airport by a screaming crowd of over 2,000 people led by Mayor Tate. While an impromptu band played "Hail, Hail, the Gang's All Here," the Phillies' wives and their adoring fans greeted the players. The city of Philadelphia suddenly was caught up in a baseball frenzy not seen since the glory days of the Whiz Kids. World Series tickets were due to go on sale that week. Box seats went for $25, a great deal of money in those days, while reserved seats were listed at $17 and general admission at $9. It was expected that they would be bought up in a couple of days.

One of Philadelphia's most exclusive hotels, the Warwick, was designated as Major League Baseball's headquarters for the World Series. The hotel estimated that it would take in over $50,000 during the World Series. Other Philadelphia establishments such as restaurants, bars and taxi services were counting on making a killing also.[1]

The scheduled seven-game home stand pitted the Phillies against two teams, the Cincinnati Reds and Milwaukee Braves, they had winning records against: 7–6 with the Reds; 8–6 versus the Braves. The three-city road trip had been a difficult one but the Phillies actually managed to add one game to their lead in the National League, returning to the City of Brotherly Love with a seemingly safe 6½-game margin over the second place Reds.

Beginning in mid-September the three major Philadelphia papers, the staid but highly influential *Evening Bulletin*, Walter Annenberg's aggressive morning *Inquirer* and the racy *Daily News* all prominently carried a box with a number in it. Philadelphia fans were introduced to the magic number, the combination of Phillies wins and Cincinnati losses that would give Phillies the pennant. The number had dropped throughout the Phillies' last road trip from 11 to 7 when they arrived home.

There were no sports talk shows in those days but various radio stations tried to cash in on the popularity of the Phillies by hiring players, past and present, to do commentary about the teams chances in the coming World Series. Frank Thomas, recovering from his hand injury, appeared on a morning show headed by a popular local celebrity, "Uncle Phil" Sheriden. Thomas filled in as the "weather girl" and exchanged jokes with the host. An example of Thomas' humor: "Why does it take longer to run from second to third than from first to second. Because there's a shortstop in between."

One of the new UHF TV stations even brought back former Whiz Kids to compare the 1964 team with their club. Sitting around a table in their ill-fitting suits and bad haircuts, most of the Whiz Kids thought the 1964 team superior to the 1950 pennant winners. The current Phillies, they believed, had greater depth and wouldn't suffer from the late season fatigue that overtook the Whiz Kids. So much for the insight of former players.

One area of concern for the Phillies was the lack of post-season experience. Only four Phillies players— Covington, Roebuck, Shantz and Triandos— had appeared in a World Series. The Cardinals hadn't been in a World Series since 1946, while the Reds had been there as recently as 1961. But the Cardinals did have the experience of being in a heated pennant race as recently as 1963 when they made a run at the pennant-winning Dodgers.

Signs of support sprung up throughout the city. Along Chestnut Street, then one of the elite shopping areas in the city, the local businessmen's association (it was businessmen in those pre-feminist days) put up large signs reading: "Go, Phillies, Go." Gimbels' department store on Market Street unfurled a huge banner declaring: "Go Phillies: We're For You." A local singer recorded a most forgettable ditty about being in love with the Phillies.[2]

Phillies players were everywhere doing advertisements. Especially popular was the Hollywood handsome Johnny Callison. Callison already had been on the cover of the *Sporting News* and was used to advertise the Bayuk Cigar Company's popular brand, called appropriately enough, Phillies cigars. Jim Brosnan, the relief pitcher-turned journalist, was hired by *Life Magazine*, then at the height of its popularity, to follow the

Phillies for an article on their clinching of the pennant. It would never appear. *Sports Illustrated* was preparing a cover with Jim Bunning on it for its World Series issue.[3] That never appeared either.

Philadelphia was enthused about a sports team in a way it hadn't been in years. True, the Eagles had won the NFL title game in 1960 but that was before pro football had become America's most popular sport. The Eagles-Green Bay Packers playoff game that year wasn't even televised into Philadelphia.

The Phillies' season boiled down to two weeks and 12 games, 7 at home, 5 on the road. Since moving into first place on July 16th, the Phillies had been an amazingly consistent team. Between July 16th and September 8th, their longest losing streak was three games, and that happened only one time.

The Phillies entered their last home stand with the best home record in the National League, 46–28, a .616 winning percentage. They had experienced one losing home stand all season. No Phillies fan's worst nightmare envisioned them losing every game in the home stand. There were worries to be sure. After all this was Philadelphia — but the Phillies' true believers thought their heroes might even clinch the pennant before going on the road.

Mauch tried to put the last two weeks in perspective for the younger Phillies players. Remember what happened to the Whiz Kids he told them. They had a 7½ game lead with 11 to go. "But they lost eight of their last ten and had to win the last game of the season to save the pennant."[4] It didn't make much of an impression. The Phillies players weren't cocky but some of them, like Chris Short, were already spending their World Series money on expensive hunting rifles.

There were some disturbing signs not noted at the time. Since the beginning of September, the Phillies had not been hitting with their usual authority. In August they had averaged 5.6 runs a game; in September this figure dropped to 3.3. The Phillies also were not doing well in one-run games. From April to the end of August, the Phillies record in one-run games was 21 victories versus 12 defeats for a superb .636 percentage. In the last month of the season, their record would be just over .500 at seven wins versus six losses. The large number of close games in September was another reflection of the Phillies' lack of hitting. These games also took a heavy toll on the pitching staff, especially the bullpen, which had been heavily used by Mauch all season.

The home stand opened on a cold, windy fall night before 20,000 happy but nervous fans with a game that is now famous, or better infamous, in the long history of Phillies' disasters. Cincinnati, 6½ games out of first and playing decent baseball, wanted to hold onto second place which was then worth about $2,000, a lot of money in the days when average baseball salaries were around $15–16,000. The Reds manager, former Whiz Kid Dick Sisler, filling in for the cancer stricken Fred Hutchinson who would die that November, sent right-hander John Tsitouris to the mound against the Phillies' inconsistent starter, Art Mahaffey. It was Mahaffey's first start in 12 days, which says something about Mauch's confidence in him. It also was a match up of two right-handers who had struggled all season. Tsitouris was 7–11 with no shutouts but a reputation for beating the Phillies— he had won four of seven decisions over them dating back to the 1962 season. Mahaffey was 12–8 but hadn't won a game in over three weeks. Mahaffey normally pitched well against the Reds' predominantly right-handed hitting lineup. He had beaten them 4–2 in late April in one of his best starts all season.

Sandy Grady, then writing one of the best sports columns in the *Evening Bulletin*, described Tsitouris as "having the pitching motion of your Aunt Maud swatting a mosquito."[5] Aunt Maud tormented the Phillies all night with an assortment of slow stuff mixed in with an occasional fastball, not allowing more than one hit in any inning and striking out eight. Mahaffey pitched well also, and neither team mounted much of threat for the first five innings. It looked like one of those games where whoever scored first would win.

In the top of the sixth with Mahaffey cruising along, fate stepped in and began the unraveling of the Phillies' magical season. With one out, the outcome of the game was set. Chico Ruiz, a lifetime reserve player and something of a baseball hot dog, slapped a single to right. The next batter, Vada Pinson, in the midst of a down year for him — he was batting just over .260 — hit a ground ball up the middle that Mahaffey nearly caught but instead deflected past Tony Taylor into center field. If he had caught the ball, Mahaffey may have been able to turn a double play. Instead Ruiz easily made it to third. The Phillies got a break when Pinson was thrown out trying to stretch his hit into a double on a perfect throw from Tony Gonzalez.

With two out, the next batter was Frank Robinson, who Mauch regarded as one of the most dangerous clutch hitters in baseball. Mauch had a standing order with his pitchers not to knock Robinson down as it only made him mad and a better hitter.

Normal procedure called for walking Robinson, setting up a force at second base and taking your chances on the next hitter, Deron Johnson, a 26-year-old playing his first full season in the majors. Since he had decent success against Robinson in the past, Mahaffey decided to pitch to him. It is strange that Mauch, who was often accused of overmanaging, didn't order the dangerous Robinson put on base. Perhaps this was one of the first signs that Mauch was managing differently than he had during the season.

Interestingly if he walked Robinson, Mahaffey would have had to pitch from the stretch and there was no way a runner could have stolen home with the pitcher looking right at him.

Mahaffey's first pitch to Robinson was a called strike. Ruiz was dancing off third, watching Mahaffey's big windup. It was rare then for a pitcher to use the stretch motion with a man on third base as it was believed that the windup gave you better movement on your pitches. Windups also were bigger, more elaborate back in the 1960s.

With the count one strike, Ruiz decided to break for home on the next pitch. Again Mahaffey went into his big windup. There is no way he should have been caught off guard when Ruiz started for home. Unlike a left-hander, a right-handed pitcher is angled in the direction of the third base line. Mahaffey says he picked up sight of Ruiz at the last split second and hurried his throw to the plate just a bit. Cincinnati players were yelling "no, no" as they saw their $2,000 checks going down the drain in Ruiz's reckless play.

Mahaffey's pitch was high and wide with the surprised Robinson watching it sail past Dalrymple and roll all the way to the stands. Robinson said the ball reached the plate before Ruiz. "I thought he would have been out" if Dalrymple caught the ball, Robinson told reporters in the locker room after the game.[6] Robinson also said he never remembered anyone trying to steal home while he was at bat. Dalrymple had no chance to make the tag. He claimed that if he caught the ball he would have tagged Ruiz out easily. It was just Ruiz's seventh steal of the season and his first steal of home.

Sisler's reaction put the idea of stealing home with his cleanup hitter at bat in perspective: "if he didn't make it," Sisler said, "he might as well have continued on to San Diego" home of the Reds farm team.[7]

Dalrymple believes that Mahaffey simply came apart. "I think he completely drew a blank on what he was supposed to do. Losing a game is one thing," Dalrymple lamented. "When you lose one like that, the whole world starts to crumble around you pretty quickly. That's when we started to crumble."[8]

Still the Phillies had four shots at Tsitouris who was no mystery to

6—The Blue Snow Melts

National League hitters. All season the Phillies had proven to be one of the most resilient clubs in the league, staging late game rallies and comebacks. For the last four innings, the Phillies failed to mount any threats save for a two-out double by Covington in the bottom of the sixth. Then in the bottom of the ninth, they came alive. Covington, leading off the inning, hit one of his patented line drives off the scoreboard in right and beat Robinson's throw with a headfirst slide into second base. The speedy rookie Adolfo Phillips was sent in to run for him.

Now came the turning point of the game and perhaps the season for the Phillies. The next batter was John Herrnstein. Herrnstein had started the season well but had tailed off badly during the second half, especially once the Phillies got Thomas to play first base. Mauch seemed to have lost faith in him and was using him sparingly until Thomas got hurt when Herrnstein occasionally spelled Power at first. A left-handed batter, Herrnstein had two options—try to hit the ball to the right side and move the runner to third or bunt him over. Mauch, who loved to play "little ball," normally would call for the sacrifice in this situation and play for the tie at home. He usually played for one run, arguing that one often led to many. For some reason, perhaps because he believed that Herrnstein could pull Tsitouris' slow stuff, Mauch let him hit away. Herrnstein popped to short. This was the first of four times during the ten-game losing streak that Herrnstein would fail to deliver. The next batter, Dalrymple, grounded to second, with Phillips easily moving to third. But now there were two out and it would take a hit, error, passed ball or wild pitch to score the tying run.

Tony Taylor, batting seventh, worked Tsitouris for a walk on a tough 3–2 pitch and became the winning run. That brought up the light hitting shortstop, Ruben Amaro. On his bench Mauch had any number of possible pinch hitters, Alex Johnson, Gus Triandos, Costen Shockley, Danny Cater, Vic Power, Cookie Rojas, but for some reason he let Amaro bat. Amaro struck out feebly.

The entire inning was not typical of Mauch's approach to managing. He normally would have sacrificed to get the runner to third. Then with two out and the speedy Taylor on first, Mauch might even have gambled and tried a steal with the speedy Taylor, hoping that the catcher's throw would sail into center field. If Taylor succeeded in stealing second then at the very least the Phillies would have the winning run in scoring position. Instead the man usually accused of overmanaging did nothing. It was as if Mauch began to change his managerial style now that he could almost taste the pennant.

The loss hurt. Mahaffey had pitched his best game in weeks and the bullpen had kept the score 1–0, giving the Phillies a chance to get back into the game. Still it was only one game and didn't seem to mean that much. The Reds, it is true, picked up a game but that was no big deal — they were still a distant 5½ back with only 11 games to play. The Cardinals, enjoying a rare off day in September, picked up a half game to move within six games of the Phillies.

Allen Lewis, in a front-page piece for the morning *Inquirer* the next day, wrote that there was no cause for alarm over losing one game. But the fact that the Phillies had lost two games in three days on a steal of home bothered him. "If the Phillies should lose the pennant it might be correct to say the flag was stolen from them."[9]

Entering the second game of the Reds' series, the Phillies seemed uncharacteristically tight. They had finished their last road trip losing three of their last five games and had not been hitting with any authority, having scored only 15 runs in those five games. In the loss to the Reds they had been shut out for the second time in their last 19 games. They also had failed to hit a home run for the seventh consecutive game. Something was wrong, but it wasn't time to panic yet.

Short started the second game of the series having had his normal three days rest. He had pitched well in his previous start on Friday against the Dodgers, a game which the normally reliable bullpen allowed to get away. This night before a crowd of 21,000, Short had his roughest outing of the year. He was hit hard, giving up six runs along with five walks in just 4⅔ innings. Among the runs he surrendered was a long upper deck homer to Frank Robinson. Deron Johnson knocked Short out of the game with a two-run single in the fifth inning. A 6–0 game became a rout when Morrie Steevens gave up three runs in relief. The Phillies scored two meaningless runs late in the game. The 9–2 pasting was the first Phillies game in a week that wasn't decided by one run. The Phillies' fans booed their hometown heroes unmercifully.

What made this loss hard to take was not just the shabby performance by Short but also the fact that the Phillies played so sloppily. Richie Allen made a crucial error, while Gus Triandos threw a ball into center field for an error and also allowed two passed balls.

Mauch dismissed the loss as insignificant. "Everything's fine," he told the assembled press after the game in a voice that was barely audible because of a sore throat, hoarse from yelling at the umpires over the weekend. But everything wasn't fine. The Phillies were tight, not playing the loose brand of ball that had brought them to the top since July.

Having suffered their fifth loss in seven games, it was obvious that something was wrong. The Reds had reduced the Phillies lead to 4½ games and were starting to believe that they had a chance. In the Reds' clubhouse, Joe Nuxhall told the reporters that Mauch was beginning to crack. "The Little General," he chuckled "will begin to push the panic button."[10] To make matters worse the Cardinals behind Phillie killer Curt Simmons had beaten the Mets 2–1 to put them five games out of first. Even the Giants, seemingly dead, were drawing close, having beaten the Colts 7–1. They were now six back. The pennant race was suddenly tightening.

Bunning and Short

The Phillies were feeling the pressure of the pennant race for the first time. After they had taken over first place on July 16th, they had slowly built their lead. During this two-month stretch, there few games that fell into the category of "must win" contests. The Phillies' longest losing streak during this period was three games, and they rarely lost two games in a row. But now something had happened. The team was uneasy, as were the fans. People were beginning to talk about the Phillies blowing the pennant for the first time. The situation suddenly took on a disturbing similarity to what happened to the Whiz Kids. People tried to cheer themselves by saying, one victory would change the entire atmosphere of gloom that hung over the team and the city.

The last game against the Reds saw Mauch send Dennis Bennett to the mound against yet another lefty, Billy McCool. McCool was a 20-year-old rookie who the Reds had to keep under the first year rule then in effect. He pitched surprisingly well all season but had never been in a game as important as this one. For McCool it was one of his rare starts— he only had three starts in 40 appearances. The Reds' pitching staff wasn't stretched as thin as the Phillies' but the fact that they had to resort to a rookie in a game as crucial as this one says something about their pitching problems.

Bennett had won three of his last four starts— two of them crucial 1–0 shut outs over the Giants and the Colts. The Phillies hoped that he was back to the Bennett of the first three months of the season. But now he was almost in constant pain from his inflamed shoulder and arm. The Phillies' team doctors wanted to give him a cortisone shot but were afraid to because he had a rash on his left shoulder. Stan Hochman of the *Daily*

News noted that this was the first time acne played a role in a pennant race.[11]

Both McCool and Bennett pitched well with each lasting six innings. McCool gave up four hits and three runs while Bennett allowed eight hits and four runs. The Phillies scored first but the Reds took a 2–1 lead on solo homers by Vada Pinson and Chico Ruiz. For Ruiz it was his second of the season. Then in the bottom of the sixth, the Phillies regained the lead when, with two outs and Callison on base with a single, Alex Johnson hit a mammoth 430-foot homer to the roof in left center. Phillies fans thought maybe the tide had changed.

With a 3–2 lead, when Bennett gave up back-to-back hits to start the seventh inning, Mauch turned the game over to the bullpen in the person of Ed Roebuck. Pete Rose immediately tied the game with a single, but Roebuck got the next two batters out. Then Vada Pinson hit a three-run homer over the right-field fence to give the Reds a 6–3 lead.

Still, as they had throughout the season, the Phillies bounced back in the bottom of the seventh. Fireballing right-hander Sammy Ellis, who entered the game in relief of McCool, got the first batter, Tony Gonzalez, on strikes and then lost the strike zone, walking the bases loaded. This brought up the Phillies' most dangerous clutch hitter, Johnny Callison. With 23,000 fans screaming and pounding their feet, Shibe Park shook with cheers of "Go, Go." Ellis admitted after the game that he was so scared that "My knees were knocking and my hands were perspiring."[12] All season in these situations, Callison had come through when the Phillies needed a lift. In fact, he was the top clutch hitter in the majors in 1964. Five of his homers, six singles and a two-run sacrifice fly, either tied games for the Phillies or put them in the lead.

Sisler decided to let Ellis face Callison despite having the left-handed Phillie killer Joe Nuxhall warming up in the bullpen.

With 23,000 fans screaming, Callison ran the count to 3–2. A double would tie the score while even a long fly or a walk would put the Phillies back in the game. Callison struck out on a borderline pitch. The next hitter, Tony Taylor, for some reason batting third in one of Mauch's many lineup maneuvers, also struck out on a two-ball, two-strike fastball. The Phillies managed a run in the bottom of the eighth, but it didn't matter as Herrnstein struck out with the tying run on base. The lead was now down to 3½ as a result of the Reds' sweep of the series.

The sense of gloom now was pervasive. For the Phillies nothing was working. The pitching was shaky and the offensive was struggling. On the day that the Phillies received 63,000 requests for World Series tickets, peo-

6—The Blue Snow Melts

Catcher John Edwards congratulates right-hander Jimmy Ellis, who snuffed a Phillies' rally during the third game of the ten-game losing streak. Stopping the rally was a pivotal moment in the streak, and the win lifted Cincinnati to 3½ games out of first place. (Urban Archives, Temple University, Philadelphia Pennsylvania.)

ple in Philadelphia began talking about the unthinkable: maybe the Phillies are going to blow this pennant. Phillies fans talked about something to change the team's mood. Maybe Mauch should throw one of his patented tantrums to stir the team up. If only the Phillies had a flake like Phil Linz whose harmonica playing had relaxed the New York Yankees during their stretch run in September. Alas the Phillies had no clubhouse flake.

The well-known sports writer Red Smith penned an important piece about the Phillies' struggle that appeared in the *Inquirer*. It was time for Mauch to show he is more than a tactical genius. Now he has to be a spiritual leader, argued Smith. "He's got to keep the young Phillies on an even gait because they haven't experienced pressure like this."[13]

The Cards lost a chance to pick up a game when their ex-teammate Roger Craig and the Mets beat them 2–1. The Giants behind Juan Marichal's 20th victory, a 3–1 triumph over the Colts, moved to five games out. The National League pennant suddenly no longer looked settled.

Having lost six of their last eight games, the Phillies desperately needed a victory with the always-dangerous hard-hitting Milwaukee Braves coming to town for four games. The Phillies had won 8 of the 14 meetings between the two teams and had been particularly tough on Warren Spahn, beating him three times. But the Braves were loose, and some of their players talked of sweeping the swooning Phillies.[14]

For the first game, Braves' manager, Bobby Bragan, an old friend of Mauch from their young days with the Dodgers, named Wade Blasingame as his pitcher. Blasingame, a 20-year-old lefty, was another of those journeymen southpaws that teams used to quiet the Phillies' left-handed bats. He had already beaten the Phillies twice in three decisions. Mauch countered with Jim Bunning starting for the fourth time in 12 days. All season Bunning had been the teams' ace, the pitcher that Mauch turned to when things were going badly. Three times he had gotten the Phillies out of one of their losing streaks. He had won 10 of his last 11 decisions and 6 in a row at Shibe Park.

Mauch made two uncharacteristic lineup changes for this game. He installed Alex Johnson in left field instead of Covington and put Adolfo Phillips in center in place of left-handed hitting Tony Gonzalez. Mauch gave as his reason "Johnson and Philips had beaten Blasingame two games in the Pacific Coast League" that season.

This night Bunning didn't have his good stuff and the Braves built a 5–0 lead with Bunning surrendering three of the runs in six innings. Jack Baldschun gave up the other two runs in relief of Bunning. The Braves scored on two triples by the lead footed Joe Torre. Both balls could have been caught. Adolfo Phillips charged Torre's ball only to watch it take a strange bounce over his glove and roll to the wall for a triple. Torre's second triple was almost caught by Callison, but the ball skipped under the glove of the sure-handed right fielder. The bounces that had gone the Phillies' way all season and Mauch's inspired hunches now suddenly were going against them. Johnson and Phillips went 0–6 against Blasingame. Contrary to what Mauch had told the reporters before the game, Phillips and Johnson had not faced Blasingame in the minors. Phillips had one at bat against him, Johnson none.

Meanwhile Blasingame was stifling the Phillies' hitters, retiring the first 14 batters he faced. He eventually allowed just three hits. The Phillies were not the loose crew that raked mediocre pitching all season. Finally in the eighth inning, the Phillies knocked Blasingame out, scoring three runs to make the game competitive. But the Braves' bullpen in the person of 38-year-old Chi Chi Olivo silenced the Phillies. He came on in the eighth inning with two runs in and a man on base. He struck out Covington, gave up a single to Allen, which brought in the third run, and then struck out Gonzalez to end the inning. He retired the side easily in the sixth inning.

The Phillies' fourth loss in a row combined with a doubleheader sweep by the Cardinals over the Pirates further tightened the pennant race. The Cards now moved to 3½ games out of first. The Giants 4½ back and Reds now 3 behind the Phillies had an off day as the pennant race tightened.

Phillies	90–64	
Reds	86–66	3 games behind
Cardinals	86–67	3½
Giants	85–68	4½

Warren Giles, president of the National League, now began to give serious thought to the unthinkable, a possible four team deadlock.

The Phillies seemed to be unraveling before their hometown fans. Richie Allen, who had been booed unmercifully for making a couple of errors in the home stand, spoke for many of his teammates when he told the press: "we'd be better off on the road." This about a team that started the home stand with the best home record in the National League. It was obvious that the Phillies were rattled and had lost their self-confidence.

Game five of the losing streak was heartbreaking, the one loss that sent the Phillies into a total funk. Chris Short on just two days' rest made his second start of the losing streak as Mauch once again skipped Mahaffey's turn. For his opponent Short drew a journeyman right-hander, Hank Fischer, who for some reason gave the Phillies fits. Back in May he shut them out, 1–0, although the Phillies had beaten him badly a week later.

For the fifth game in a row, Mauch juggled his lineup again. Gonzalez was back leading off with Allen in the second spot in the batting order. Frank Thomas, defying his doctors' orders, took the cast off his thumb and offered to play for the first time in three weeks. He batted fifth in the order and went hitless in four at bats. It was apparent that he could hardly swing the bat.

Short pitched well, giving up six hits and three runs in 7⅔ innings. Fischer was better, holding the Phillies to one run and three hits in six innings. The Braves took a 3–1 lead in the seventh inning when they scored two runs in a bizarre fashion. Denis Menke, playing second, was awarded first base when Dalrymple tipped his bat for catcher's interference. Menke went to third on a double by reserve infielder Mike de la Hoz and then scored on a sacrifice fly. De la Hoz scored on a two out single by Felipe Alou.

It looked like a repetition of the Phillies' previous losses when, with Allen on base, John Callison hit a dramatic homer in the eighth inning to tie the game. Neither team scored in the ninth, but in the top of the 10th the Braves scored twice to retake the lead. Again, in the bottom of the inning, Rojas singled and Allen rocked a ball off the scoreboard in right for an inside-the-park home run. The score was tied 5–5.

Neither team scored in the 11th inning. In the top of the 12th with John Boozer on the mound, the Braves got two runs without hitting a ball out of the infield and took a 7–5 lead. Bragan brought in rookie Clay Carroll who shut the Phillies down in the bottom half of the inning for his first win in the majors.

After the game a visibly tired Bragan told reporters that this was one of the most tension filled games he had ever managed. "It was like a World Series game."[15]

What made this game so hard to take for the 30,000 Phillies fans in attendance was the way the team had come back only to lose in extra innings and then to an unknown rookie. In just a few games, young untried pitchers victimized the Phillies: McCool, Blasingame, now Carroll. The Phillies seemed as if they were jinxed and were coming unglued. Even reliable players, like the sound defensive catcher Dalrymple, were making mistakes. He made two errors in this game and only five others all season.

The Phillies had now topped their longest losing streak of the season, four games, with no end in sight. They were not hitting, they were playing sloppy, hesitant baseball and the pitching staff looked exhausted with no fresh arms available. To make matters worse, all of the Phillies' challengers had won, the Reds taking a doubleheader from the Mets while the Cards beat the Pirates and the Giants edged the Cubs. The Phillies lead over the Reds was now down to 1½ games, an almost unheard of five-game decline in five days.

Instead of getting better, matters continued to spin out of control for the Phillies who now were playing with a sense of desperation. The sixth game of the home stand was scheduled for Saturday afternoon, a day when for some reason the Phillies had played poorly all season. Their record was 10 wins versus 13 losses on Saturdays at this point despite playing .600 baseball for most the year. When the Phillies got off to a fast start early in the season, NBC's Game of the Week began to feature them on their Saturday game. The Phillies didn't rise to the occasion and instead played some of their worst games before a national television audience. The superstitious Mauch hated it when he discovered that the Phillies were on national television.

This Saturday seemed different. Art Mahaffey got the Braves out easily in the first two innings, while the Phillies unloaded on the Braves starter, left-hander Denny Lemaster for three runs. The big hits were a triple by Allen followed by a home run from Alex Johnson. They knocked Lemaster out in the second inning, scoring their fourth run on a sacrifice fly by Johnny Callison. For the first time in their slide, the Phillies had a decent lead. Unfortunately it was still early and the Braves were the best hitting team in the National League.

Although he was in and out of trouble, Mahaffey pitched effectively until the fifth inning when he surrendered a homer to shortstop Dennis Menke and back-to-back doubles to Felipe Alou and Lee Maye to halve the Phillies' lead.

The big problem for the Phillies at this point wasn't Mahaffey's pitching but the team's lack of hitting again. After knocking Lemaster out of the game, they got exactly four more hits the rest of the game as the Braves' bullpen, led by journeymen like Bob Sadowski, Dave Eilers and American League reject, Frank Lary, shut them down. Still it looked as if the Phillies finally might eke out a win.

Then in the top of the eighth, with the Phillies up 4–2 and six outs away from ending their nightmare, Mahaffey tired and gave up hits to the first two Braves hitters, Joe Torre and Rico Carty. Mauch took him out in favor of Jack Baldschun. Baldschun got a force out at third but then reserve infielder, Mike de la Hoz, beat out an infield hit to load the bases. With the dangerous left-handed Ed Bailey at the plate, Mauch took out Baldschun in favor of lefty Bobby Shantz who was making his fourth consecutive appearance, a lot of work for a 39-year-old veteran in his last year in the majors. It could be argued that Mauch should have left Baldschun in the game since his best pitch was a screwball that broke away from left-handed batters. This would give him an edge over Bailey. On the other hand, Shantz had pitched effectively for the Phillies ever since they got him from the Cubs in August. Also arguing in favor of Shantz was the fact that he was the premier fielding pitcher of his era (he would win the Gold Glove for 1964) and might turn a double play on anything hit back to him.

With Bailey coming up, the Phillies' coach Peanuts Lowery, noticing how much catcher Gus Triandos was hobbling around on two bad legs, asked Mauch: "do you want to get Dalrymple in the game?" Mauch said no, "my daughter could catch Shantz."[16] It was one of those fateful decisions that Mauch made during the ten game slide that failed to work.

Shantz worked the count to 2–2 then threw a curveball that bounced in the dirt. Gus Triandos was unable to handle the pitch as the third run scored. Shantz struck out Bailey and got out of the inning without further damage with the Phillies' lead cut to 4–3.

The Phillies failed to score in their half of the eighth against their nemesis, Wade Blasingame, despite getting two runners on base via a hit by Gonzalez and a walk. In the top of the ninth, Hank Aaron led off with a single and Eddie Matthews followed with another hit. Mauch left Shantz in and he got pinch hitter Frank Bolling to hit a routine grounder to Amaro at short. The smooth fielding Amaro— he would win a Gold Glove for his defensive work in 1964 — tossed the ball to the sure-handed Tony Taylor. It was at the very least a force out and a possible double play but Taylor dropped the ball. Instead of one out or two with any luck, the bases were loaded with the dangerous Rico Carty coming to bat. Carty, a .330 hitter, had three hits in the series so far and was deadly against left-handed pitching.

For some reason Mauch decided to stay with Shantz. On his first pitch, Carty drove the ball to deep center over Tony Gonzalez's head for a bases clearing triple. The Braves had turned a 4–3 Phillies lead into a 6–4 Braves advantage.

The Phillies went out meekly in the bottom of the ninth as manager Bobby Bragan called on Warren Spahn for a rare relief appearance. Spahn, who the Phillies had beaten three times in 1964, got a measure of revenge. After the Phillies' nightmare was over, Mauch said that this loss to the Braves hurt the most.[17]

"Help"

That day the Reds moved to a half game behind the Phillies when Tsitouris beat the Mets 6–1. The normally erratic Tsitouris had pitched back-to-back gems, allowing just one run in 18 innings. The Cardinals also won as Curt Simmons tied his career high in victories, 17, set when he was with the Whiz Kids, as he beat the Pirates 6–3. The Cardinals were now just 1½ games out of first.

The Phillies players were furious with the Pirates who, in this five game series with the Cardinals, seemed to be going through the motions. The Pirates' first two starters in the series were rookies Wilbur Wood and Tom Butters. Bob Friend, one of the Pirates' key starters, did not appear in any game in this crucial series that the Cardinals swept, possibly because he had already lost 18 games and didn't want any more defeats on his record. The two losses to the Braves, in games that the Phillies had a chance to win, seemed to have taken the life out of them. They looked and played like a beaten team.

Sunday's game, the last of the awful home stand that had begun with so much promise, was one of the worst the Phillies played during the losing streak. Jim Bunning had started two days earlier but he asked Mauch to let him pitch. Looking back 30 years later, Bunning explained

The "HELP" banner hanging in the right field stands sums up the Phillies fans' frustrations during the final game of their ten-game collapse.

why he wanted to pitch this crucial game. "Hindsight dictates that we (referring to Short and himself) should have been rested.... But the emotions of the moment dictated that we try for it.... To say no, to refuse the ball...was to go against every impulse superior athletes have."[18] That Sunday Bunning had nothing and was bombed by the Braves in one of his worst starts of the season.

After the Phillies took a brief 3–2 lead in the second inning, the Braves knocked Bunning out, batting around and scoring six runs in the fourth inning. They then scored four more runs the next inning, batting around once again against Dallas Green making his first appearance during the losing streak.

20,000 Phillies fans sat in stunned silence as the Braves banged out 22 hits and poured 14 runs across the plate. Even three home runs by Callison late in the game couldn't dent the gloom that settled over Shibe Park. A couple of miles away that Sunday, the Philadelphia Eagles were playing the Cleveland Browns before 60,000 fans at Franklin Field. Many of the fans carried transistor radios tuned into the Phillies game. They roared their approval at each of Callison's three homers but had little to cheer about at the end.

Back at Shibe Park the scoreboard in right field showed that the Reds were winning. The Phillies and their fans knew what that meant. For the first time since July 16th, 73 consecutive days, the Phillies were not in first place. One sign in the outfield captured the moment perfectly. It read simply: "Help."

The Braves offensive was devastating. Led by Joe Torre, who had 11 hits including two homers and two triples in the series, the Braves battered the Phillies staff for a .359 batting average. The Phillies' average, on the other hand, was over 100 points lower at .257. Other Braves who feasted on Mauch's tired staff were Felipe Alou who went eight for 19, Hank Aaron who had seven hits and outfielder Lee Maye who hit .467. The Braves averaged eight runs in the four games. No wonder the fans were crying for help.

After the series Bobby Bragan told the press that he hated seeing what was happening to the Phillies. "Look, Mauch has done the best job of managing baseball has seen in years. Who else ever came this close without an All Star on his team. I hate to see it all go down the drain for him" Bragan's pitching coach, Whit Wyatt, also an old friend of Mauch's, agreed. The Phillies' pitching he told the press "looks sorta tired."[19] Bragan and Wyatt were saying in a nice way that the Phillies were dead.

Not only had the Reds moved into first place by capturing a doubleheader from the Mets but the Cardinals also won their fifth consecutive game against the Pirates. They were now a half game behind the Phillies and only 1½ out of first place.

The Phillies now had five games remaining on the road, three in St. Louis and two in Cincinnati. A sense of resignation, a fatalistic belief that all was lost hung over the team and their fans. There was little optimism that the Phillies could somehow rebound as they had done so often in the past and regain first place. Whatever momentum the Phillies had had when they arrived home seven days earlier was gone in this week to be forgotten.

On the plane to St. Louis, the Phillies players talked about how happy they were to get away from Shibe Park, which suddenly had turned into a Chamber of Horrors for them. Baldschun spoke for many of the Phillies when he said: "It has got to help for us to get away. You don't hear the boos when you are out there pitching, but down in the bullpen you hear the comments and the cuss words...."[20]

A dispirited Phillies team flew to St. Louis to play the surging Cardinals three night games. When the Phillies arrived in St. Louis, they were told that 90,000 requests for World Series tickets had been received so far — requests that increasingly looked as if they wouldn't have to be filled. With the Cardinals in the midst of a winning streak, the Reds now in first, it looked grim for the Phillies. If they were to regain first place, they would have to vault past two teams not one, a near impossible task with only five games left in the season. To make matters worse the Phillies would have to face the Big Three of the Cardinals pitching staff: Gibson, Sadecki and Simmons. Keane had avoided overworking them and they were overpowering from mid-August on. The three of them went an incredible 22–4 for the last month and a half of the season. Gibson, who was 10–10 on August 15, finished by winning 9 of his last 11 starts.[21]

Before the first game of the series, some of the Cardinal players watched the Phillies in the pre-game practice. The Phillies seemed lifeless. Bill White, the Cardinal first baseman, thought they were a beaten down bunch of players. Keane agreed. Ever since the Phillies had begun to struggle in the Reds' series, he had told his players to not let up. We have a chance. "We play them three more times, all at home. Then they must play their last two games in Cincinnati."[22]

Bob Gibson, the Cardinals starter for the first game, was going after his 18th victory of the season. Mauch countered with Short for his second start with just two days' rest and his fourth in 11 games. Short didn't pitch badly. He gave up single runs in the second, fourth and sixth innings but allowed only seven hits before being relieved with one out in the sixth. In the meantime, Gibson was overpowering. He gave up just five hits, four singles and one double. At one point he retired 13 Phillies hitters in a row.

In the top of the eighth, the Phillies finally scored on a sacrifice fly by Johnny Callison. With one runner on base, Covington almost tied the game with a 400-foot blast to dead center that Curt Flood caught up to at the last second. It didn't matter as the Cardinals scored two runs in the bottom of the eighth off Jack Baldschun to solidify their lead. Once again the Phillies' defense broke down as they made two errors, including one by the sure-handed Ruben Amaro.

The Cardinals win moved them ½ game ahead of the Phillies, who now dropped to third place for the first time since May 6th. Other than that one day, the Phillies had never been lower than second at any time during the season until now. The Reds, with a day off, led the Cardinals by one game, the Phillies by 1½ games.

In the second game of the series, lefty Ray Sadecki won his 20th victory of the season 4–2. Dennis Bennett was picked to start for the Phillies despite his badly inflamed left shoulder. He was his usual cocky self. After he warmed up he told Mauch not to worry: "I've got it. I'll give you five, six, seven good innings."[23] He lasted just an inning and a third.

Before the game a surprisingly relaxed Mauch joked with the sportswriters and played pepper with some of his players. Mauch may have seemed relaxed but there was a strong element of whistling in the dark about his behavior. His players watched and waited for one of his famous explosions but it never took place.

After Bennett was knocked out, the Cardinals built up a 3–0 lead but the Phillies bullpen did a good job of keeping the game close. In the fourth inning Sadecki suddenly lost the plate and walked the bases loaded. Triandos singled for two runs but the rally ended when pinch hitter Frank Thomas grounded out.

The Cardinals scored the fourth run of the game on a homer by Bill White off John Boozer. The Phillies had a chance in the top of the seventh inning. Callison, who was suffering from the flu and had a bad case of the shakes, singled as a pinch hitter. He was so weak that Cardinal first baseman Bill White had to zip up his windbreaker. With two out he got to third base. With Richie Allen up, representing the tying run

Cardinal manager, Johnny Keane, yanked Sadecki and brought in Barney Schultz. Schultz, a 38-year-old knuckleball pitcher, had come up from the minors in late August and stabilized the Cardinals' one weak spot, the bullpen. He was appearing in his fifth consecutive game and had become the Cardinals' number one man out of the bullpen. He was virtually unhittable in September.

Allen worked the count to 3–2 but then popped out. Over the next two innings, Schultz completely shut the door on the Phillies, allowing them no hits and retiring seven of the eight men he faced. Mauch tried everything to win the game, using six pitchers and sending up seven pinch hitters. Nothing was working. The great pitching feats, the clutch hits of the first five months of the season had disappeared. After the game one of the local sportswriters interviewing Mauch speculated that the Phillies would have to win their remaining three games to win the pennant. A weary Mauch laughed: Yes that would be a good idea. "In fact, it's the best idea I've had all season."[24]

The Cardinal victory combined with a Reds loss at Pittsburgh gave them a tie for first place. The Phillies remained in third, 1½ games back but two behind in the important loss column.

The last game of the series pitted the Phillies against their nemesis, Curt Simmons, who had beaten them 15 times versus 2 defeats since the Phillies' released him in April 1960. Bunning started for the Phillies for his second start during the slide on two days' rest. Once again he faltered. He didn't have his usual sharp stuff. The Cardinals had an easy time with him, scoring six runs in his three innings. They built up an invincible 8–0 lead with Simmons pitching no-hit baseball into the seventh inning. The Phillies finally got to him for five runs, but by then it was too late and the Cardinal bullpen shut them down in the ninth inning with Gordon Richardson, the lefty who had beaten them in mid-season, getting the last two outs. What made this game so frustrating was the sloppy play of the Phillies. They made four errors, including misplays by the usually reliable Bobby Wine, Tony Taylor and Johnny Callison. The Phillies simply self-destructed as they fell 2½ games back of the Cardinals.

After the game Simmons was asked if he got any special pleasure out of beating his former team. He said no. "I feel for them a little bit. I just hope it never happens to us like that. It would stay with you the rest of your life."[25] How right he was.

A weary Phillies team left for Cincinnati to run out the schedule. Various scenarios were trotted out to explain how the Phillies could tie for the pennant, but outright victory was gone. A sense of pessimism settled over the team. For the Phillies to tie, they would have to beat the Reds both games while the Cardinals somehow lost all three games to the woeful Mets—not very likely and yet it almost came true.

The Phillies broke their losing streak on a come from behind victory. With the Reds' Jim O'Toole ahead 3–0 against Chris Short pitching with his normal three days' rest and the Phillies seemingly on the verge of losing their 11th consecutive game, fate stepped in. Short hit Reds shortstop Leo Cardenas in the middle of the back in the bottom of the seventh inning. Short was frustrated and may have thrown at Cardenas on purpose. Cardenas waved his bat menacingly at Short as players from both teams poured onto the field.

Nothing happened until the Phillies went to bat in the top of the eighth. They scored four runs when Cardenas, who was sulking, failed to catch a pop up to shallow left field off the bat of Thomas. Rojas walked and Taylor singled home Johnny Briggs who was running for Thomas. Allen then tripled in two more runs and scored the go ahead run on a sharp single up the middle by Alex Johnson. Just like that the Phillies had taken a late inning lead, something that eluded them through their 10-game slide.

The Reds' players were furious at Cardenas for losing his concentration, especially when they found out that the Mets had ended the Cardinals eight-game winning streak. The Reds had lost a chance to move into first place by ½ game. In the Reds' clubhouse after the game, O'Toole threw Cardenas against the wall. Cardenas responded by picking up a screwdriver and had to be restrained by his teammates from trying to stab O'Toole.

The Phillies and Reds were off the next to last day of the season and they watched the Mets thump the Cardinals 15–5. Everything now depended on the outcome of the last games of the season. If the Phillies won and St. Louis lost, there would be a three-way tie for the pennant. If the Reds beat the Phillies and St. Louis lost, then the Reds would be the National League pennant winners. The league president Warren Giles had to plan for a possible round robin playoff that was incredibly confusing. If three teams tied, then there would a series of playoff games with two losses leading to elimination.

The Reds started John Tsitouris, believing that he still had the Phillies' number, instead of fireballing Jim Maloney who had pitched 11 innings in a tough game three days before. He had a stiff shoulder but had not allowed a run in his last 20 innings pitched. The Reds players wanted him to start but he backed off. Bunning, now pitching on his normal three days' rest, took the mound for the Phillies. He was over-

Approximately 8,000 fans welcomed the Phillies home at the end of the season. (Urban Archives, Temple University, Philadelphia Pennsylvania.)

powering, and the Reds never had a chance as the Phillies knocked Tsitouris all over the field. Richie Allen hit homers number 28 and 29 as the Phillies' bats came alive in a 10–0 romp. While the Phillies' game was in progress, the scoreboard showed the Mets leading the Cardinals early in the game. Once the Cardinals took the lead, Crosley Field emptied out until there were just 5,000 diehards in attendance for the funeral of the Phillies and Reds.

The Phillies and Reds tied for second place, one game behind the pennant-winning Cardinals. The Phillies' record of 92–70 was their best since the Whiz Kids, but that was no consolation. They had blown a pennant that was all but theirs and they would have to live with that memory. After the game a visibly shaken Mauch tried to lift the burden from his players for the collapse, telling the writers that he didn't feel sorry for himself but for the players who had tried so hard to win: "I wish I could have done as good a job as the players. They did a great job. That's all I have to say." Frustrated at the questions that implied that he had blown the pennant, Mauch said: "I'm not going to defend myself to anybody. Inside I know I did everything I could to win."[26]

That night a dejected Phillies team flew home to Philadelphia. They were shocked to find 8,000 fans (four times the number that greeted them when they flew home to begin their last home stand) gathered at Philadelphia International Airport to greet them, not with boos, but with cheers. Mauch said he wanted to be the first one off the plane in case there was any ugliness. "You guys didn't lose it," he told the players, "I did."[27] There was a strange party-like atmosphere as fans waved banners telling of their love for the players. But as the players got into their cars, it was clear that this was a wake, a good old-fashioned Philadelphia wake with lots of crying and a sense that a golden moment was gone forever.

The Phillies fans were angry and hurt. They felt that a pennant was taken from them by dame fortune. Something had gone wrong, and the memory of those 10 awful losses washed away all the wonderful things that had happened in 1964: Bunning's perfect game, Callison's game-winning homer in the All-Star Game, Richie Allen's incredible rookie season. All was for naught. The Phillies fans of 1964 had their hearts broken, and they would be reluctant to invest their emotions in another Phillies team for years.

7
What Went Wrong

When the season ended with a whimper not a bang, Phillies players and fans were in a state of shock. The collapse had happened too quickly to be fully absorbed. A 6½-game lead disappeared while people were sending in their checks for World Series tickets. Every day the major Philadelphia papers, The morning *Inquirer*, *Evening Bulletin* and the afternoon *Daily News*, had carried a large box with the figure 7 inside. It was the magic number of Phillies' victories and/or Reds' and Cardinals' losses that would give the Phillies the pennant. About six games into the slide, the box disappeared along with the fans hopes.

Larry Merchant, then the sports editor of the *Daily News*, captured the city's confusion perfectly. "Future generations," he wrote, "will be told this incredible horror story September after September.... Children will shriek, adults will shiver, managers will faint. The legend will take its place alongside such classics as the Dodgers of '51 and Frankenstein and the Wolfman."[1]

Many Phillies fans, me among them, couldn't bring themselves to watch the 1964 World Series. It just didn't seem right. Neither, it seems, could Mauch. He and Quinn attended the first two games in St. Louis, but when the games started Mauch walked out of the park in a kind of daze. Quinn had to drag him back. The World Series should have been the Phillies, not the Cardinals, in there against the hated Yankees. All season, Phillies' fans had been hoping for a Yankee win in the American League so that they could watch their heroes get a measure of revenge for the four-game sweep of the Whiz Kids in 1950. Philadelphia sports fans have long memories.

What went wrong? How could a team that played so well for 90 percent of the season suddenly and ignominiously collapse the way the Phillies did? A couple of thoughts, not explanations or excuses, stand out.

Such collapses are not all that rare in baseball although few have been as deadly as that which happened to the 1964 Phillies. In 1950 the Whiz Kids had a 7½-game lead over the Brooklyn Dodgers with 11 games remaining and still almost blew the pennant. They had to win the last game of the year or face a three-game playoff that they almost surely would have lost due to the worn out state of their pitching staff. But at least that Phillies team won their "must win" game even if they did get swept in four games by the Yankees.

Just two years before the Phillies' nightmare in 1964, the Los Angeles Dodgers were four games ahead of the Giants with 13 games left. The Dodgers won three of their remaining games but were tied with the Giants at the end of the season. They then proceeded to lose the playoffs despite having a two-run lead going into the last inning of the third game.

None of this would satisfy the Phillies' fans. They were humiliated and wanted an explanation. Even more than that, they wanted a scapegoat. They got the latter in "The Little General," Gene Mauch.

In 1964 Mauch had been the most popular manager or coach of any sports team in the city. The press loved him because he was colorful and always quotable. He gave interviews that showed a deep knowledge of baseball and the nuances of the game — Stan Hochman, long time sportswriter for the Philadelphia *Daily News* who covered the 1964 Phillies, today still describes Mauch as the most intense student of baseball he ever met.[2] Bill Conlin, who first started covering the Phillies for the *Daily News* in 1965, agreed. "He taught me most of what I know about the fundamentals and technical side of the game."[3]

Mauch had his flaws, however. He was better at strategy than in handling his players. He also created tension around the team. It was often hard for the players to relax and play their own game. Instead they seemed to be trying too hard to please him. In effect, he intimidated his own players in a counterproductive way.[4]

He was particularly tough on pitchers, who he really didn't understand. He seemed to believe that they were not athletes like everyday players and were given to a bewildering number of ailments. He thought some of his pitchers, Culp in particular, were soft.

When it came to the everyday regulars, as a player of limited ability, Mauch couldn't understand those who he believed failed to capitalize on their talents, players like Johnny Callison and Dick Allen. He loved both of them but could never figure out how to get the most out of them. It is also possible that Mauch forgot the advice he had been given by one of his former managers Billy Southworth. Whatever you do, Southworth told him: "Don't fall in love with your players." Mauch admitted he was aware of Southworth's advice in 1964: "How could I help it," Mauch said after the season, "For 150 days these guys gave me more thrills than I had in a lifetime."[5]

Philadelphia fans had adopted Mauch and his feisty yet cerebral style of play dating back to the 23-game losing streak when they rallied to the underdog quality of his Phillies team. By 1963 Mauch's Phillies were on the rise as the fans embraced the edgy quality of his managing. Mauch loved to outsmart the opposition, playing inside baseball, hit and running, all the while trying to keep your opponents off balance. He once protested a game because a player, pitcher Elroy Face, left the bullpen and went to the bathroom on the scoreboard in Forbes Field. Mauch pointed out to the umpires that since the scoreboard was in the field of play, this was in violation of rule 1.01, "baseball is a game between two teams of nine players," which meant that Face constituted a 10th player on the field. The protest was rejected but these kinds of actions irritated his opponents. The downside of Mauch's combativeness was that the opposition players like Frank Robinson, Ron Santo, Joe Nuxhall, and Orlando Cepada would do anything to beat him.

Mauch knew that he was unpopular with some of the players and other managers around the league. He once told Sandy Grady that if a popularity test was held for National League managers he would come in last. Grady thought it was a dangerous way to manage, but Mauch said he didn't care as long as his players wanted to win.[6]

At some point during the losing streak, the fans' love affair with Mauch began to fade. Toward the end of the losing streak, banners appeared in the stands at Shibe Park saying, "Fire Mauch." The hero of the spring and summer was suddenly being fitted for goat horns. The notoriously fickle fans and sportswriters of Philadelphia alike began dissecting his handling of the team, not only during the losing streak but also throughout the season.

Their major indictment of Mauch's responsibility for the ten-game collapse centered around his handling of the pitching staff, especially his reliance on Short and Bunning during the ten-game slide. Each pitched twice on two days' rest. In Mauch's defense the issue is more complex than that. One has to keep in mind the state of the Phillies pitching staff in September. In effect by then Mauch was reduced to two reliable starters, Short and Bunning. Mahaffey did not win a game after August 29th; Culp's last victory was July 22nd and he didn't start a game after

August 15th. Nor did Culp appear in any of the games of the collapse. Mauch claimed that Culp did not want the ball, something the chunky Texan vehemently denied. Culp said he was injured and unable to pitch effectively. By August Dennis Bennett was pitching on sheer nerve. His loss of effectiveness robbed the Phillies of that third solid starter behind Short and Bunning and unsteadied the rotation. Rookie Rick Wise won his fifth and last game August 20th. In September and early October, the Phillies' record was 14–19, their only losing month of the season. Short and Bunning accounted for eight of these victories, while the sore armed Bennett added three. No other starter won a game—a difficult way to win a pennant.

Still the question was asked, why not start someone else during the 10-games slide—how about Wise who pitched surprisingly well through early August? What about using Shantz who had shown he could still pitch deep into a game? Mauch also could have risked using the inconsistent Boozer. He was capable of cranking up a solid effort. These are reasonable questions in retrospect but only on the assumption that Mauch knew that the Phillies were going to lose 10 in a row. He admitted after the season that "if I'd known after 150 games that we only had to win four more, I might have given Bunning and Short a little more rest."[7]

In considering these points it should also be remembered that in two of their starts during the collapse Short and Bunning pitched well enough to win. In the fourth game of the slide, Bunning went six innings and gave up six hits and three runs to the hard-hitting Braves lineup. The next day, Short, on two days' rest, in $7\frac{2}{3}$ innings allowed the Braves six hits and three runs, only one earned.

Mauch also started Mahaffey and Bennett twice during the 10-games losing streak. Mahaffey pitched effectively in both his starts, losing the infamous 1–0 game to the Reds and giving up just three runs, of which two were earned, to the Braves in the sixth game of the slide. Bennett pitched well in the third game against the Reds but was totally ineffective against the Cardinals in the ninth game of the losing streak.

Another way of looking at the Phillies' pitching dilemma is to compare Mauch's handling of his starters with the Cardinals' Johnny Keane. Keane was by no means Mauch's match as a baseball strategist, but he handled his pitching staff brilliantly. He had his Big Three, Bob Gibson, Ray Sadecki and Curt Simmons, ready for the pennant run in late August-early September. He also found a reliable reliever in veteran knuckleball pitcher, Barney Schultz, to stabilize his bullpen. As a result the Cardinals were primed for a pennant drive. In contrast the Phillies' pitching woes surfaced when the team could least afford such a breakdown.

You could also make a similar comparison to Mauch's handling of his staff in the final weeks of the season with Yogi Berra's. Berra may not have been a managerial genius, but he had the Yankee pitching lined up to beat back a serious challenge from the Baltimore Orioles and the Chicago White Sox. In the critical months of September-October, the Yankees won their pennant by compiling a remarkable 24–9 record. Berra, who would be fired after the season, kept his big four starters healthy: Whitey Ford, Al Downing, Jim Bouton and rookie Mel Stollemyre. He also got a big assist from Pedro Ramos who stabilized the Yankee bullpen, which had been erratic most of the season after he came over to them in trade with the Indians on September 5. In 21 innings with the Yankees, Ramos saved seven games, winning one while striking 21 batters and walking none. Mauch could have used a reliever like Ramos in September.

Pitching wasn't the only thing that cost the Phillies so dearly. The major problem the Phillies faced during these 10 games was an almost total offensive meltdown. A team that hit all season, and was particularly effective in the clutch, suddenly found their bats cold.

At the same time the Phillies stopped hitting, they began to make rookie blunders. During their seven consecutive losses at home and the previous weeks' games in Houston and Los Angeles, Phillies players had been thrown out 10 times trying to take an extra base. This was totally uncharacteristic of the way the team had played all season. They took advantage of other team's mistakes and made few of their own. That all changed during the losing streak.

Going into the final weeks of the season, Wes Covington had said that now was the time for the veterans, the players who had been through the pressure of a pennant race, to step up and carry the burden for the team. Well the vets, especially Covington, failed the test.

Of the Phillies' regulars only Allen and Callison hit better than their 1964 season average during the ten-game losing streak. Allen was simply incredible, hitting .366 in those ten games. Callison hit .275 but added four homers, including his three-homer game against Milwaukee. The remaining Phillies' averages were terrible. Taylor hit .229, Dalrymple .222, Alex Johnson .191 although with three homers, Rojas .200, and Amaro a disastrous .050. Tony Gonzalez hit .279 but drove in no runs.

The old pro Covington "stepped up" to relieve the young players at a puny .150 clip. Vic Power, Thomas' replacement, hit .263 but drove in no runs. Thomas took the cast off his thumb and tried to play. But he was a shadow of the player he had been in August and early September. He went 2 for 13 with no RBIs. What was worse the Phillies failed to get an RBI from any of the first basemen that Mauch used in these 10 games.

In essence the Phillies lost these 10 games not just because of poor pitching—it was sub par—but largely because they failed to score. In the 10 games the Phillies scored 34 runs, an average of 3.4 per game, a figure that is distorted by the 8 runs they put on the board in the 14–8 drubbing at the hands of the Braves. Subtracting the 8 runs the Phillies scored in that game, their average was even worse, 2.9 runs per game. The Phillies scored 3 or fewer runs in half of their 10 defeats, a hard way to win a game much less a pennant. Even at that, John Herrnstein believes that a clutch hit here or there might have won seven of the ten games.[8] Herrnstein may be exaggerating, but it is true that the Phillies had a realistic chance to win games number 1, 3, 4, 5 and 6 of the losing streak with a big hit here or there. They led in three of these games. Interestingly Herrnstein himself failed to get a hit during the losing streak. He was used a number of times by Mauch as a left-handed pinch hitter but with no success.

The Phillies' defense, one of the strongest in the league, also turned shaky in the last two weeks. Solid position players like Taylor, Wine, Amaro, Callison and Dalrymple made key errors or turned in sloppy play that gave the opposition extra outs at the wrong time.

During the last two weeks of the season the Phillies, young and inexperienced, went into a team funk probably brought on by the pressure of the pennant race. This funk deepened once they lost the first couple of games to the Reds. For Dalrymple this was the key to the collapse: "we were a young ball club which found itself in first place and didn't know how to handle it."[-9]

The Phillies still might have survived if they hadn't had to play two of the hottest teams in the National League as well as the two teams closest to them in the standings, the Reds and Cardinals. Even the Braves, who the Phillies had to face four times during the losing streak, were red hot in September and October, winning 23 and losing 10.

While the Phillies added one game to their lead between September 1st and September 20th, the Cardinals went 12–7, the Reds 10–9. At that point both these teams were launched on winning streaks that coincided with the Phillies' collapse. The Reds won nine in a row, the Cardinals eight straight victories. Even the Giants briefly surged back in the race by winning seven of nine games. The Phillies, who hadn't had a serious losing streak all season, picked a bad time to have one.

One criticism that emerged after the collapse is easy to dispel — that Mauch stopped using Jack Baldschun and started relying on untested relief pitchers like Bobby Locke and Morrie Steevens in key situations. In fact, Steevens appeared in three games of the losing streak, Locke two. Steevens was adequate, while Locke was bombed both times.

The story has it that Mauch said when he looked into Baldschun's eyes he saw fear. Mauch had keen eyesight, but I doubt that from the dugout he could see Baldschun's eyes in the bullpen warming up. Leading up to the crucial Reds series, Baldschun had made six appearances in September. If Mauch no longer trusted Baldschun then how do you explain that he used him in seven of the team's ten losses?

The real problem with the bullpen was simple. It was worn out through overuse, especially once the starting pitching began to break down in mid-August. Roebuck, who had been instrumental in the Phillies' early success, was almost useless by the end of the season. Roebuck made a great comeback with the Phillies in 1964, appearing in 60 games, while compiling a 2.22 ERA, the lowest in his career. But he had had arm problems in the past that forced him to miss almost all of one season, 1961, and led the Dodgers to give up on him midway through the 1963 season. Mauch had gotten him in April and liked his willingness to take the ball. Ever the gambler, Mauch played the hot hand and used Roebuck constantly especially for the first three months of the season. When the Phillies needed him most, Roebuck was worn out, barely able to lift his right arm. Still Roebuck was used in half the games during the losing streak and pitched fairly effectively. The one time he pitched, however, in a crucial situation in the third game, he surrendered the game-winning homer to Vada Pinson.

Some idea of the state of the Phillies' bullpen can be gleaned from this simple fact. During the seven losses at home, Mauch went to the bullpen 23 times to stem the tide of defeat. The failure of the Phillies' relievers was at least as much a factor in the losing streak as was the ineffectiveness of the starters or Mauch's overuse of Bunning and Short.

A fairer criticism of Mauch may be that he failed to react during the 10-game slide the way one would have expected the volatile manager to do. Mauch was amazingly quiet throughout the collapse. There were no blow-ups save one 20-minute tirade after the sixth game of the slump, no confrontations with the umpires, and no fights with the opposition.

Instead Mauch was almost serene, something which shocked the players. Baldschun was surprised at Mauch's reaction. Instead of "bringing down the clubhouse" and "jumping on the players" Mauch didn't raise hell. Baldschun wonders "if he had jumped on us it might have put us back on the right track."[10] There may be something to Baldschun's point but it is also self-serving. It shifts the burden for the collapse from the players to the manager.

While the disaster was unfolding, one anonymous Phillies player described Mauch as being "the nicest he was all year."[11] Niceness wasn't Mauch's strong suit.

Looking back maybe the answer to the Phillies' failure to win the pennant is simpler than pitching problems, lack of hitting, poor defense or Mauch's limitations. Perhaps the Phillies were not the best team in the National League. This was certainly the view of Ed Roebuck who knew something about winning teams, having pitched for the Dodgers. He believed that the Phillies were essentially "a shaky club…a team with a lot of flaws."[12]

If you compare their starting eight to the Reds, Cardinals, or even Braves regulars, the Phillies probably were no better than third or fourth in the league. From a statistical standpoint, they ranked fourth in batting average, fourth in home runs and third in runs scored. After the Cardinals won the pennant, Stan Musial made a shrewd observation about the Phillies. "I know it's tough on the people of Philadelphia to lose like this," the future Hall of Famer said, "but all year, the pros in the league felt the Phils had the talent of a third or fourth team. Gee, Mauch almost got away with it."[13]

What the Phillies had in 1964 was four genuine stars—pitchers Short and Bunning, plus everyday players Allen and Callison. The rest of their lineup was average or below average. You could argue that instead of criticizing Mauch, maybe he deserved credit for keeping a team with so many flaws in the pennant race. Some of his moves worked perfectly. Platooning the light hitting Wine and Amaro at short and getting the maximum out of them, including eight homers and 68 RBIs, was a stroke of genius. During the rest of their careers, they never came close to those figures. Only two shortstops in the National League, Dick Groat and Leo Cardenas drove in more runs that the Phillies duo. Despite having no first baseman until he got Thomas, Mauch managed to get 18 homers and 80 RBIs out of the nine men who played that position in 1964, a figure close to what Roy Sievers achieved in 1962 and 1963.

In retrospect the Phillies loss in 1964, heartbreaking as it was for

Philadelphia, was not all that surprising. They had played heady, even inspirational, baseball all season, raising the hopes of their victory-starved fans. But when crunch time came the team just lacked the depth to win. It wasn't Mauch, bad luck, or the "breaks." It wasn't even injuries although they may have particularly hurt a vulnerable team that lacked depth. Mauch had gone to the whip at different times during his career in Philadelphia, but I doubt if that would have worked during the slide.

The real tragedy of 1964 is that it created unrealistic aspirations on the part of the fans and even Quinn and Mauch. The latter came to believe that they were one or two pieces away from succeeding where they had failed in 1964. The Phillies began searching for that missing ingredient, not in their organization, but in getting the right veteran to fill the gaps in the team. According to Bill Conlin, longtime baseball writer for the *Philadelphia Daily News*, if Mauch had a weakness it was his admiration for former stars. A mediocre player himself, he had a soft spot for veterans and valued pedigree more than performance.[14]

After the 1964 season, Quinn made two trades that failed to pan out, getting Bo Belinsky from the Angels and Dick Stuart from the Red Sox for the sore-armed Bennett. The two trades were designed to plug holes that hurt the Phillies so badly in 1964. Belinsky was to replace Bennett in the starting rotation, while Stuart was to give the Phillies a right-handed bat and provide power at first base. As it turned out both moves backfired badly.

Belinsky was a flop, winning just four games, eight less than the sore-armed Bennett had won in 1964, while Stuart hit 28 homers and drove in 95 runs but his defense was as bad as his reputation as "Dr. Strangeglove" indicated. Belinsky lasted just nine games for the Phillies in 1966. Some idea of Stuart's value can be inferred from what the Phillies got for him after the 1965 season. He went to the Mets for catcher Jim Schaeffer, infielder Bobby Klaus and the same Wayne Graham the Phillies had traded to the Mets for Frank Thomas in 1964. The 1965 Phillies wound up in sixth place with seven fewer wins than in 1964.

The following season the Phillies again traded for veterans, sending the talented but enigmatic Alex Johnson and the increasingly disgruntled Art Mahaffey to the Cardinals for 36-year-old Dick Groat and Bill White who was 32. Both men had good years in 1966 with the Phillies — Groat hit a tough .260 and drove in 53 runs, while White hit 22 homers to go along with 103 RBIs. White was the first Phillies first baseman to drive in 100 runs since Dolf Camilli in 1936. Both Groat and White unfortunately broke down quickly. Groat was out of baseball after the 1967 season and White, having torn his Achilles tendon before spring training in 1967, was never a regular again.

In another controversial move, early in 1966 Quinn, at Mauch's urging, traded future Hall of Famer, Ferguson Jenkins to the Cubs for two aging veterans, 38-year-old Bob Buhl and Larry Jackson who was 36. Mauch believed that the two ex-Cubs would join Bunning and Short to give the Phillies a starting rotation second to none in the National League. Quinn and Mauch once again were looking for a quick fix and didn't get it as the Phillies won 87 games but finished fourth, a distant eight games out of first.

A more serious sign of trouble for the Phillies was the fact that in neither 1966 nor 1967 did their farm system produce an everyday player or starting pitcher other than Jenkins, Johnson and Phillips who they traded away. The Phillies' farm system, so productive in 1962 through 1964, had dried up.

The near pennant in 1964 in some ways was the worst thing that could have happened to the Phillies. By getting so close it created the false impression that the team was a genuine pennant contender. It led the organization to neglect the farm system and rely too much on trades instead of building from within as they had in the early 1960s.

For Phillies fans the disillusion of 1964 was even worse. It soured them on the team and on Mauch in particular. The man who had guided the Phillies to respectability now became a target of boos. He was eventually let go in June 1968 unlamented by both the fans and the sportswriters of the city.

When the team slipped into mediocrity and even worse in the late 1960s, the Phillies fans deserted them in droves. Attendance, which set an all time record of 1.4 million in 1964, dropped to just over 500,000 five years later.

Even the great success of the Paul Owens rebuilt Phillies teams of the 1970s and early 1980s couldn't make the painful memories of 1964 fade away for many fans. The pain and anguish of that bleak moment was too deep, although Tug McGraw's strikeout of Willie Wilson to win the World Series in 1980 made the loss in 1964 bearable even if it didn't completely erase it. But the memories of the Year of Blue Snow will never fade.

8
Where Are They Now

The collapse of the 1964 Phillies, while a devastating blow to the team and the city, didn't necessarily have to be fatal. After all, teams had recovered from worse collapses. The Dodgers in 1951 had blown a huge lead to the Giants in what is probably the most famous collapse in baseball history. The next year the Dodgers rallied to win the pennant with ease. In fact, they won pennants in four of the next five years as well as their only World Series while in Brooklyn.

A similar situation took place a decade later. The Dodgers in 1962 again saw a large lead disappear and were overtaken by the Giants. The next year the Dodgers not only won the pennant, but they went on to win the World Series by sweeping the vaunted New York Yankees in four straight games in which the Bronx Bombers scored just four runs. The Phillies had hopes that they could recover their poise and become a powerhouse in the National League. It wasn't to be.

A cloud seems to hang over the survivors of the '64' disaster—some kind of awful jinx that denied them what was so close that year. Nothing seemed to go right for them after the 1964 fiasco. Two of the team's free spirits, Short and John Boozer both died at a young age. Frank Thomas, who almost single-handedly carried the Phillies for a month late in the season, was relegated to the bench by the trade for Dick Stuart. Stuart proved a flop, batting .234, almost 50 points lower than in 1964 and striking out frequently. Bo Belinsky, Dennis Bennett's replacement, never got untracked, quickly earned a spot in Mauch's doghouse and was let go the next year. Wes Covington also feuded with Mauch, claiming that he had lost control of the team. He was traded away after the 1965 season and held on in the majors for one more season.

A taunting incident in early July between Dick Allen and Frank Thomas, whose nickname "The Big Donkey" says all you need to know about his sense of humor, led to a scuffle in which Thomas hit Allen on the shoulder with a bat. That night Thomas was released despite hitting a dramatic home run. The Phillies overreacted and should have forgotten the entire incident. They made matters worse by telling Allen not to talk to the press. Fans took sides, some for racial reasons and blamed Allen for Thomas' firing. The first signs of the cold war between Allen and the Phillies fans began with the Thomas incident.

Of the 39 players who made an appearance with the Phillies in 1964, only a handful went on to greater success in baseball. Just two of them reached baseball's Valhalla, the World Series. Rick Wise, saw a distinguished career in which he won 188 games overshadowed by his trade for future Hall of Famer, Steve Carlton. At least Wise reached the World Series with Boston in 1975. In that exciting seven-game battle with the Big Red Machine of Cincinnati, Wise won a game in relief. He was the only pitcher on the Phillies' roster to ever win a World-Series Game. (Ryne Duren who pitched for the Phillies a few weeks in 1964 had a Series victory with the Yankees in 1958).

Clay Dalrymple remained with the Phillies until 1968 with decreasing playing time and then was traded to the Baltimore Orioles in 1969. He served as a pinch hitter and back up to the Orioles' regular catchers, Elrod Hendricks and Andy Etchebarren. In the year the "Miracle Mets" defeated the hugely favored Orioles, Dalrymple went two for two in the World Series.

The best the rest of the survivors of '64' could do was get to the playoffs when they first were introduced in 1969. From the 1964 Phillies only Tony Gonzalez with the Atlanta Braves in 1969, Tony Taylor with the Detroit Tigers in 1972 and Cookie Rojas with Kansas City in 1976–77 reached post-season play. Of these three, Rojas and Gonzalez had a modicum of success. In two League Championships Rojas hit .308, while Gonzalez hit a lusty .357 with one home run for the Braves in a losing effort against the Miracle Mets of 1969.

The record of the other survivors of 1964 was checkered to say the least. Robert R. M. "Bob" Carpenter stayed on as president of the Phillies with decreasing enthusiasm until November 1972 when he turned the team over to his son, Robert "Ruly" Carpenter. Bob Carpenter never really recovered from the collapse in 1964 and seemed to be preparing to pass on the club's presidency in the years that followed. Under Ruly Carpenter the Phillies went through an impressive revival and became one of the National League premier dynasties in the mid-1970s to the early 1980s. He saw the Phillies win three National League East titles

(1976–78) but suffer frustration due to their inability to gain a pennant. In 1977 his Phillies lost in a manner that bore some resemblance to the 1964 collapse. The Phillies had split the first two games of the playoffs with the Los Angeles Dodgers and had a two-run lead with two out and nobody on base in the top of the ninth inning. They were one out away from a two games to one lead with their ace Steve Carlton ready to start the next night. Then the roof fell in and the Dodgers scored three runs in the top of the ninth to win 6–5.

Eventually the Phillies got out from under their cloud by winning the World Series in 1980, the only one in Phillies' history. Overall, during the Carpenter era the Phillies won five National League East titles, counting the split season in 1981, and one World Series in six years.

In 1981 Ruly Carpenter surprised the baseball world by announcing that the Phillies were for sale. He gave as his reason a growing disenchantment with the direction that baseball had taken in the free agent era. The last straw apparently came when Braves' owner Ted Turner signed journeyman outfielder Claudell Washington to a five year $3.5 million contract.

John Quinn never recovered from the disastrous finish in 1964. He continued as general manager until June 1972, but it was increasingly clear that he was growing out of touch with the direction baseball took in the early years of Marvin Miller's reign as head of the Players Union. A tough, harsh bargainer, Quinn irritated many of the Phillies' players with his dealings with them and raises were hard to come by. What also hurt the Phillies was that none of the trades he made, often at Mauch's urging, after 1964 worked out. By the last years of his tenure as general manager, the Phillies had slipped back to the second division. The farm system was in the good hands of Paul Owens and would begin to produce in the early 1970s, but Quinn would not be around to bask in that glory. Before he was let go he did make one final trade, easily the best in his career. In spring training 1972 he heard that the Cardinals were angry with pitcher Steve Carlton over his contract demands. Quinn arranged a trade for Carlton giving up Rick Wise, then coming off his best year, 17–14 with a no hitter, in the process. In June 1972, while the Phillies were heading for their worst record since the late 1950s, Bob Carpenter announced that Quinn had "retired" and would be replaced by Owens.

Of all the personnel connected to the fateful 1964 team, none was as identified with it as the manager Gene Mauch. Mauch continued to manage the Phillies until June 1968, but the 1965 through 1967 teams, although competitive, lacked the sense of destiny that the 1962 through

1964 teams had possessed. The Phillies of Mauch's later years, although highly professional, played without a sense of direction and leadership. The Phillies of 1965–67 looked like a bunch of individualists, not a team as had been the case in 1964.

The Phillies in Mauch's last three full seasons averaged 85 victories but they were never serious contenders for the pennant. Mauch personally seemed to have lost his magic touch with the playing personnel. He became restless, constantly tinkering to find the right mix to get back into the pennant chase. Questionable veterans like Jackie Brandt or Don Lock were brought in only to be discarded after a season or two.

Mauch's handling of pitching was questioned again. He had two superb starters in Bunning and Short, who continued to be big winners for the Phillies. Culp bounced back in 1965 to win 14 games but he and Mauch still rubbed each other the wrong way. After a poor 1966 season, Mauch had him sent to the Cubs for left-hander Dick Ellsworth. The trade didn't benefit either club. It was another case of Mauch trying to get a veteran to recapture the greatness he had shown in the past. Ellsworth, a 22-game winner in 1963, went 6–7 with the Phillies and was sent on to the Red Sox in 1968 where he joined Culp, who lasted just one season with the Cubs. Both saw their careers revive although in Ellsworth's case it was just for one year. Culp had four good years for the Red Sox, winning 64 games at a time when the Phillies were struggling for pitching and could have used him. He finished his career with a decent 122–101 record.

Mauch's handling of the relief core also was erratic after 1964. He lost faith in Baldschun during the 1965 season and began using rookie Gary Wagner as his closer. But Wagner was always suspect in Mauch's eyes. He had some odd ideas about pitchers: "I never saw a pitcher worth a shit who sweated a lot. This guy (Wagner) goes through three shirts a workout."[1] He believed that pitchers who sweated too much were afraid. When Wagner developed arm problems in 1966, Mauch turned to lefty Darrold Knowles as his prime reliever and got a decent year out of him. Then Knowles was used in the trade for Don Lock, who flopped badly in two years with the Phillies. In 1967 Mauch scrambled and finally found capable relievers in veterans Dick Farrell in his second tour with the Phillies and a Baltimore reject, Dick Hall. Through those three years, 1965–67, the Phillies' bullpen was in constant turmoil.

What soured many Philadelphia fans on Mauch was the trade for Larry Jackson and Bob Buhl that led to Ferguson Jenkins going to the Cubs. When Jenkins, who Mauch believed didn't possess a major league make up, had six consecutive 20-game victory seasons beginning in 1967, Phillies fans felt robbed. To many of them the Jackson-for-Jenkins trade epitomized what was wrong with Mauch's approach — preferring the veterans to developing the younger players. Mauch seemed to be looking for the quick fix rather than patiently waiting for the talent to mature.

After his release by the Phillies in June 1968, Mauch took over as the manager of the Montreal Expos in their inaugural season in the majors. In the early 1970s he brought the Expos to the brink of respectability, proving in the process that he could still nurture young talent such as Gary Carter, Bob Bailey, Mike Marshall, Mike Torrez and Steve Rogers.

After seven years with the Expos, Mauch took over the Minnesota Twins for five years and then had two terms with Gene Autry's California Angels. He got the most out of the Twins. Working with the chronically financially tight-fisted Calvin Griffith didn't allow Mauch much leeway in building a pennant contender. Still his Twins played better than .500 baseball in three of Mauch's years with them.

With the Angels, Mauch reached the playoffs twice but lost out in a fashion reminiscent of what happened in 1964. In 1982 his Angels had a two to zero game lead over the Milwaukee Brewers only to lose the last three games of the playoffs. He was criticized for his pitching selections once again. But the Angels' second chance at a pennant was in some ways more agonizing than the collapse of 1964.

The Angels were up three games to one over the Red Sox in the 1986 playoffs and led by three runs with two outs in the ninth inning. With Mauch standing on the top step of the dugout, poised to rush on to the field to celebrate his first trip to the World Series, the Red Sox rallied to tie the game and then win it in extra innings. In effect, Mauch never recovered from that setback, retiring from managing at age 62 during spring training 1988.

Mauch's statistics as a manager are impressive and probably deserve consideration for a place in the Hall of Fame. His 1,902 victories rank him 11th among major league managers. Of those managers with more career victories, all are in the Hall of Fame except for the two active managers, Bobby Cox and Tony LaRussa. Today Mauch lives in Rancho Mirage California where he keeps in shape playing golf.

Of the 1964 Phillies Jim Bunning had the most unusual and successful post-baseball career. After the 1964 season he had three more brilliant seasons with the Phillies, winning 55 games before being traded to the Pittsburgh Pirates. After spending a couple of years with the Pirates and Dodgers, he returned to the Phillies to finish his career.

In April 1971 Bunning was the winning pitcher in the first game in the Phillies' new home, Veterans Memorial Stadium. Later that season he won his 100th game in the National League to become one of the few pitchers to win 100 games in both major leagues. When retired after the 1971 season he had a record of 224–184.

Bunning served for a couple of years as a manager in the Phillies minor league system but he was fired in 1976. He eventually opted for a career in politics. Returning to his home state of Kentucky he was eventually elected to the House of Representatives. In 2000 he won a Senate seat, becoming the first major league baseball player to sit in the United States Senate. In 1996 the veteran's committee elected him to the Hall of Fame.

Dallas Green, a fringe player during his years as a pitcher, probably had the most baseball success of any survivor of the 1964 collapse. After retiring in 1967 with a record of just 20 wins versus 22 defeats, Green became part of the Phillies' organization. When Paul Owens was named general manager, Green took over as director of the farm system. Under Green a steady stream of players were sent to the majors, among them Lonnie Smith, Keith Moreland, Bob Walk, Julio Franco, Ryne Sandberg and Dickie Noles.

In 1979 when the Phillies fell from pennant contention for the first time in three years, Green took over from Danny Ozark as Phillies manager. He inherited a veteran team that was not playing to its potential and in 1980 led, some would say drove, them to the pennant and the World Series in 1980. It is still the only World Championship any Phillies team has ever won.

Green left the Phillies after 1981 and took over as general manager of the Chicago Cubs. During his tenure he led the Cubs to the playoffs in 1984 only to lose the pennant to the San Diego Padres. He left the Cubs after the 1987 season and spent time managing both New York teams, the Yanks in 1989 and the Mets from 1993 through 1996. Green returned to the Phillies in 1998 and currently serves as senior adviser to general manager Ed Wade.

A number of the members of the 1964 team continued in baseball after their playing days were over. Tony Taylor was a coach for the Phillies in the mid-1970s. He also managed in the Phillies' minor league system. He presently serves as a coach with the World Champion Florida Marlins.

Bobby Wine also was a longtime coach with the Phillies and Montreal Expos where he rejoined his former manager, Gene Mauch. He moved to the Atlanta Braves organization in the 1990s where he now serves as their advance scout.

Ruben Amaro Sr. was also a coach with the Phillies in their World Championship season. He followed Green to the Cubs when he took over that franchise and returned to the Phillies in the late 1990s where he helped rebuild their scouting program in Latin America.

Catcher Pat Corrales led one of the most successful post-1964 careers. Corrales was a September call up in 1964, getting into two games with one at bat. After a year with the Phillies, Corrales had a nine-year major league stint as a back up catcher with a number of teams. After he retired he managed for three different teams, Texas, Cleveland and the Phillies from 1982 through July 1983. In recent years he has served as bench coach for Bobby Cox's great Atlanta Braves teams.

The cloud that hung over the 1964 survivors is best represented in the careers of three key members of that team: Dennis Bennett, Richie Allen and Johnny Callison. All three seemed destined for greatness and, in the case of Allen, a potential place in the Hall of Fame. All were star crossed.

Bennett at one time looked like the best pitching prospect to come through the Phillies' system since Robin Roberts and Curt Simmons. Before the 1964 season Bennett predicted that he would win 20 games. Few in baseball would have disagreed with him. In the equivalent of one full season in the majors, he had won 18 games. Halfway through the 1964 campaign, it seemed his prediction would come true. Bennett was on the cusp of becoming one of the dominant left-handers in the National League. At this point his career record was 27–17. Then he suffered a flare-up of the arm and shoulder problems that he dated to a car accident before the 1963 season. He lost 10 of his remaining 13 decisions for the Phillies in 1964. After his trade to the Red Sox, he never regained the form that made him such a dominant presence on the mound. He was finished as major leaguer at age 28, just when most left-handers begin to blossom. His post–Phillies pitching record was 13 wins and 19 losses.

Richie Allen, or Dick as he prefers to be known, had one of the greatest rookie years in baseball history. He handily won the Rookie of the Year Award for hitting .318 with 29 homers and 91 RBIs while leading the National League in runs scored, total bases and tying for the lead in triples. Three more impressive seasons followed, including hitting 40 homers in 1966, the first Phillies player to reach that mark since Chuck Klein.

Allen became increasingly alienated from the Philadelphia fans and the Phillies' organization. Allen had a serious accident in August 1967, severely cutting his hand while pushing his car. Phillies fans were suspicious and rumors flew that he had been injured in a fight. After 1967 the Phillies gradually lost Allen, who became a victim of racial intolerance on the part of the city's fans as well as his own unreliability. He began to miss games, drink too much and show little interest in the team.

The conflict between Allen and Mauch eventually led to the latter's firing as manager in June 1968. There was an ugly element of racism in the fans' treatment of Allen, the Phillies' first great African American player. At the same time Allen never seemed totally focused on baseball. His off the field behavior — missing games, getting into fights, rumors of drinking etc. — didn't win him any friends in baseball circles.

After the 1969 season Allen, despite his immense talent, was traded by the Phillies to the Cardinals and began a gypsy career that saw him traded three times in three years despite putting up impressive offensive statistics. Only Chuck Tanner, manager of the White Sox for whom Allen played for three years, was able to harness his talent. In 1972 Allen won the American League's MVP Award. Then late in 1974 Allen seemed to have lost interest in baseball and retired at the young age of 32. He was lured back by the Phillies for whom he had two indifferent seasons in 1975 and 1976. His incredible skills had eroded and he left baseball never achieving the great things he was capable of. Always his own man no matter the cost to himself, Allen's personal journey of isolation began in 1964. He was shocked when his hometown fans booed him so unmercifully for his errors and his strikeouts. Allen has never found a home for himself in the sport he played so well. In recent years he has resolved his differences with the Phillies for whom he occasionally works. Allen today seems more at ease with his baseball past.

In a sense the saddest of the all post-1964 careers was Johnny Callison's. Under Mauch's handling — he was regarded good naturedly by his teammates as Mauch's pet-Callison had become by 1963 one of the best right fielders in the National League. His 31 homers in 1964 were the most any left-handed hitter ever hit in Shibe Park with its high right field wall. Callison had another great year in 1965, driving in 100 runs for the second consecutive year and hitting 32 homers including three in a game for the second time.

Suddenly at the young baseball age of 27, Callison lost his hitting stroke. In 1966 he finished with 11 home runs and just 55 RBIs. He never again hit more than 19 home runs or drove in more than 68 runs in a career that literally petered out. No one could figure out what went wrong. Callison tried everything to recapture his hitting stroke. He took to wearing glasses; he adopted an exercise program that Red Sox great Carl Yastrzemski used. But nothing worked. Callison claims that injuries took their toll, but to many baseball people it looked like a case of loss of confidence.

After he retired Callison never found himself. He drifted into a number of jobs—selling cars, bartending-and then experienced health problems. In a sense Callison is the symbol along with Alex Johnson, Richie Allen, and Dennis Bennett of a team that showed so much potential and then faded away, a victim of expectations that were never fulfilled.

Appendix 1
The 1964 Phillies Statistics

	Name	Games	AB	R	H	2b	3b	HR	RBI	BA
1B	J. Herrnstein+	125	303	38	71	12	4	6	25	.234
	F. Thomas	39	143	20	42	11	0	7	26	.294
	R. Sievers	49	120	7	22	3	1	4	16	.183
	C. Shockley	11	35	4	8	0	1	1	2	.229
2B	T. Taylor	154	570	62	143	13	6	4	46	.251
SS	R. Amaro	129	299	31	79	11	0	4	34	.264
	B. Wine	126	283	28	60	8	3	4	34	.212
3B	R. Allen	162	632	125*	201	38*	13*	29	91	.318
LF	W. Covington	129	333	37	95	18	0	13	58	.280
	D. Cater	60	152	13	45	9	1	1	13	.296
	A. Johnson	43	109	18	33	7	1	4	18	.303
CF	T. Gonzalez	131	421	55	117	25	3	4	40	.278
RF	J. Callison	162	654	101	179	30	10	31	104	.274
C.	C. Dalrymple	127	382	36	91	16	3	6	46	.238
	G. Triandos	73	188	17	47	9	0	8	33	.250
Reserves										
	C. Rojas	109	340	58	99	19	5	2	31	.291
	V. Power	18	48	1	10	4	0	0	3	.208
	J. Briggs	66	61	16	17	2	0	1	6	.258

*led league
+Herrnstein played 69 games at first and 68 in the outfield

Pitchers

	Games Starters	Innings	Wins	Losses	Saves	ERA
J. Bunning	41	284	19	8	2	2.63
C. Short	42	221	17	9	2	2.20
D. Bennett	41	208	12	14	1	3.68

Appendix 1

	Games Starters	Innings	Wins	Losses	Saves	ERA
R. Culp	30	135	8	7		4.13
A. Mahaffey	34	157	12	9		4.53
R. Wise	25	69	5	3		4.04
J. Boozer	22	60	3	4	2	5.10
C. McLish	2	5	0	1		3.60

	Games Relievers	Innings	Wins	Losses	Saves	ERA
J. Baldschun	71	118	6	9	21	3.13
E. Roebuck	60	77	5	3	12	2.22
D. Green	25	42	2	1		5.79
B. Shantz	14	32	1	1		2.25
J. Klippstein	11	22	2	1		4.09
M. Steevens	4	3	0	0		3.00
B. Locke	8	19	0	0		4.53

Appendix 2
The 1964 Phillies Season

Team	Date	Score	Starting Pitcher	W/L Pitcher
Mets	4/14	3	A. Jackson	Jackson
Phils		5	D. Bennett	Klippstein
Mets	4/15	1	T. Stallard	Stallard
Phils		4	Bunning	Bunning

Bunning's first victory in Shibe Park. He will not lose a game there until the Reds beat him on July 11.

Team	Date	Score	Starting Pitcher	W/L Pitcher
Phils	4/17	10	Mahaffey	Klippstein
Cubs		8	D. Ellsworth	Ellsworth
Phils	4/18	0	Culp	Culp
Cubs		7	B. Buhl	Buhl
Phils	4/19	8	Bennett	Bennett
Cubs		1	L. Jackson	Jackson
Pirates	4/23	6	Mahaffey	Baldschun
Phils		5	J. Gibbon	Face
Cubs	4/24	10	Bunning	Bunning
Phils		0	Buhl	Buhl
Cubs	4/25	4	Jackson	Jackson
Phils		1	Bennett	Bennett
Cubs	4/26	1	F. Norman	Norman
Phils		5	Culp	Culp
Phils	4/28	4	Mahaffey	Mahaffey
Reds		2	J. O'Toole	O'Toole
Phils	4/30	3	Bennett	Bennett
Reds		1	J. Nuxhall	Nuxhall

Phils finish April 9–2 for one of their best starts in team history. Six lefthanders started against them in their first eleven games.

Team	Date	Score	Starting Pitcher	W/L Pitcher
Phils	5/1	5	Bunning	Bunning
Braves		3	W. Spahn	Spahn
Phils	5/2	2	Culp	Culp
Braves		11	B. Sadowski	Sadowski
Phils	5/3	0	Mahaffey	Mahaffey

Team	Date	Score	Starting Pitcher	W/L Pitcher
Braves		1	Fischer	Fischer

Phillies are shut out for the first time.

Team	Date	Score	Starting Pitcher	W/L Pitcher
Phils	5/4	2	Bennett	Bennett
Cards		9	B. Gibson	R. Craig
Phils	5/5	1	Bunning	Bunning
Cards		2	R. Washburn	Washburn

Phils lose four games in a row and drop to third place — their lowest position for the season.

Team	Date	Score	Starting Pitcher	W/L Pitcher
Braves	5/6	6	Sadowski	B. Tiefenauer
Phils		7	Culp	E. Roebuck
Braves	5/7	6	Fischer	Fischer
Phils		9	Mahaffey	Mahaffey
Reds	5/8	3	J. Tsitouris	Tsitouris
Phils		11	Bennett	Bennett
Reds	5/9	4	B. Purkey	Purkey
Phils		5	Bunning	D. Green
Reds	5/10	2	J. Nuxhall	Nuxhall
Phils		0	C. Short	Short

Short's first start of the season.

Team	Date	Score	Starting Pitcher	W/L Pitcher
Cards	5/11	3	R. Sadecki	Sadecki
Phils		2	Culp	Culp
Cards	5/12	4	C. Simmons	Simmons
Phils		2	Mahaffey	Mahaffey

Simmons improves his record to 13–2 versus Phils since they released him in April 1960. Phils release Don Hoak.

Team	Date	Score	Starting Pitcher	W/L Pitcher
Cards	5/14	2	E. Broglio	Broglio
Phils		3	Bunning	Bunning
Phils	5/15	4	Bennett	Bennett
Colts		0	D. Nottebart	Nottebart
Phils	5/16	3	Culp	Culp
Colts		4	D. Farrell	Farrell
Phils	5/17	2	Short	Short
Colts		0	J. Owens	Owens

Short wins his first game as a starter.

Team	Date	Score	Starting Pitcher	W/L Pitcher
Phils	5/18	4	Bunning	Bunning
Colts		0	K. Johnson	Johnson
Phils	5/19	0	Bennett	Bennett
Giants		3	J. Sanford	Sanford
Phils	5/20	7	Mahaffey	Baldschun
Giants		2	J. Marichal	Marichal

Dick Allen hit his eighth home run of the season and Johnny Callison went 5–5 as Phils ended Marichal's 12-game winning streak.

The 1964 Phillies Season

Team	Date	Score	Starting Pitcher	W/L Pitcher
Phils	5/21	4	R. Wise	Klippstein
Giants		9	B. Hendley	B. Bolin

Wise makes his first start in the majors. Phillies start someone other than Bunning, Bennett, Culp, Mahaffey and Short for the first time.

Team	Date	Score	Starting Pitcher	W/L Pitcher
Phils	5/22	2	Short	Short
Dodgers		0	D. Drysdale	Drysdale

Short's second consecutive shutout. Phils beat Drysdale for the fifth time in a row.

Team	Date	Score	Starting Pitcher	W/L Pitcher
Phils	5/23	4	Bennett	Bennett
Dodgers		2	P. Ortega	Perranoski
Phils	5/24	0	Bunning	Bunning
Dodgers		3	J. Moeller	Moeller
Phils	5/26	4	Short	Short
Pirates		13	V. Law	Law
Phils	5/27	2	Mahaffey	Mahaffey
Pirates		0	B. Friend	Friend
Phils	5/28	5	Bennett	Baldschun
Pirates		6	B. Veale	A. McBean
Colts	5/29	6	B. Bruce	Woodeshick
Phils		7	Bunning	Bennett
Colts	5/30	1	Nottebart	Nottebart
Phils		5	Short	Short
Colts	5/31	1	Owens	Owens
Phils		4	Mahaffey	Mahaffey
Dodgers	6/2	3	Ortega	Ortega
Phils		4	Bennett	Bennett
Dodgers	6/3	0	Drysdale	Drysdale
Phils		1	Bunning	Baldschun
Dodgers	6/4	3	Koufax	Koufax
Phils		0	Short	Short

Koufax pitches no hitter. Faces just 27 batters when he walks Allen who is thrown out trying to steal second base.

Team	Date	Score	Starting Pitcher	W/L Pitcher
Giants	6/5	5	Marichal	Shaw
Phils		3	Mahaffey	Baldschun
Giants	6/6	4	Sanford	B. O'Dell
Phils		2	Bennett	Roebuck

Roebuck surrenders a two-run homer to Tom Haller for the first runs he allowed in 18 2/3 innings pitched.

Team	Date	Score	Starting Pitcher	W/L Pitcher
Giants	6/7	4	B. Hendley	Shaw
Phils		3	Bunning	Roebuck
Pirates	6/9	3	J. Gibbon	Gibbon
Phils		4	Mahaffey	Mahaffey

Dick Allen hits a homer, ending a drought of 75 innings for the Phils without a home run.

Appendix 2

Team	Date	Score	Starting Pitcher	W/L Pitcher
Pirates	6/9	4	S. Blass	Blass
Phils		0	Culp	Culp

Culp making his first start since May 16 sees his record drop to 1–5.

Team	Date	Score	Starting Pitcher	W/L Pitcher
Pirates	6/10	1	Friend	Friend
Phils		4	Short	Short
Mets	6/12	11	Stallard	Stallard
Phils		3	Bennett	Bennett
Mets	6/13	2	F. Lary	Lary
Phils		8	Bunning	Bunning
Mets	6/14	5	G. Cisco	Cisco
Phils		9	Short	Culp
Mets	6/15	2	Jackson	Jackson
Phils		4	Mahaffey	Mahaffey
Phils	6/16	4	Bennett	Bennett
Cubs		2	L. Jackson	Jackson
Phils	6/17	5	Bunning	Baldschun
Cubs		9	Buhl	Buhl
Phils	6/18	6	Short	Short
Cubs		3	Ellsworth	Ellsworth
Phils	6/19	2	Mahaffey	Mahaffey
Mets		1	C. Willey	Bearnarth
Phils	..	7	Culp	Culp
Mets		2	G. Cisco	Cisco
Phils	6/20	3	Bennett	D. Green
Mets		7	J. Fisher	Fisher
Phils	6/21	6	Bunning	Bunning
Mets		0	Stallard	Stallard

Bunning's perfect game, the first in regular season since 1922.

Team	Date	Score	Starting Pitcher	W/L Pitcher
Phils		8	R. Wise	Wise
Mets		2	F. Lary	Lary

Eighteen-year-old Wise's first start in the majors. He was the first Phils pitcher other than the five starters to start a game.

Team	Date	Score	Starting Pitcher	W/L Pitcher
Cubs	6/23	2	Ellsworth	Ellsworth
Phils		0	Short	Short
Cubs	..	0	S. Slaughter	Slaughter
Phils		9	Culp	Culp

Culp had a no hitter for 5 2/3 innings and gave up his only hit in the seventh inning.

Team	Date	Score	Starting Pitcher	W/L Pitcher
Cubs	6/24	8	E. Broglio	Broglio
Phils		9	Mahaffey	Green
Phils	6/26	6	Bunning	Roebuck
Cards		5	B. Gibson	Taylor

The 1964 Phillies Season

Team	Date	Score	Starting Pitcher	W/L Pitcher
Phils	6/27	4	Bennett	Wise
Cards		9	C. Simmons	Simmons
Phils	6/28	5	Short	Short
Cards		0	M. Cuellar	Cuellar
Phils	..	2	Culp	Culp
Cards		8	R. Sadecki	Sadecki
Phils	6/29	1	Mahaffey	Mahaffey
Colts		6	B. Bruce	Bruce
Phils	6/30	8	Bunning	Bunning
Colts		1	K. Johnson	Johnson
Phils	7/1	2	Bennett	Bennett
Dodgers		3	S. Koufax	Koufax
Phils	7/2	3	Short	Short
Dodgers		2	P. Ortega	Ortega
Phils	7/3	5	Culp	Culp
Giants		1	R. Herbel	Herbel
Phils	7/4	5	Bunning	Bunning
Giants		2	J. Sanford	G. Perry
Phils	7/5	2	Bennett	Bennett
Giants		1	J. Marichal	Marichal

Bennett's ninth victory. He would not win another game for almost two months as he began to suffer arm miseries.

Going into the All Star break, the Phils were in first place with a ½ game lead over the Giants.

Reds	7/9	3	J. Tsitouris	Tsitouris
Phils		4	Culp	Culp
Reds	7/10	5	J. O'Toole	O'Toole
Phils		1	Bennett	Bennett
Reds	7/11	3	J. Nuxhall	Nuxhall
Phils		1	Bunning	Bunning

Bunning's first loss at home.

Braves	7/12	4	W. Blasingame	Blasingame
Phils		3	Short	Short
Braves	..	6	H. Fischer	B. Hoeft
Phils		2	Mahaffey	Mahaffey
Braves	7/13	2	W. Spahn	Spahn
Phils		3	Culp	Culp
Phils	7/14	3	C. McLish	McLish
Pirates		4	B. Veale	Veale

McLish's only start for the Phils. He was released a couple of days later.

Phils	7/15	0	Bunning	Bunning
Pirates		3	B. Friend	Friend
Phils	7/16	7	Mahaffey	Mahaffey
Pirates		5	J. Gibbon	Gibbon

Phils regain first place and will remain there for 73 consecutive days.

Appendix 2

Team	Date	Score	Starting Pitcher	W/L Pitcher
Phils	7/17	5	Short	Short
Reds		4	J. Jay	Jay
Phils	7/18	4	Culp	Culp
Reds		14	Tsitouris	Tsitouris
Phils	7/19	4	Bunning	Baldschun
Reds		7	J. Maloney	McCool
Phils	..	4	J. Boozer	Boozer
Reds		3	J. O'Toole	R. Duren
Phils	7/20	2	Bennett	Bennett
Reds		6	Nuxhall	Nuxhall

Bennett's first start in 10 days.

Team	Date	Score	Starting Pitcher	W/L Pitcher
Phils	7/21	6	Mahaffey	Mahaffey
Braves		3	Blasingame	Blasingame
Phils	7/22	4	Culp	Culp
Braves		1	Spahn	Spahan

Culp's eighth victory and last win for the Phils in 1964.

Team	Date	Score	Starting Pitcher	W/L Pitcher
Phils	7/23	13	Bunning	Baldschun
Braves		10	D. Lemaster	B. Tiefenauer
Cards	7/24	1	Gibson	Gibson
Phils		9	Short	Short
Cards	7/25	10	Simmons	Simmons
Phils		9	Bennett	Bennett

Phils fall short, scoring seven runs in the ninth.

Team	Date	Score	Starting Pitcher	W/L Pitcher
Cards	7/26	6	G. Richardson	Richardson
Phils		1	Boozer	Boozer
Cards	..	4	Sadecki	Sadecki
Phils		1	Mahaffey	Mahaffey
Giants	7/28	0	B. O'Dell	O'Dell
Phils		4	Bunning	Bunning
Giants	7/29	6	Marichal	Marichal
Phils		3	Bennett	Baldschun
Giants	7/30	3	Hendley	G. Perry
Phils		4	Culp	Mahaffey
Dodgers	7/31	1	J. Moeller	Moeller
Phils		6	Short	Short

After 100 games, the Phillies are playing .590 baseball. Over the course of 162 games, this would add up to 96 wins.

Team	Date	Score	Starting Pitcher	W/L Pitcher
Dodgers	8/1	6	Drysdale	Drysdale
Phils		10	Bunning	Wise
Dodgers	8/2	6	L. Miller	Miller
Phils		1	Boozer	Boozer
Colts	8/5	1	Bruce	Bruce

Team	Date	Score	Starting Pitcher	W/L Pitcher
Phils		4	Bunning	Bunning
Colts	..	1	Johnson	Woodeshick
Phils		2	Culp	Roebuck
Colts	8/6	2	D. Farrell	Farrell
Phils		1	Short	Short
Mets	8/7	4	A. Jackson	Wakefield
Phils		9	Mahaffey	Roebuck

Before game the Phils get Frank Thomas from the Mets.

Team	Date	Score	Starting Pitcher	W/L Pitcher
Mets	8/8	5	Cisco	Cisco
Phils		12	Wise	Wise
Mets	8/9	0	Stallard	Stallard
Phils		6	Bunning	Bunning
Phils	8/11	13	Culp	Boozer
Cubs		5	Ellsworth	Ellsworth
Phils	8/12	6	Short	Short
Cubs		5	L. Jackson	Jackson
Phils	8/13	1	Bennett	Bennett
Cubs		3	Broglio	Broglio
Phils	8/14	6	Bunning	Bunning
Mets		1	A. Jackson	Jackson
Phils	..	6	Wise	Wise
Mets		4	Stallard	Stallard
Phils	8/15	8	Culp	Boozer
Mets		1	J. Fisher	Fisher
Phils	8/16	4	Mahaffey	Mahaffey
Mets		12	Cisco	Cisco
Cubs	8/17	1	Broglio	Broglio
Phils		8	Short	Short
Cubs	8/18	4	Buhl	F. Burdette
Phils		3	Bennett	Boozer
Cubs	8/19	5	Ellsworth	L. McDaniel
Phils		9	Bunning	Baldschun
Pirates	8/20	0	Friend	Friend
Phils		2	Mahaffey	Mahaffey
Pirates	..	2	D. Schwall	Schwall
Phils		3	Wise	Wise
Pirates	8/21	0	Veale	Veale
Phils		2	Short	Short
Pirates	8/22	9	F. Bork	Bork
Phils		4	Bennett	Bennett
Pirates	8/23	3	Gibbon	Gibbon
Phils		9	Bunning	Bunning
Phils	8/24	9	Mahaffey	Bennett
Braves		12	B. Sadowski	Sadowski
Phils	8/25	5	Wise	Wise
Braves		7	T. Cloninger	Cloninger
Phils	8/26	6	Short	Short
Braves		1	D. Lemaster	Lemaster

Team	Date	Score	Starting Pitcher	W/L Pitcher
Phils	8/28	2	Bunning	Roebuck
Pirates		4	Gibbon	E. Face
Phils	8/29	10	Mahaffey	Mahaffey
Pirates		8	Friend	Friend

Mahaffey's 12th win and last of the season.

Team	Date	Score	Starting Pitcher	W/L Pitcher
Phils	8/30	2	Short	Short
Pirates		10	Veale	Veale
Colts	9/1	3	H. Brown	Brown
Phils		4	Bunning	Bunning
Colts	9/2	1	Nottebart	Nottebart
Phils		2	Short	Short
Colts	9/3	6	D. Larsen	Larsen
Phils		0	Bennett	Bennett
Giants	9/4	3	D. Estelle	O'Dell
Phils		5	Mahaffey	Baldschun
Giants	9/5	3	B. Bolin	Bolin
Phils		9	Bunning	Bunning
Giants	9/6	4	Marichal	Marichal
Phils		3	Short	Baldschun
Dodgers	9/7	1	L. Miller	Miller
Phils		5	Bennett	Bennett

Bennett's first win since July 5th.

Team	Date	Score	Starting Pitcher	W/L Pitcher
Dodgers		3	P. Richert	Richert
Phils		1	Wise	Wise
Dodgers	9/8	3	J. Brewer	Brewer
Phils		2	Mahaffey	Mahaffey
Cards	9/9	10	Simmons	B. Humphreys
Phils		5	Bunning	Bunning
Cards	9/10	1	Sadecki	Sadecki
Phils		5	Short	Short
Phils	9/11	1	Bennett	Bennett
Giants		0	Marichal	Marichal
Phils	9/12	1	Mahaffey	Mahaffey
Giants		9	G. Perry	Perry
Phils	9/13	4	Bunning	Bunning
Giants		1	D. Estelle	Estelle
Phils	9/14	4	Short	Short
Colts		1	Bruce	Bruce
Phils	9/15	1	Bennett	Bennett
Colts		0	K. Johnson	Johnson
Phils	9/16	5	Bunning	Bunning
Colts		6	Nottebart	H. Brown

Bunning pitching on two days' rest, see his eight-game winning streak end. Mauch criticized for trying to steal a win.

Team	Date	Score	Starting Pitcher	W/L Pitcher
Phils	9/17	4	Wise	B. Shantz
Dodgers		3	Drysdale	Drysdale
Phils	9/18	3	Short	Baldschun
Dodgers		4	Richert	R. Miller
Phils	9/19	3	Bennett	Baldschun
Dodgers		4	L. Miller	Ortega
Phils	9/20	3	Bunning	Bunning
Dodgers		2	Brewer	Brewer
Reds	9/21	1	Tsitouris	Tsitouris
Phils		0	Mahaffey	Mahaffey
Reds	9/22	9	O'Toole	O'Toole
Phils		2	Short	Short
Reds	9/23/	6	McCool	McCool
Phils		4	Bennett	Bennett
Braves	9/24	5	Blasingame	Blasingame
Phils		3	Bunning	Bunning
Braves	9/25	7	Fischer	C. Carroll
Phils		5	Short	Boozer
Braves	9/26	6	Lemaster	Blasingame
Phils		4	Mahaffey	Shantz
Braves	9/27	13	Cloninger	Cloninger
Phils		8	Bunning	Bunning

After 73 days in first place, the Phils drop to second.

Team	Date	Score	Starting Pitcher	W/L Pitcher
Phils	9/28	1	Short	Short
Cards		5	Gibson	Gibson
Phils	9/29	2	Bennett	Bennett
Cards		4	Sadecki	Sadecki
Phils	9/30	5	Bunning	Bunning
Cards		8	Simmons	Simmons
Phils	10/2	4	Short	Roebuck
Reds		3	O'Toole	McCool
Phils	10/4	10	Bunning	Bunning
Reds		0	Tsitouris	Tsitouris

Phils record by month:

April	9 — 2
May	16 — 13
June	18 — 12
July	16 — 14
August	19 — 10
Sept/Oct	14 — 19
Total	92 — 70

Appendix 3
The Ten Game Collapse

Game One: September 21

Cincinnati Reds	Ab.	r.	h.	bi.		Phillies	Ab.	r.	h.	bi.
Rose 2B	4	0	0	0		Gonzalez CF	4	0	1	0
Ruiz 3B	4	1	1	0		Allen 3B	2	0	1	0
Pinson CF	3	0	1	0		Callison RF	4	0	0	0
Robinson RF	4	0	2	0		Covington LF	4	0	2	0
Johnson 1B	4	0	0	0		Phillips pr	0	0	0	0
Edwards C	4	0	0	0		H'r'stein 1B	4	0	0	0
Keough RF	4	0	2	0		Dalrymple C	4	0	1	0
Card'as SS3	0	0	0			Taylor 2B	3	0	0	0
Tsit'ris P2	0	1	0			Amaro SS	4	0	1	0
	32	1	7	0		Mahaffey P	2	0	0	0
						Briggs ph	1	0	0	0
							32	0	6	0

Cincinnati 0 0 0 0 0 1 0 0 0–1
Phillies   0 0 0 0 0 0 0 0 0–0

Errors: Cardenas. LOB—Cincinnati 7, Phillies 8. 2B Allen, Covington 2, Keough. SB. Ruiz Sacrifice Allen.

	IP	H	R	ER	BB	So
Tsitouris (8-11)	9	6	0	0	2	8
Mahaffey (12-9)	6.2	6	1	1	2	5
Locke	1.3	1	0	0	1	0
Shantz	1	0	0	0	0	0

Passed Ball Dalrymple Time 2:30 Att. 20,067.

Game Two: September 22

Cincinnati	AB	H	R	BI		Phillies	AB	H	R	BI
Rose 2B	4	2	2	0		Rojas CF	4	0	0	0
Ruiz 3B	2	1	0	0		Taylor 2B	4	0	2	1
Pinson CF	5	1	0	1		Callison RF	3	0	0	0
Rob'son RF	4	2	2	2		Allen 3B	4	0	1	0
Johnson 1B	5	0	2	2		Power 1B	4	0	2	0
Harper LF	4	0	0	0		Johnson LF	4	1	1	0
Edwards C	5	1	2	0		Amaro SS	3	0	0	0
Car'nas SS	4	1	1	1		Triandos C	4	0	0	0
O'Toole P	3	1	0	0		Short P	1	0	0	0
						Cater ph	1	0	1	1
	36	9	9	6		Phillips ph	1	1	1	0
							33	2	8	2

Cincinnati 0 0 4 0 2 2 1 0 0–9
Phillies   0 0 0 1 0 0 0 1 0–2

Error: Triandos, Allen. DP Cincinnati 2 LOB-Cincinnati 8, Phillies 6 2B A. Johnson (P), Taylor, Power. HR-Robinson (20) SB-Pinson, Ruiz.

	IP	H	R	ER	BB	SO
O'Toole (16-7)	9	8	2	2	2	6
Short (17-8)	4.2	4	6	6	5	4
Boozer	1 3	0	0	0	0	1
Steevens	1.1	5	3	1	1	2
Roebuck	1.2	0	0	0	1	2
Wise	1	0	0	0	0	1

HBP Ruiz; PB Triandos 2; Time 2:37; Att: 21,232

Game Three: September 23

Cinncinati	AB	R	H	BI		Phillies	AB	R	H	BI
Rose 2B	5	1	2	1		Rojas CF	3	0	0	0
Ruiz 3B	4	1	1	1		e) Covington	0	0	0	0
Pinson CF	4	2	3	4		Amaro SS	1	0	0	0
Rob'nson RF	4	0	0	0		Callison RF	5	1	2	0
Johnson 1B	4	0	1	0		Taylor 2B	4	0	1	0
Harper LF	2	0	1	0		Allen 3B	4	1	1	0
Ellis P	1	0	1	0		Johnson LF	4	1	2	2
Edwards C	4	1	1	0		Power 1B	4	0	0	0
Car'nas SS	4	0	1	0		Wine SS	1	1	0	0
McCool P	2	0	0	0		c) Gonzalez	1	0	0	0

Cinncinati	AB	R	H	BI		Phillies	AB	R	H	BI
a)Helms	0	0	0	0		Baldschun	0	0	0	0
b)Keough	2	1	0	0		f) Herrnstein	1	0	0	0
						Shantz P	0	0	0	0
						Dalrymple C	2	0	1	1
						Bennett P	1	0	0	0
						Roebuck P	0	0	0	0
						d)Briggs CF	1	0	0	0
Totals	36	6	11	6			32	4	7	3

a) batted for McCool in 7th
b) batted for Helms in 7th
c) struck out for Wine in 7th
d) walked for Roebuck in 7th
e) walked for Rojas in 7th
f) struck out for Baldschun in 8th

```
Cincinnati  0 0 0  1 0 1  4 0 0-6
Phillies    0 1 0  0 0 2  0 1 0-4
```

2B-Allen, Callison. 3B-Dalrymple. HR-Ruiz, Pinson, A. Johnson. SAC-Ruiz, Taylor. DP-Ruiz,Rose, Johnson. Dalrymple, Wine. LOB-Cincinnati 5, Phillies 8.

	IP	H	R	ER	BB	SO
McCool (6-3)	6	4	3	3	2	3
Ellis	3	3	1	0	3	5
Bennett(12-13)	6	8	4	4	1	6
Roebuck	1	2	2	2	0	0
Baldschun	1	1	0	0	0	0
Shantz	1	0	0	0	0	0

HBP Bennett by McCool. Time: 2:50 Att: 23,247.

Game Four: September 24

Braves	AB	R	H	BI		Phillies	AB	R	H	BI
Alou 1B	4	0	1	1		Phillips CF	3	1	0	0
Maye CF,LF	4	0	1	0		Callison RF	4	0	1	2
Aaron RF	4	1	2	0		Taylor 2B	2	0	0	0
Mathews 3B	1	2	0	0		d) Covington	1	0	0	0
Torre C	4	0	2	3		Dalrymple C	0	0	0	0
Carty LF	3	1	1	0		Allen 3B	4	0	3	1
Cline CF	1	0	0	0		Johnson LF	3	0	0	0
Menke 2B	3	0	0	0		a) Gonzalez	1	0	0	0
Alomar SS	4	0	1	0		Boozer P	0	0	0	0
Blas'game P	3	1	1	1		Power 1B	4	0	1	0
Olivo P	1	0	0	0		Triandos C	2	0	0	0

Braves	AB	R	H	BI	Phillies	AB	R	H	BI
Totals	32	5	9	5	b) Her'stein	1	1	0	0
					Wine SS	3	0	1	0
					f) Briggs	1	0	0	0
					Bunning P	1	0	0	0
					a) Cater	1	0	0	0
					Baldschun P	0	0	0	0
					Shantz	0	0	0	0
					c) Rojas 2B	1	1	0	0
					Totals	32	3	6	3

a) Grounded out for Bunning in 6th
b) Ran for Triandos in 8th
c) Hit into force play for Shantz in 8th
d) Fouled out for Taylor in 8th
e) Struck out for Johnson in 8th
f) Flied out for Wine in 8th

3B-Torre 2. SB-Alomar SAC-Menke   DP-Wine, Taylor, Power LOB-Braves 4, Phillies 5

	IP	H	R	ER	BB	SO
Blasingame (7-5)	7.1	5	3	3	3	6
Olivo	1.2	1	0	0	0	1
Bunning (18-6)	6	6	3	3	2	1
Baldschun	1.2	3	2	2	1	0
Shantz	.1	0	0	0	0	1
Boozer	1	0	0	0	0	1

Time: 2:29   Att: 17,342

Game Five: September 25

Braves	AB	R	H	BI	Phillies	AB	R	H	BI
Alou CF,RF	5	0	2	1	Gonzalez CF	6	0	0	0
Carty LF	4	0	1	0	Allen 3B	6	2	4	2
Cline CF	2	1	1	0	Callison RF	5	2	3	2
Aaron RF	4	1	1	0	Covington	5	0	1	0
Kolb 1B	1	1	1	0	g) Phillips	0	0	0	0
Torre C	6	1	3	3	I) Her'stein	1	0	0	0
Oliver 1B	5	1	0	0	Thomas 1B	4	0	0	0
Mathews 3B	6	0	2	1	Dalrymple C	4	0	0	0
Menke 2B,SS	2	1	1	0	Taylor 2B	4	0	0	0
Alomar SS	2	0	0	0	Amaro SS	3	0	0	0
a) DelaHoz 2B	3	1	2	0	Locke P				
					e) Briggs	1	0	0	0
Woodward 2B	0	0	0	0	h) Johnson	1	0	0	0

Braves	AB	R	H	BI		Phillies	AB	R	H	BI
b)Maye	0	0	0	1		Boozer P	0	0	0	0
Fischer P	2	0	0	0		Short P	2	0	0	0
Olivo P	0	0	0	0		Wine SS	0	0	0	0
a)Klim'shk	1	0	0	0		c)Rojas SS	3	1	1	0
Hoeft P	0	0	0	0		Baldschun P	0	0	0	0
Sadowski P	0	0	0	0		Shantz P	0	0	0	0
f)Bailey	1	0	0	0		Totals	45	5	9	4
Carroll P	0	0	0	0						
Cloninger P	0	0	0	0						
Totals	44	7	14	6						

a) hit double for Alomar in 7th
b) Sac fly for Fischer in 7th
c) Grounded out for Wine in 8th
d) Grounded out for Hoeft in 9th
e) Struck out for Locke in 10th
f) Grounded out for Sadowski in 11th
g) Ran for Covington in 11th
h) Fouled out for Shantz in 11th
i) Grounded out for Phillips in 11th

```
Braves    0 0 0 0 0 2 1 0 2 0 2–7
Phillies  0 0 1 0 0 0 2 0 2 0 0–5
```

2B-Carty, DelaHoz. HR-Torre, Callison, Allen. SAC-Kolb, DelaHoz, Thomas. SF-Maye. DP-Taylor, Amaro, Thomas LOB-Braves 10, Phillies 8.

	IP	H	R	ER	BB	SO
Fischer	6	3	1	0	1	4
Olivo	1.2	1	1	1	0	0
Hoeft	.1	1	1	1	0	0
Sadowski	2	2	2	2	0	2
Carroll (1-0)	1.1	0	0	0	0	0
Cloninger	.2	0	0	0	0	0
Short	7.1	6	3	1	2	6
Locke	2.2	4	2	2	0	1
Baldschun	.1	1	0	0	0	0
Shantz	.2	0	0	0	1	0
Boozer (3-4)	1	2	2	1	2	1

Game Six: September 26

Braves	AB	R	H	BI		Phillies	AB	R	H	BI
Alou 1B	4	1	2	0		Rojas CF,LF	4	1	2	0
Maye CF	5	0	1	1		Cater LF	1	0	0	0
Aaron RF	5	1	2	0		Callison RF	4	0	1	1
Mathews 3B	5	1	1	0		Allen 3B	5	1	1	1

The Ten Game Collapse

Braves	AB	R	H	BI
Torre C	4	0	3	0
a)Kolb	0	0	0	0
b)Bolling 2B1	1	0	0	
Carty Lf	4	1	2	3
Menke 2B,SS	5	1	1	1
Alomar SS	2	0	1	0
c)Cline	0	0	0	0
Woodward 2B	0	0	0	0
DelaHoz 2B	2	0	1	0
Lemaster P	0	0	0	0
e)Kim'chk	1	0	0	0
f)Blackaby	1	0	0	0
g)Oliver	1	0	0	0
h)Bailey	1	0	0	0
Totals	41	6	14	5

Phillies	AB	R	H	BI
Thomas 1B	3	0	1	0
Power 1B	1	0	0	0
Johnson LF	3	1	1	2
Gonzalez CF	1	0	1	0
Taylor 2B	4	0	1	0
Triandos C	2	0	0	0
d)Covington	0	0	0	0
Dalrymple C	0	0	0	0
Amaro SS	4	1	1	0
Mahaffey P	3	0	0	0
Shantz P	1	0	0	0
Totals	36	4	9	4

```
Braves    0 0 0 0 2 0 0 1 3–6
Phillies  3 1 0 0 0 0 0 0 0–4
```

a) Ran for Torre in 8th
b) Safe on error in 9th
c) Hit by pitch in 6th
d) Walked for Triandos in 8th
e) Flied out in 3rd
f) Grounded out in 5th
g) Struck out in 6th
h) Struck out in 8th

2B-Alou, Maye. 3B-Carty, Allen. HR-Menke, Johnson. SF-Callison. LOB-Braves 11, Phillies 8.

	IP	H	R	ER	BB	SO
Lemaster	1.1	6	4	4	0	2
Sadowski	.2	0	0	0	0	0
Eilers	2	2	0	0	1	0
Carroll	1	0	0	0	0	1
Olivo	2	0	0	0	0	3
Lary	.1	1	0	0	0	0
Blas'game(8-5)	.2	1	0	0	0	0
Spahn	1	0	0	0	0	0
Mahaffey	7	10	3	2	1	3
Baldschun	.1	1	0	0	0	0
Shantz (1-1)	.2	3	3	2	1	1
Roebuck	1	0	0	0	0	0

Game Seven: September 27
Phillies Fall Out of First Place

Braves	AB	R	H	BI	Phillies	AB	R	H	BI
Alou 1B	6	3	3	3	Gonzalez CF	5	1	2	0
Maye CF,LF	6	2	5	2	Allen 3B	5	1	3	1
Aaron RF	4	0	2	2	Callison RF	5	3	3	4
Kolb RF	2	0	1	0	Covg'ton LF	4	0	0	0
Mathews 3B	5	0	0	0	Thomas 1B	4	1	1	0
Olivo P	1	0	0	0	Dalrymple C	4	1	1	0
Torre C	5	2	3	1	Taylor 2B	4	1	2	2
Carty LF	2	1	1	0	Amaro SS	4	0	0	0
Woodward 2B	3	0	1	0	Bunning P	0	0	0	1
Menke 2B,SS	4	2	2	1	Steevens P	0	0	0	0
Alomar SS	1	0	0	0	a) Shockley	1	0	0	0
b) Cline	3	2	2	1	Wise	0	0	0	0
Cloninger P	4	2	2	2	c) Briggs	0	0	0	0
d) Klim'cok 3B	1	0	0	0	e) Rojas	1	0	0	0
Totals	47	14	22	12		37	8	12	8

a) Flied out for Steevens in 7th
b) Doubled for Alomar in 4th
c) Walked for Wise in 7th
d) Flied out for Baldschun

```
Braves    2 0 0 6 4 0 1 1 0–14
Phillies  1 2 0 0 0 1 0 0 2–8
```

Error-Thomas. 2B-Maye, Aaron, Gonzalez, Dalrymple, Cline, Alous 2, Thomas, Allen. 3B Taylor. HR-Callison 3, Torre SF-Bunning. DP-Amaro, Thomas. Mathews, Menke, Alou. Taylor, Thomas. LOB-Braves 8, Phillies 5.

	IP	H	R	ER	BB	SO
Cloninger (18-14)	7	7	4	4	2	3
Olivo	2	5	4	4	0	3
Bunning (18-7)	3	10	7	7	0	0
Green	1.2	7	5	5	1	0
Steevens	.1	0	0	0	0	0
Wise	2	3	1	1	0	1
Baldschun	2	2	1	1	1	2

Time: 3:00. Attendance 20,569.

Game Eight: September 28

Phillies	AB	R	H	BI	Cardinals	AB	R	H	BI
Gonzalez CF	3	1	2	0	Flood CF	4	0	0	0
Allen 3B	4	0	1	0	Brock LF	4	0	1	0
Callison RF	4	0	0	1	Groat SS	4	1	1	0
Covington LF	4	0	0	0	Boyer 3B	4	2	2	0
Baldschun P	0	0	0	0	White 1B	4	2	3	1
Shockley 1B	4	0	1	0	Javier 2B	4	0	1	1
Taylor 2B	3	0	1	0	Shannon RF	3	0	1	3
Dalrymple C	2	0	0	0	McCarver C	4	0	0	0
Amaro SS	3	0	0	0	Gibson P	3	0	0	0
b)Her'stein	1	0	0	0	Schultz P	0	0	0	0
Short P	2	0	0	0	Totals	34	5	9	5
Roebuck P	0	0	0	0					
a)Briggs	1	0	0	0					
Totals	31	1	5	1					

Flied out for Roebuck in 8th
B) Popped up for Amaro in 9th

Phillies   0 0 0 0 0 0 1 0–1
Cardinals 0 1 0 1 0 1 0 2 x–5

2B-Gonzalez, Boyer 2. 3B-Brock. SF-Shannon. DP-Groat, Javier. White. Amaro, Allen. White, Groat, White. LOB-Phillies 7, Cardinals 6.

	IP	H	R	ER	BB	SO
Short (17-9)	5.1	7	3	3	0	2
Roebuck	1.2	0	0	0	0	1
Baldschun	1	1	2	2	0	1
Gibson (18-11)	8	5	1	1	4	4
Schultz	1	0	0	0	0	0

Time: 2:13 Attendance 24,146

Game Nine: September 29

Phillies	AB	R	H	BI	Cardinals	AB	R	H	BI
Rojas LF, 2B	5	0	1	0	Flood CF	4	1	1	1
Taylor 2B	3	0	1	0	Brock LF	3	0	1	0
Baldschun P	0	0	0	0	Groat SS	3	0	1	1
Allen 3B	3	1	0	0	Boyer 3B	3	0	0	0
Johnson RF	3	0	0	0	White 1B	4	2	2	1
Shantz P	0	0	0	0	Javier 2B	4	1	2	0
Gonzalez CF	1	0	0	0	Shannon RF	4	0	1	0
Phillips CF	2	1	0	0	McCarver C	3	0	1	1

Phillies	AB	R	H	BI		Cardinals	AB	R	H	BI
Power 1B	3	0	2	0		Sadecki P	1	0	0	0
e)Covington	1	0	0	0		Schultz	1	0	1	0
Wine SS	0	0	0	0		Totals	30	4	10	4
Amaro SS	2	0	0	0						
f)Her'stein	1	0	0	0						
Dalrymple C	1	0	0	0						
b)Triandos C	3	0	1	2						
Bennett P	0	0	0	0						
Roebuck P	0	0	0	0						
a)Cater	1	0	1	0						
Mahaffey P	0	0	0	0						
c)Thomas	1	0	0	0						
Boozer P	0	0	0	0						
d)Callison	2	0	1	0						
Totals	32	2	7	2						

a) Singled for Roebuck in the 3rd
b) Singled for Dalrymple in the 4th
c) Grounded out for Mahaffey in the 4th
d) Singled for Boozer in the 7th
e) Struck out for Power in the 8th
f) Flied out for Amaro in the 8th

```
Phillies   0 0 0 2 0 0 0 0 0–2
Cardinals  1 2 0 0 0 1 0 0 x–4
```

2B-Rojas, Groat, Javier. HR-White. SB-Taylor. SAC-Brock, Sadecki. DP-Taylor, Power. Dalrymple, Taylor. Boyer, Javier, White 2. LOB-Phillies 3, Cardinals 6.

	IP	H	R	ER	BB	SO
Bennett (12-14)	1.1	5	3	3	1	0
Roebuck	.2	0	0	0	0	0
Mahaffey	1	1	0	0	1	1
Boozer	3	1	1	1	0	4
Shantz	.2	0	0	0	0	0
Baldschun	1.1	1	0	0	0	1
Sadecki (20-10)	6.2	7	2	2	4	2
Schultz	2/1	0	0	0	1	1

Time:2:32 Attendance 27,423.

Game Ten: September 30

Phillies	AB	R	H	BI		Cardinals	AB	R	H	BI
Rojas CF	4	0	1	1		Flood CF	5	2	3	0
Taylor 2B	4	0	0	0		Brock LF	4	2	2	0
Callison RF 4	1	0	0			White 1B	5	1	2	2

The Ten Game Collapse

Phillies	AB	R	H	BI	Cardinals	AB	R	H	BI
Allen 3B	4	2	0	0	Boyer 3B	5	1	3	1
Johnson LF	3	1	0	2	Groat SS	4	1	3	1
c)Cov'ton	1	0	0	0	McCarver C	4	1	1	2
Power 1B	3	0	0	0	Javier 2B	4	0	0	0
d)Dalrymple	1	0	1	2	Shannon RF	4	0	0	0
Triandos C	3	0	0	0	Simmons P	4	0	0	0
a)Gonzalez	0	0	0	0	Taylor P	0	0	0	0
f)Thomas	1	0	0	0	Richardson P	0	0	0	0
Wine SS	4	0	1	0	Totals	39	8	14	6
Bunning P	1	0	0	0					
Locke P	0	0	0	0					
a)Cater	1	0	0	0					
Wise P	0	0	0	0					
b)Phillips	1	1	0	0					
Steevens P	0	0	0	0					
Totals	35	5	6	5					

a) Flied out for Locke in 6th
b) Grounded out for Wise in 8th
c) Popped up for Johnson in 9th
d) Singled for Power in 9th
e) Announced for Triandos in 9th
f) Flied out for Gonzalez in 9th

```
Phillies    0 0 0 0  0 0 2 1 2–5
Cardinals   0 2 2 4  0 0 0 0 x 8-2b
```

Allen, Flood, White. 3b-Rojas. HR-Johnson, McCarver. SAC-Brock. LOB-Phillies 3, St. Louis 8.

	IP	H	R	ER	BB	SO
Bunning (18-8)	3	8	6	5	0	2
Locke	3	5	2	2	0	1
Wise	2	1	0	0	0	1
Steevens	1	0	0	0	0	1
Simmons (18-9)	8	5	5	4	4	2
Taylor	.1	1	0	0	0	0
Richardson	.2	0	0	0	0	0

Time 2:25 Attendance 29,920.

Chapter Notes

Chapter 1

1. There is no single history of Philadelphia at mid-20th century, but for an overview see Russell Weigley, *Philadelphia: A Bicentennial History*. Philadelphia, 1976 and chapter nine of John A. Lukacs, *Philadelphia: Patricians and Philistines*. New York, 1981.
2. A good analysis of the Philadelphia Reform Movement can be found in *Philadelphia's Political Reform Movement, 1946-1961*. The Historical Society of Pennsylvania, A Symposium February 27, 1988.
3. For an in-depth history of the Big Five see Robert S. Lyons, *Palestra Pandemonium: A History of the Big Five*. Philadelphia, 2004.
4. Bruce Kuklick, *To Every Thing a Season: Shibe Park and Urban Philadelphia*. Princeton, N.J., 1991, p. 119.
5. Two good surveys of the history of the Phillies are: David M. Jordan, *Occasional Glory: The History of the Philadelphia Phillies*. Jefferson, N.C., 2002 and Rich Westcott and Frank Bilovsky, *The New Phillies Encyclopedia*, Philadelphia, 1993.
6. The best portrait of Baker Bowl can be found in: Rich Westcott, *Philadelphia's Old Ballparks*. Philadelphia, 1996, pp. 27-98.
7. Frank Fitzpatrick, *You Can't Lose 'Em All: The Year the Phillies Finally Won the World Series*. Dallas, 2001.
8. Kuklick, *Shibe Park*, p. 90.
9. See David M. Jordan, Larry Gerlach and John P. Rossi, "A Baseball Myth Exploded: Bill Veeck and the 1943 Sale of the Phillies," *The National Pastime*, #18, 1998, pp. 3-13.
10. Robin Roberts and C. Paul Rogers III, *The Whiz Kids and the 1950 Pennant*. Philadelphia, 1996, pp. 96-97.
11. Ibid., p. 346.
12. John P. Rossi, *A Whole New Game: Off the Field Changes in Baseball, 1946-1960*. Jefferson, N.C., 1999, pp. 96-97.

Chapter 2

1. There is no biography of John Quinn. See Westcott & Bilovsky, *The New Phillies Encyclopedia*, for a sketch of his career with the Phillies.

2. Lee E. Lowenfish, "A Tale of Two Cities: Baseball Moves West in the 1950s," *The Journal of the West*, Vol. XVII, nu. 3, 1978, pp. 71-82.
3. William Leggett, "A Hot Team in the Old Town," *Sports Illustrated*, April 29, 1963, p. 19-20.
4. *The Sporting News Official Baseball Guide*, 1961, St. Louis, 1961, p. 191.
5. No biography of Mauch has appeared but a good overview of his career and managing style can be found in Ed Richter, *View from the Dugout*, Philadelphia, 1963, and Leonard Koppett, *The Man in the Dugout*, New York, 1993.
6. Myron Cope, "The Whip Who Puts the Snap in the Phillies," Saturday Evening Post, CCXXXVI, August 8, 1964, p. 79.
7. Furman Bisher, "The Many Moods of Mauch," in Richard Orodenker (ed.), *The Phillies Reader*, Philadelphia, 1996, p. 126.
8. Ibid., 130.
9. Cope, "The Whip," SEP, p. 79.
10. Bisher, "The Many Moods of Mauch," p. 134.
11. Cope, "The Whip," SEP, p. 79.
12. Ibid., p. 74.
13. Leggett, "A Hot Team," SI, p. 20.
14. Ibid., p. 20.

Chapter 3

1. Street & Smith's *Baseball Yearbook*, 1962, p. 49.
2. Ibid. p. 49.
3. Skip Clayton, "Don Demeter Led Phis Out of the Cellar," *Phillies Report*, October 6, 1983, p. 10.
4. *Sports Illustrated, Baseball Annual*, 1964, April 13, 1964, p. 57.
5. Leggett, "Hot Team," *Sports Illustrated*, p. 20.
6. Ibid., p. 20.
7. Stan Hochman, Daily News baseball writer to John Rossi, December 21, 2003.
8. *Street & Smith Baseball Yearbook*, 1963, p. 40.
9. Westcott & Bilovsky, *Phillies Encyclopedia*, p. 119.
10. Michael Sokolove, "It Hurt Like the Devil," *Philly Sport*, Vol. II, nu. 6, June 1989, p. 46.
11. For Mauch's hurling spare ribs and chicken, see Cope, "The Whip," SEP, p. 79. The Hutchinson quote is from, Bernard McCormick, "Little Napoleon," *Philadelphia Magazine*, April 1967, p. 76.

Chapter 4

1. The *Sporting News Official Guide*, 1964, St. Louis, p. 80.
2. *Sports Illustrated, Baseball Annual*, April 13, 1964, p. 57.
3. The *Sporting News*, April 18, 1964, p. 4.
4. The *Philadelphia Bulletin*, January 24, 1964, p. 23.
5. Ibid. Sunday Sports Section, January 25, 1964, p. 9; The *Sporting News*, February 8, 1964, p. 14.
6. Maria Gallagher, "The Boys of 64," *Philadelphia Magazine*, September 1976, p. 69.
7. The *Philadelphia Bulletin*, June 23, 1964, p. 24.

Chapter Notes

8. Ibid., p. 24.
9. Gallagher, "The Boys of 64," *Philadelphia Magazine*, p. 71.
10. The *Philadelphia Bulletin*, April 30, 1964, p. 28.
11. Ibid. Sunday Sports Section, January 26, 1964, p. 2.
12. Ibid. March 11, 1964, p. 24; March 26, 1964, Sunday Sports Section, p. 2.
13. The *Sporting News*, February 8, 1964, p. 14; *Daily News*, April 4, 1974, p. 43.
14. Rick Wise to John Rossi, telephone conversation, November 20, 2003.
15. Bill Conlin quoted in Bernard McCormick, "Little Napoleon," *Philadelphia Magazine*, April 1967, p. 48. Conlin believed that Mauch had a "soft spot for old guys."
16. John Herrnstein to John Rossi, October 26, 2003.
17. Herrnstein to Rossi, October 26, 2003.
18. Bob Oldis to John Rossi, October 24, 2003.
19. Roy Sievers to John Rossi, March 1, 2004.
20. The *Sporting News*, April 18, 1964, p. 29.
21. William Leggett, "An Epic That Ended in Tragedy," *Sports Illustrated*, March 6, 1965, p. 58.
22. Ibid. p. 58.
23. The *Philadelphia Inquirer*, April 23, 1964, p. 42.
24. Arthur Daley, "Sports of the Times," The *New York Times*, August 8, 1964, p. 231.
25. Sievers to Rossi, March 1, 2004.
26. The *Sporting News Official Guide*, 1965, p. 238.
27. Danny Peary (ed). *We Played the Game*. New York, 1994, p. 594.
28. The *Sporting News Official Guide*, 1965, p. 235.
29. The *Philadelphia Bulletin*, June 22, 1964, p. 24. The complete story of his perfect game can be found in Jim Bunning (as told to Ralph Bernstein), *The Story of Jim Bunning*. Philadelphia, 1965.

Chapter 5

1. Gallagher, "Boys of '64," *Philadelphia Magazine*, p. 66.
2. Leonard Koppett, *The Man in the Dugout*, New York, 1993, p. 265-266.
3. *New York Times*, August 8, 1964, p. 32.
4. *Philadelphia Bulletin*, June 28, 1964, p. 21.
5. Don Bostrom, "Johnny Callison's Memorable Moment," http://home.one-main.com
6. *Philadelphia Bulletin*, June 27, 1964, p. 13.
7. *Daily News*, April 4, 1974, p. 44.
8. Ibid. p. 45.
9. Ibid. p. 45.
10. Dalrymple to Rossi, October 27, 2003.
11. Gallagher, "Boys of '64," *Philadelphia Magazine*, p. 66.
12. Steve Wulf, "The Year of Blue Snow," *Sports Illustrated*, September 25, 1989, p. 82.
13. *Philadelphia Bulletin*, August 8, 1964, p. 21.
14. Dalrymple to Rossi, October 27, 2003.
15. David Halberstam, *October 1964*. New York, 1994, p. 253-266.
16. *New York Times*, August 23, 1964, p.
17. Kuklick, *Everything*, see Chapter 9, "Race Relations" for a discussion of the

area around Shibe Park and the complex problems that racial change created for the Phillies. A. Hano, "A Week With the Phillies," in Orodenker, *Phillies Reader*, p. 147.
   18. Ibid. p. 153.
   19. The *Sporting News*, September 9, 1964, p. 5.
   20. Leggett, "An Epic That Ended in Tragedy," *Sports Illustrated*, March 6, 1965, p. 60.
   21. Ibid. p. 60.
   22. Ibid. p. 61.
   23. Dave Anderson, *Pennant Races*. New York, 1994, p. 261.
   24. Ibid. p. 257-258.
   25. Ibid. p. 262.

Chapter 6

   1. Leggett, "An Epic," p. 61.
   2. Charles McNamara, "Pennant Fever," *Philadelphia Magazine*, October 1964, p. 95.
   3. Halberstam, *October 1964*, p. 304.
   4. Dave Anderson, *Pennant Races*, p. 262.
   5. Sandy Grady, quoted in John Rossi, "The 1964 Phillies Collapse," *Phillies Report*, October 8, 1992, p. 20.
   6. *Philadelphia Inquirer*, September 22, 1964, p. 36.
   7. Rossi, "The 1964 Phillies Collapse," p. 21.
   8. Michael Sokolove, "The Big Swoon," *Philly Sport*, June 1989, p. 59.
   9. *Philadelphia Inquirer*, September 22, 1964, p. 36.
   10. Leggett, "An Epic," p. 60.
   11. Sokolove, "The Big Swoon," p. 36.
   12. Leggett, "An Epic," p. 61.
   13. *Philadelphia Inquirer*, September 24, 1964, p. 49.
   14. Leggett, "An Epic," p. 61.
   15. Ibid. p. 61.
   16. Anderson, *Pennant Races*, p. 270.
   17. The *Sporting News*, October 17, 1964, p. 6.
   18. Halberstam, October 1964, p. 306.
   19. Sandy Grady, "Out With a Whimper," in Orodenker, *Phillies Reader*, p. 167.
   20. Leggett, "An Epic," p. 62.
   21. Halberstam, October 1964, p. 306.
   22. Anderson, *Pennant Races*, p. 265.
   23. Ibid. p. 275.
   24. The *New York Times*, September 29, 1964, p. 23.
   25. Anderson, *Pennant Races*, p. 278.
   26. The *Sporting News*, October 17, 1964, p. 6.
   27. Anderson, *Pennant Races*, p. 284.

Chapter 7

   1. Michael Sokolove, "The Big Swoon," *Philly Sport*, June 1989, p. 45.
   2. Stan Hochman, *Daily News* sportswriter to Rossi, December 27, 2003.
   3. Bill Conlin, *Daily News* baseball writer to Rossi, February 19, 2004.
   4. Koppett, *The Man in the Dugout*, p.367.

5. John McDermott, "Mauch of the Calamity Phils Says: Wait Till This Year," *Life Magazine*, Vol. LVIII, March 26, 1965, p. 78.
6. The *Sporting News*, August 8, 1964, p. 8.
7. Gallagher, "The Boys of '64," *Philadelphia Magazine*, p. 73.
8. John Herrnstein to Rossi, October 26, 2003.
9. Gallagher, p. 71.
10. Hochman, *Daily News*, April 4, 1974; Roebuck to Rossi, October 20, 2003.
11. Gallagher, p. 69.
12. *Daily News*, April 4, 1974, p. 45; Ed Roebuck to Rossi, October 20, 2003.
13. Sandy Grady, "Out With a Whimper," in Orodenker, *Phillies Reader*, p. 168.
14. Bill Conlin, *Daily News, Baseball Supplement*, April 1983; Bernard McCormick, "Little Napoleon," *Philadelphia Magazine*, May 1967, p. 48.

Chapter 8

1. Bill Conlin to Rossi, February 19, 2004.

Bibliography

Allen, Dick, and Tim Whitaker. *Crash: The Life and Times of Dick Allen.* New York: Ticknor & Fields, 1989.
Anderson, Dave. *Pennant Races.* New York: Doubleday, 1994.
Bostrom, Don. "Johnny Callison's Memorable Moment." http:/home.onemain.com
Callison, John, with John Austin Sletten. *The Johnny Callison Story.* New York: Vantage, 1991.
Clayton, Skip. "Don Demeter Led Phils Out of the Cellar." *The Phillies Report*, October 6, 1983.
Conlin, Bill. "Up from the Cellar." Baseball Supplement, *Philadelphia Daily News*, April 1983.
Cope, Myron. "The Whip Who Put the Snap in the Phillies." *Saturday Evening Post*, August 6, 1964.
Fitzpatrick, Frank. *You Can't Lose 'Em All: The Year the Phillies Finally Won the World Series.* Dallas TX: Cooper Square, 2001.
Gallagher, Maria. "The Boys of '64." *Philadelphia Magazine*, September 1976.
Golenbock, Peter. *Dynasty: The New York Yankees, 1949–1964.* Englewood Cliffs NJ: Prentice Hall, 1975.
Halberstam, David. *October 1964.* New York: Villard, 1994.
Hochman, Stan. "Ten Years After the Year of the Blue Snow." Baseball Supplement, *Philadelphia Daily News*, April 4, 1974.
Honig, Donald. *The Phillies: An Illustrated History.* New York: Simon & Schuster, 1992.
Jordan, David M. *Occasional Glory: The History of the Philadelphia Phillies.* Jefferson NC: McFarland, 2002.
____, Larry Gerlach, and John P. Rossi. "Bill Veeck and the 1943 Sale of the Phillies: A Baseball Myth Exploded." *The National Pastime*, 1998.
Koppett, Leonard. *The Man in the Dugout.* New York: Crown, 1993.
Kuklick, Bruce. *To Every Thing a Season: Shibe Park and Urban Philadelphia.* Princeton NJ: Princeton University Press, 1991.
Leggett, William. "The Big Red Surge." *Sports Illustrated*, October 6, 1964.
____. "An Epic That Ended in Tragedy." *Sports Illustrated*, March 6, 1965.
____. "A Hot Team in the Old Town." *Sports Illustrated*, April 29, 1963.
Lukacs, John A. *Philadelphia: Patricians and Philistines.* New York: Farrar, Straus & Giroux, 1981.
Lyons, Robert S. *Palestra Pandemonium: A History of the Big Five.* Philadelphia: Temple University Press, 2004.

McCormick, Bernard. "Little Napoleon." *Philadelphia Magazine*, April 1967.
McDermott, John. "Mauch of the Calamity Phillies Says 'Wait Til This Year.'" *Life*, March 26, 1965.
McFarland, Bill. "Shantz Could Have Played With the Whiz Kids." *Northeast Times*, May 29, 1903.
McNamara, Charles. "Pennant Fever." *Philadelphia Magazine*, October 1964.
"1964 Philadelphia Phillies." Baseballlibrary.com.
Orodenker, Richard (ed). *The Phillies Reader*. Philadelphia: Temple University Press, 1996.
Peary, Danny (ed). *We Played the Game*. New York: Hyperion, 1995.
Porter, David L. (ed). *Biographical Dictionary of American Sports: Baseball*. Westport CT: Greenwood, 2000.
Richter, Ed. *View from the Dugout: A Season with Baseball's Amazing Gene Mauch*. Philadelphia: Chilton, 1964.
Roberts, Robin, and Paul Rogers III. *The Whiz Kids and the 1950 Pennant*. Philadelphia: Temple University Press, 1996.
Rossi, John. "The 1964 Collapse." *The Phillies Report*, October 8, 1992.
Sokolove, Michael. "The Big Swoon." *Philly Sport*, June 1989.
Weigley, Russell. *Philadelphia: A Three Hundred Year History*. New York: W.W. Norton, 1982.
Westcott, Rich. *Philadelphia's Old Ballparks*. Philadelphia: Temple University Press, 1996.
____, and Frank Bilovsky. *The New Phillies Encyclopedia*. Philadelphia: Temple University Press, 1993.
Whicker, Mark. "Richie Allen: The Prodigal Phillie." *Daily News* Supplement, *The Phillies: One Hundred Years*, April 1983.
Wulf, Steve. "The Year of Blue Snow." *Sports Illustrated*, September 25, 1989.

Newspapers and Magazines

Life
The New York Times
The Philadelphia Daily News
The Philadelphia Evening Bulletin
The Philadelphia Morning Inquirer
The Phillies Report
The Sporting News
The Saturday Evening Post
Sports Illustrated
Time

Encyclopedia and Annuals

The Baseball Encyclopedia. 8th Edition, 1984.
The Sporting News Official Baseball Guide, 1965. St. Louis, 1965.
Who's Who in Baseball, 1965. Allan Roth, editor.

Correspondence

Bill Conlin, baseball writer, *Philadelphia Daily News*
Clay Dalrymple
Alvin Dark
Dallas Green
John Herrnstein
Stan Hochman, baseball writer, *Philadelphia Daily News*
Bob Oldis
Roy Sievers
Ed Roebuck
Rick Wise, telephone interview

Index

Aaron, Henry 16, 20, 26, 70, 86, 91, 111, 126, 128
Adcock, Joe, Braves first baseman 19, 20
Alexander, Grover Cleveland 1, 10, 22
Allen, Richie 58, 59, 70, 72, 74, 76, 81, 82, 83, 84, 85, 95, 96, 99, 101, 103, 106, 118, 123, 124, 125, 130, 133, 134, 136, 139, 145, 151–52
Alou, Felipe, Braves outfielder 124, 128
Alston, Walter, Dodger manager 73
Amaro, Ruben 30, 41, 44, 74, 81, 95, 117, 126, 140, 142, 151
Anderson, Harry 20, 22, 27, 41
Anderson, "Sparky" 23
Arizin, Paul 9
Ashburn, Richie 13

Bacon, Ed 8
Baker, William, owner of Phillies 11
Baker Bowl, home of the Phillies (1887–1938) 11
Baldschun, Jack 43, 70, 71, 72, 73, 75, 77, 86, 91, 106, 109, 110, 122, 125, 129, 141–42, 148
Bavasi, Buzzy, Dodger GM 2, 17
Belinsky, "Bo," Angels pitcher 143, 145
Bennett, Dennis 40, 42, 43, 47, 48, 50, 52, 66, 72–3, 74, 76, 77, 77, 82, 86, 88, 90, 98, 101, 107, 109, 119–20, 130, 138, 145, 151
Berra, Yogi, New York Yankees manager (1964) 139
"Big Five" 9
Blasingame, Wade, Braves pitcher 71, 122, 126
Blass, Steve, Pirate pitcher 75
Bolin, Bob, Giants pitcher 106
Bolling, Frank, Braves infielder 126

Boozer, John 90, 92, 94, 98, 99, 100, 109, 110, 130
Bork, Frank, Pirate pitcher 101, 102
Bouchee, Ed 20, 22
Boudreau, Lou 18
Bragan, Bobby, Braves manager 122, 124; on Mauch's managing in 1964 128
Brewer, Jim, Dodger pitcher 107
Briggs, Johnny 61
Brock, Lou, Cubs/Cardinal outfielder 76, 98
Broglio, Ernie, Cards and Cubs pitcher 76, 98, 100
Bruce, Bob, Houston pitcher 74
Buhl, Bob, Cubs pitcher 20, 36, 67, 148
Bunning, Jim 55, 56, 63, 66, 70, 72, 73, 74, 75, 78–79, 84, 89, 92, 96, 98, 99, 108, 110, 111, 122, 127–28, 132, 137, 149–50
Burdette, Lou, Braves pitcher 19
Burgess, "Smokey," Pirates catcher 15, 41, 102
Busch, Gussie, Cardinals owner 100
Buzhardt, John 23, 30, 33

Callison, Johnny 2, 22, 26, 30–1, 38, 40, 44, 47, 49, 69, 72, 74, 76, 81, 82, 83, 84, 85, 86–87, 94, 100, 106, 109, 113, 120, 124, 125, 128, 130, 136, 140, 152
Cardenas, Leo, Reds shortstop 142
Cardwell, Don, Phillies pitcher 20, 25
Carey, Andy, White Sox third baseman 39
Carlton, Steve 146, 147
Carpenter, Robert, Phillies owner 2, 13, 15, 17, 20, 23, 31, 79, 146
Carpenter, Ruly 146, 147
Carroll, Clay, Braves pitcher 124

185

Carty, Rico, Braves outfielder 125, 126
Cater, Danny 59, 70, 77
Cepada, Orlando, Giants first baseman 57, 82, 84, 88, 109
Clark, Joseph Sill, mayor of Philadelphia (1951–55) 8
Clemente, Roberto 26, 86
Cochrane, Mickey 10
Coker, Jim 25
Conley, Gene 21, 23, 28
Conlin, Bill, Philadelphia *Daily News* baseball writer 61, 136
Corrales, Pat 56, 151
Covington, Wes 16, 31, 38, 40, 52, 69, 70, 98, 100, 103, 117, 123, 130, 139
Cox, Bobby, Braves manager 149, 151
Cox, William, owner of Phillies 1943, 12
Culp, Ray 46, 48, 50, 66, 67, 72, 76, 81, 82, 83, 84, 88, 89, 90, 91, 97, 98, 99, 136, 148
Curry, Tony 22, 26, 30

Daley, Arthur, *New York Times* sports columnist 103
Dalrymple, Clay 25–26, 30, 41, 49, 50, 56, 66, 69, 81, 83, 91, 94, 116, 117, 124, 139 140, 146; on trade for Frank Thomas 97
"Dalton Gang" 27
Dark, Alvin, Giants manager 18, 22, 71, 75, 82, 94, 106
Davis, Tommy, Dodger outfielder 111
Davis, Willie, Dodger outfielder 110, 111
De la Hoz, Mike, Braves infielder 124
Del Greco, Bobby 22, 26, 31
Demeter, Don 30, 31, 32, 38, 44, 49, 55
Devine, "Bing," Cardinals GM 100
Dilworth, Richardson, mayor of Philadelphia (1944–62) 7
Drysdale, Don, Dodgers pitcher 39, 54, 56, 72, 75, 94, 110
Durocher, Leo, Dodger coach (1964) 29, 44, 100, 111

Ellis, Sammy, Reds pitcher 120
Ellsworth, Dick 77, 85, 148
Ennis, Del 13, 14, 15, 41

Fain, Ferris 10
Farrell, Dick, Houston pitcher 35, 72, 97, 148
Finnegan, Jim 8
Fischer, Hank, Braves pitcher 123–24

Flood, Curt, Cardinals outfielder 27, 54, 77, 94, 130
Fowler, Dick 10
Foxx, Jimmie 9
Freese, Gene 22, 32
Friend, Bob, Pirate pitcher 73
Fulks, Joe 9

Gibson, Bob, Cardinal pitcher 42, 54, 56, 94, 129, 139
Giles, Warren, President of the National League 123
Gola, Tom 9
Goliat, Mike 14
Gomez, Ruben 16, 30
Gonder, Jesse, Mets catcher 79
Gonzalez, Tony 2, 27, 30–31, 40, 47, 49, 50, 70, 81, 95, 102, 122, 123, 139, 146
Grady, Sandy, Philadelphia *Bulletin* sports columnist 53, 56, 57, 115
Graham, Wayne, Phillies farmhand 143
Green, Dallas 50, 62, 70, 77, 83, 128, 150
Greengrass, Jim 15
Griffith, Calvin, Minnesota Twins owner 149
Groat, Dick, Cardinals shortstop 36–37, 54, 87, 142

Hall, Dick, Phillies pitcher 148
Haller, Tom 75
Hamey, Roy, Phillies GM (1958–59) 14, 15
Hamilton, Jack 43, 55
Hamner, Granny 13, 14, 15
Harris, "Bucky," Phillies manager (1943) 12
Hart, Jim Ray, Giants third baseman 82, 84
Hendley, Bob, Giants pitcher 72, 82
Herrara, "Pancho" 22, 25, 30, 31, 45
Herrnstein, John 59, 70, 73, 94, 110, 117, 140
Hochman, Stan, Philadelphia *Daily News* baseball writer 65, 119–20, 136
Holmes, Tommy, Braves outfielder 18, 19
Hutchinson, Fred, Reds manager 41–42

Jackson, Al, Mets pitcher 57, 67
Jackson, Larry, Cubs pitcher 37, 67, 77, 144, 148
Jay, Joey, Reds pitcher 89
Jenkins, Ferguson, Phillies pitcher 37, 144, 148

Index

Jethroe, Sam, Braves outfielder 19
Johnson, Alex 94, 122, 125, 139
Johnson, Deron, Reds outfielder 118
Jones, Willie 13, 21, 30

Kashatus, William 3
Keane, Johnny, Cardinals manager 85, 100 129, 138
Kellner, Alex 10
Kelly, John B. 7–8
Kelly, Ray, Philadelphia *Bulletin* baseball writer 44, 65
Klaus, Bobby 143
Klein, Chuck 12, 41, 58, 151
Klippstein, John 48, 50, 66, 67, 72, 81
Knowles, Darrold 148
Konstanty, Jim 14
Koufax, Sandy 42, 52, 54, 57, 71, 84, 100, 107

Landis, Kenesaw Mountain, Commissioner of Baseball 12
Larsen, Don, Houston pitcher 106
LaRussa, Tony, Cardinals manager 149
Lemaster, Denver, Braves pitcher 125
Lewis, Allen, Philadelphia *Inquirer* baseball writer 65, 118
Locke, Bobby 141
Lombardi, Vince 29
Lopata, Stan 13, 21, 41
Lowery, "Peanuts," Phillies coach 91, 126
Lynch, Jerry, Pirates outfielder 75, 89, 102

Mack, Connie 9, 10, 11, 13
Mahaffey, Art 2, 27, 28, 30, 32, 43, 47, 52, 66, 73, 74, 76, 81, 83, 89, 94, 100, 101, 102, 103, 106, 109, 137, 138; loses first game of ten game streak 115–16
Mantle, Mickey 22, 56, 86
Marchildon, Phil 10
Marichal, Juan, Giants pitcher 28, 32, 53, 72, 84, 106
Martin, Billy 28–29
Matthews, Eddie 70, 126
Mauch, Gene 1, 2, 21, 24–25 (hiring of), 26–28 (and the 1960 Phillies), 30–34 (and the 1961 Phillies), 35–45 (and the 1962 Phillies), 53 (chances of the 1964 team), 58 (optimism about Allen as a thirdbaseman), 73–74 (concern over Sievers' leg injury), 91 (views Culp as

"soft"), 96 (presses Quinn to trade for a right handed hitter), 101–2, 114, 117, 133, 135–39 (criticism of his actions during losing streak), 141–42, 147–49 (Mauch is fired as manager), 149 (his post Phillies career)
Mays, Willie, Giants outfielder 53, 82, 106–7
McCool, Billy, Reds pitcher 90, 119–20
McCovey, Willie 53, 57, 82
McGraw, Tug, Phillies pitcher 144
McLish, Cal 39, 43, 47, 50, 65, 89
Merchant, Larry, Philadelphia *Daily News* sports editor 135
Miller, Larry, Dodger pitcher 71, 96, 107
Moeller, Joe, Dodger pitcher 73, 95
Morgan, Joe, Houston infielder 50
Musial, Stan 142

Northey, Ron 13
Nottebart, Don, Houston pitcher 110
Nugent, Gerry, owner of Phillies (1932–43) 11–12
Nuxhall, Joe, Reds pitcher 54, 69, 71, 88, 119, 120

O'Doul, Lefty 12, 41
Oldis, Bob 63
Olivo, Chi Chi, Braves pitcher 123
O'Toole, Jim, Reds pitcher 28, 54, 88, 132
Owens, Jim 21, 23, 27, 40, 45
Owens, Paul 144, 147, 150
Ozark, Danny, Phillies manager (1972–79) 150

Pennock, Herb, Phillies GM (1943–48) 15, 22
Perry, Gaylord, Giants pitcher 82, 84, 109
Philadelphia, City of 5–10, 64–66, 104–5 (riots of August 1964), 112–14 (prepares for World Series of 1964)
Philips, Adolfo 117, 122
Pierce, Billy, Giants pitcher 54
Pinson, Vada, Reds outfielder 55, 115, 120, 141
Post, Wally, Phillies and Reds outfielder 22, 27, 32
Power, Vic 108, 140

Quinn, John, Braves GM (1945–58); Phillies GM (1959–72) 15, 17–23, 30–34, 76, 96, 108, 135, 143, 147

Radatz, Dick 86
Ramos, Pedro, New York Yankee pitcher 139
Repulski, "Rip," Phillies outfielder 16
Richards, Paul, Houston GM 35–36
Richardson, Gordon, Cardinals pitcher 71, 94, 131
Rickert, Pete, Dodger pitcher 107, 110
Roberts, Robin 13, 14, 27, 29, 31–32
Robinson, Frank, Reds outfielder 26, 29, 55, 115–16
Roebuck, Ed, Phillies pitcher 62, 70, 71, 74, 86, 97, 102, 141
Rogers, Guy 9
Rojas, "Cookie" 3, 45, 61–62, 74, 85, 89, 92, 100, 103, 139, 146
Rose, Pete, Reds infielder 48, 120
Ruiz, Chico, Reds infielder 115, 120

Sadecki, Ray, Cardinals pitcher 54, 71, 84, 130–31, 138
Sain, Johnny, Braves pitcher 18, 19
Samuel, Barney, mayor of Philadelphia 7
Sanford, Jack 16, 28, 54, 82
Savage, Ted 38, 41, 45
Sawyer, Eddie, Phillies manager (1948–52); (1958–60) 14, 15, 23
Seminick, Andy 13
Semproch, Ray 21
Scheib, Carl 10
Schultz, Barney, Cardinals pitcher 131
Shantz, Bobby 10, 110, 125–26, 138
Shenk, Larry, Phillies Public Relations Director 110
Shirley, Bart, Dodger infielder 110
Shockley, Costen 90
Short, Chris 3, 27, 30, 32, 33, 40, 42, 43, 47, 49, 67, 69, 71, 72, 75, 77, 81, 84, 89, 94, 95, 98, 100, 101, 102, 109, 118, 123–24, 129–30, 132, 137
Sievers, Roy 36–38, 40, 44, 47, 49, 58, 63, 66, 69, 73, 77, 85, 90
Simmons, Al 9
Simmons, Curt 13, 14, 54, 57, 71, 83, 94, 108, 127, 131, 138
Sisler, Dick, acting Reds manager (1964) 115, 116

Smith, Charley, Phillies infielder 30, 36, 38
Smith, "Red," sports columnist 122
Southworth, Billy, Braves manager (1946–50) 18, 24
Spahn, Warren, Braves pitcher 57, 91, 122, 126
Stargell, Willy, Pirates outfielder 102
Steevens, Morrie 111, 141
Stengel, Casey 14, 35
Stuart, Dick 143
Sullivan, Frank 30, 32, 33

Tate, James H.J., mayor of Philadelphia (1962–71) 65, 104
Taylor, Tony 2, 25, 31, 49, 74, 86, 102, 120, 126, 139, 140, 146, 150
Thomas, Frank 57, 97, 98, 99, 103, 106, 107, 113, 124, 145–46
Torre, Frank 44
Torre, Joe, Braves catcher 70, 91, 122, 125, 128
Triandos, Gus 1, 55, 79, 85, 88, 101, 106, 118, 126
Tsitouris, John, Reds pitcher 54, 115–16, 127, 132

Van Brocklin, Norm 49
Van Buren, Steve 9
Veale, Bob, Pirates pitcher 89, 101, 103
Veeck, Bill 12
Vermeil, Dick 30
Virdon, Bill, Pirates outfielder 102

Wagner, Gary 148
Walters, Ken 22, 26
Washington, Claudell, Braves outfielder 147
White, Bill, Cardinals first baseman 27, 36, 37, 54, 130, 144
Williams, Billy, Cubs outfielder 86
Wills, Maury, Dodger shortstop 54
Wine, Bobby 41, 74, 99, 140, 142, 150
Wise, Rick 61, 72, 79, 98, 101, 102, 107, 110, 138, 145
Woodeschick, Hal, Houston pitcher 97
Wyatt, Whit, Braves pitching coach 128
Wynn, Jim, Houston outfielder 72

www.ingramcontent.com/pod-product-compliance
Lightning Source LLC
Chambersburg PA
CBHW020934230426
43666CB00008B/1680